Cartographic Sources

IN THE ROSENBERG LIBRARY

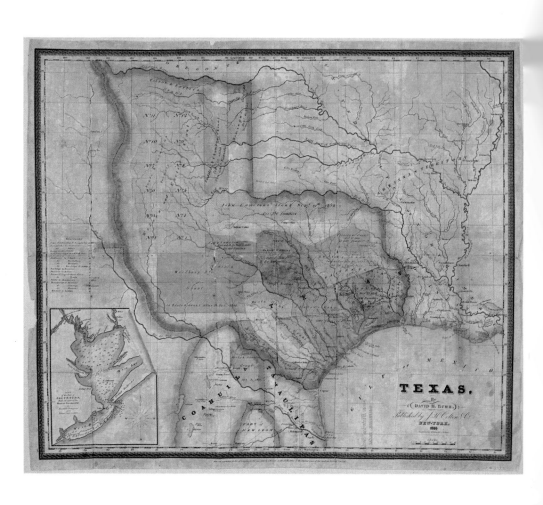

TEXAS,

By

(DAVID H. BURR)

Published by J.H. Colton & Co.

NEW-YORK.

1835.

Cartographic Sources

IN THE ROSENBERG LIBRARY

Compiled by Henry G. Taliaferro

Edited by Jane A. Kenamore

and Uli Haller

Published for the
ROSENBERG LIBRARY
by the
TEXAS A&M UNIVERSITY PRESS
College Station

FRONTISPIECE: *Texas,* by David H. Burr, 1833-35.
(See no. 247.) The first large-scale map to show all of
Texas to the Arkansas River, *Texas* includes parts of
present-day Colorado and Kansas. Alexander
Thompson's detailed manuscript map of
Galveston Bay appears as an inset.

The paper used in this book meets the minimum requirements
of the American National Standard for Permanence
of Paper for Printed Library Materials, Z39.48-1984.
Binding materials have been chosen for durability.

Library of Congress Cataloging-in-Publication Data

Rosenberg Library.
    Cartographic sources in the Rosenberg Library.
    Bibliography: p.
    Includes index.
    1. Gulf Region (Tex.)—Bibliography—Catalogs.
2. Rosenberg Library—Catalogs. I. Taliaferro, Henry G.
(Henry Garland), 1945- . II. Kenamore, Jane A.
(Jane Allen), 1938- . III. Haller, Uli, 1957- .
Z6027.U5R63 1988 [GA452]   016.912'7641   83-45095
ISBN 0-89096-161-1 (alk. paper)

*This guide is dedicated
to the late*
MARY MOODY NORTHEN
*who loved Galveston
and the sea*

and to

THE MOODY FOUNDATION
*whose generous gifts to
The Rosenberg Library
have greatly enhanced its collections
and have made the publication
of the guide possible.*

Contents

List of Maps

Preface

The cartographic collection of the Rosenberg Library focuses on Galveston, as it relates to Texas, the Gulf of Mexico, Caribbean Sea, and adjacent coasts. The maps show Galveston Bay from 1725 on; and they also illustrate European exploration of the New World during the sixteenth and seventeenth centuries and the development of Texas during the eighteenth and nineteenth centuries. The collection has been assembled for the scholar rather than the connoisseur. It contains many photostats, most of rare or otherwise inaccessible maps.

This guide is selective; there are more than 200 additional maps and map sets in the library. Some maps in extremely poor condition are omitted from this guide, as are certain types of maps published by various government agencies. For example, the library holds hundreds of United States Geological Survey maps; it simply is not feasible to include them. Maps bound into books are included only if significant. Maps acquired or cataloged after preparation of this guide began are not included.

Each description briefly relates the notable features of history of a particular map. Many standard historical and cartographic sources and checklists were consulted in preparing the map descriptions, but they are not cited unless of special interest (these sources are listed in the bibliography, however). Any cited Streeter number is from the *Bibliography,* unless otherwise noted.

The descriptions focus on developments in Galveston and along the Texas coast, but do include other relevant topics. For the purposes of this guide, on the earlier maps, the Texas coast is considered to be the area between the Bahía and Río del Espíritu Santo in the east and the Río de las Palmas or the Río Bravo in the west. If, as most scholars believe, the Río del Espíritu Santo is the Mississippi River, the easternmost place-names given for Texas in this guide apply to features in western Louisiana. The Río de las Palmas is the Soto de Marina River, about eighty miles north of Tampico. The Río Bravo appears on maps by the beginning of the seventeenth century, but only after the middle of the century does it clearly represent the Rio Grande (see introduction).

Most of the elements of each description are self-evident. Unless otherwise indicated, all maps are separately issued and printed in black on white paper. Ronald V. Tooley's *Dictionary of Mapmakers* served as our authority for cartographers' names. The map title given in the guide is a literal transcription of the title on the map, with the following exceptions: the Latin *v* and *i* have been written as *u* and *j* respectively when appropriate; commas and periods have been added where necessary (these usually correspond to line breaks in the title on the map).

All cited manuscripts are in the Rosenberg Library, except as noted. "Barker Texas History Center" refers to the Eugene C. Barker Texas History Center at the University of Texas at Austin. The MMNHMC acronym designates maps purchased by the Moody Foundation for the Mary Moody Northen Historical Maritime Collection.

Most of the maps are shelved in the library's Galveston and Texas History Center. The assigned map numbers are partial shelflist numbers, though they lack the location codes, which are omitted to save space and avoid confusion. The maps index with the complete shelf location is in the History Center. The maps were initially arranged in chronological order, but some later substitutions and deletions to this guide have scrambled that order a bit.

The Moody Foundation funded the preparation of this guide. Several people contributed time to this edition. Henry Taliaferro wrote the introduction and compiled the map descriptions through his own research and from the sales files of Walter Reuben, Inc. The following individuals and institutions provided suggestions or answered questions to greatly aid Taliaferro's work: Sarah Tyacke, British Library; Archibald Hanna, Beinecke Library, and Barbara McCorkle and Alex Victor, Sterling Library, Yale University; Ron Tyler, formerly of the Amon Carter Museum, Fort Worth; R. Philip Hoehn, Bancroft Library, University of California at Berkeley; Robert Martin, formerly of the University of Texas at Arlington; J. C. Martin, San Jacinto Museum, Deer Park, Texas; Mary Caldelough, Corpus Christi Public Library; John Mahe, Historic New Orleans Collection; Malcolm D. MacLean, University of Texas at Arlington; John Reps, Cornell University; Ed Dahl, National Map Collection, Public Archives of Canada; Robert S.

Weddle, Brenham, Texas; the late Coolie Verner; John Wolter, Richard W. Stephenson, John Hebert, Leonard Beck, Paul G. Sifton, Library of Congress; John Hyatt, Ruth Kelly, Robert Stephens, Van Ferguson, Michael Wilson, Margaret Schlankey, Julia Dunn, Murray Allen, Karen Walker, Rosenberg Library; Walter Reuban, Maryanne Hayes, formerly of Walter Reuban, Inc.; the British Public Records Office; the Royal Geographical Society, London; the Texas State Archives, the Records Bureau of the Texas General Land Office; the Houston Public Library; the Honnold Library, Claremont, California; the Barker Texas History Center; and the Louisiana State Museum.

Judy Young, Paula Landry, and Beverly Dawson typed and Joel Bromberg edited the first draft. Paula Pinto, a library volunteer, spent many weeks rechecking the map titles, cartographers, inset titles. We then revised and edited the descriptions, compiled the index, and prepared the final draft.

Jane Kenamore
Uli Haller
Galveston and Texas History Center
The Rosenberg Library
Galveston, Texas

Cartographic Sources
IN THE ROSENBERG LIBRARY

Introduction

EARLY CARTOGRAPHY OF THE TEXAS COAST

The Texas coast long remained one of the least-known stretches of the American Atlantic littoral. Not until the seventeenth century did maps begin to include conclusively identifiable features; and Galveston Bay, the coast's most prominent feature, remained completely unknown to commercial mapmakers until 1799. Even such a fundamental issue as the date when the Texas coast first appeared on manuscript and printed maps made in Europe cannot be answered with any certainty. Although the earliest map that conclusively shows the Texas coast is the rough sketch drawn after explorations made in 1519 by the Spaniard Alonso de Piñeda, maps of Portuguese origin had shown a rudimentary Gulf of Mexico, including Texas, as early as 1504.

The earliest manuscript and printed texts agree that a series of officially sanctioned Spanish expeditions were responsible for the discovery of the Gulf of Mexico. The first was that of Ponce de León to Florida in 1513, and the last was that of Piñeda to the western part of the present-day United States Gulf coast in 1519; however, a world map constructed by Alberto Cantino in Lisbon in 1502 shows a Florida-type landmass fully eleven years before the expedition of Ponce de León.[1] This chart is the earliest survivor in an important series of maps, all of Portuguese origin or based on Portuguese prototypes, that would dominate the cartography of the New World for a quarter of a century. The series presents a fundamentally similar, but evolving, geography, and includes the Januensis Caneiro chart, ca. 1504; Martin Waldseemüller's maps of 1507, 1513, and 1516; the Strobniza map, 1512; several globes constructed during the period 1515–30, including several attributed to Johann Schoener; and the so-called Holbein or Grynaeus world map of 1532.

The Caneiro chart[2] extends the west coast of the Cantino chart's Florida-type landmass first west and then south, forming to the west of Cuba an enclosed sea resembling the Gulf of Mexico. The southern terminus of this extended coast is not connected to any landmass, but Martin Waldsee-müller, on his great world map of 1507,[3] extends this coast farther south until it joins the mainland of South America. As a result, the American coastline from Newfoundland to southern Brazil appears continuous for the first time. The coast between the Mid-Atlantic United States and Central America is laid down with some degree of accuracy years before any of this vast region is known to have been discovered.

The most likely explanation for this seemingly premature appearance of the Gulf of Mexico is offered by Harrisse, who suggests that these early maps proceed "from a type on which had been grafted data borrowed from fragmentary surveys brought by mariners of different nations . . . who must have visited that coast several times in the course of clandestine expeditions."[4] The early narratives of American exploration, virtually all of which are Spanish in origin, mention only those voyages officially sanctioned by the Crown of Castile.[5] Anyone wishing to outfit an expedition was required to obtain a license (*asiento* or *capitulacion*) that severely restricted both activity and profit.[6] As a result, clandestine voyages probably were common, especially considering the growing number of adventurers and slave traders already in the New World. These clandestine navigators would have avoided officially discovered regions so as not to run the risk of encountering authorized ships. It is reasonable to assume, as does Harrisse, that some of the discoveries of these unknown early navigators were known to the chartmakers of Lisbon, one of the great centers for navigational science and exploration of the age.[7]

Presumably, a study of the maps of Spanish origin made during the years 1500–19 would help interpret the Texas coastal geography that was apparently a standard feature of the Portuguese charts. Unfortunately, few Spanish maps survived, and those that have are contradictory and difficult to interpret. However, at least three examples reflect prediscovery knowledge of Florida.[8] Scholars will probably never establish with any certainty the identity of the landmass on the Portuguese Cantino-type maps, so the beginning of Texas cartography must originate with the Piñeda expedition of 1519.

By 1518, the only unexplored portion of the American Atlantic littoral was the coast of the Gulf of Mexico between Pensacola, Florida, and the Río Panuco in northern Mexico.[9] It was only in this region, in the seas to the northwest of Cuba, that there remained any possibility of discovering a warm-water passage to Asia.

The purpose of the Piñeda expedition, authorized by Francisco de Garay, governor of Jamaica, was to explore these seas. Piñeda reconnoitered the greater part of the United States Gulf coast, finding it continuous, with no water passage leading to the west. Piñeda's exploration of this coast marked the first documented appearance of the areas now known as Texas and proved, as some mapmakers had suspected since 1507 or earlier, that the two American continents were contiguous.

Fortunately, a simple sketch map made of Piñeda's discoveries survives.[10] It shows the entire Gulf with a relatively accurate form, but it is, with one profound exception, almost totally devoid of detail. Just to the center of the Gulf's north coast, at approximately the site of Calcasieu Lake, Louisiana, the sketch shows a great unnamed bay into which flows a large river labeled "rio de Espiritu Santo." Between the "rio de Espiritu Santo" and the "Rio Panuco," the area approximately corresponding to the coast of Texas, the sketch shows only the mouths of three unnamed rivers. The Rio Espíritu Santo and its unnamed bay, later also called "Espíritu Santo," or "Mar Pequeno," remained the dominant feature of Gulf coast cartography until the close of the seventeenth century.[11]

There has been a great deal of debate regarding the identity of the Piñeda sketch's Río Espíritu Santo and its bay. Henry Harrisse, Justin Winsor, and Samuel Eliot Morison are just a few of the noted scholars who are confident that the Río Espíritu Santo represents the Mississippi.[12] Walter B. Scaife, William Edward Dunn, and Peter Joseph Hamilton believe the unnamed bay is Mobile;[13] Jean Delanglez and Marc de Villiers dur Terrage support Galveston Bay.[14] While scholars may never be absolutely certain of the identity of the river and bay, the case made for the Trinity River and Galveston Bay is as persuasive as any made for the Mississippi River or Mobile Bay. In Galveston's favor, the Piñeda sketch shows Espíritu Santo to the west of the center of the Gulf coast, near where the coast begins to trend dramatically to the southwest. The majority of manuscript and printed maps of the sixteenth and seventeenth centuries followed the Piñeda sketch in this respect.

The nonextant *Padron* map, kept at the Casa de Contratación at Seville, disseminated Piñeda's sketch to the mapmakers of Europe.[15] This map, or rather series of maps, was the official pattern by which, by edict, mapmakers were to copy all maps used by Spanish pilots. Furthermore, navigators and pilots were required to report all discoveries to the Casa for inclusion onto the *Padron*. Little is known concerning the evolution and development of the *Padron* after it was established in 1508. Charles V ordered the map extensively revised in 1526, but there is evidence that by 1535 the Spanish were neglecting both the improvement and the enforcement of the use of the *Padron*.[16] It is certain, however, that the Casa de Contratación kept official maps of some sort and that these maps incorporated Piñeda's discoveries and exerted a most powerful and positive influence on European geographical thought. Several maps drawn during the period 1520–45, for example, demonstrated that their prototype was a close copy of the *Padron,* or the *Padron* itself. These maps present an evolving geography, but one that invariably relies on Piñeda's form placement for the bay and river of Espíritu Santo.

The earliest maps giving place-names between Espíritu Santo and the Río Panuco (the Texas coast) are the Turin (ca. 1523)[17] and Hernando Cortés (1524)[18] maps. Although scholars have not identified the sites named on the early maps, both maps show Piñeda's Río Espíritu Santo and its unnamed bay, and they share an only slightly varying nomenclature that differs considerably from subsequent maps.[19] The Cortés map is the first printed map of the Gulf of Mexico. It is presumably based on the now lost manuscript that Cortés forwarded to Spain in 1520 and that must have provided information for the *Padron*. The undated Turin map betrays a more complicated origin, but its depiction of the western United States Gulf coast is clearly based on an unknown prototype similar to that of the printed Cortés map.[20] These maps' depiction of Texas must have borne a striking resemblance to that of the *Padron* in the years preceding 1526.

An anonymous map, ca. 1525, in the Salviati collection in the Medici Library in Florence, is the earliest such document to apply a name, Mar Pequena, to Piñeda's unnamed bay.[21] The Salviati map represents a transition between the earlier Turin and Cortés maps and the succeeding *Padron*-type maps that began to appear following the revision of the *Padron* ordered in 1526. The first of the *Padron*-type maps, an anonymous work dated 1527 and located in the Grand Ducal Library at Weimar, is the earliest surviving map that can be directly attributed to Sevilian hydrography.[22] Introduced for the first time are two Texas place-names that would long remain constant elements in Texas cartography: "Escondido" and "Madalena."[23] Very few maps constructed between the years 1527 and 1688 do not include at least one of these two names, and a great many include both. Usually cartographers applied the names to large rivers, with the Río Madalena (or Magdalena) the most westerly.

Diego Ribero, one of the royal cosmographers assigned in 1526 to revise the *Padron,* is often cited as the probable cartographer of the unsigned 1527 Weimar map,[24] and indeed that map shares many characteristics with two surviving manuscript world maps signed by Ribero. Both dated 1529, one signed map also survives at Weimar, and the other is at the Vatican Library. The Weimar Ribero map[25] shows the Río Escondido, but not the Madalena. To the south it introduces a place-name that would be significant to later Texas cartography: "Bravo," as "c. bravo." Although "Bravo" appears on few other sixteenth-century maps, Ribero locates it at the approximate site of the Rio Grande. By the early seventeenth century that river, established under the name "R. Bravo," would be the first conclusively identifiable geographical feature of Texas.[26] Immediately below "c. bravo," Ribero locates a "R. de Palmas," which one can identify as the present-day Soto la Marina, Mexico, approximately 150 miles south of the Rio Grande. The "R. de Palmas" would remain the northernmost identifiable feature on the Gulf Coast on most maps until the seventeenth century.[27]

The Sevilian cosmographer Alonso de Santa Cruz constructed many important manuscripts during the 1520s and 1540s. For the Texas coast, his maps present some differences from the Ribero-type maps, perhaps the result of subsequent discoveries or information. Among the more interesting is the introduction of the "Rio de Pescadores," a persistent feature on later maps.

Santa Cruz is generally accepted as the maker of the "DeSoto" map, ca. 1544.[28] This map represents a real advance, in that it is the first meaningful attempt to include interior details for the present-day Gulf Coast states. Using information supplied by survivors of the DeSoto expedition (1539–43), Santa Cruz supplemented a *Padron*-type outline for the coast's configuration, including details on Indian villages and courses of rivers.

The years 1550 to 1675 witnessed little real advance in the cartography of Texas. The Spanish lost interest in the region after the DeSoto expedition, and later Spanish manuscripts added little to the depiction of the Santa Cruz maps. Though great centers of mapmaking developed in Italy, the Lowlands, Germany, and France, Spanish secrecy forced other European mapmakers to rely on inferior maps for the depiction of the Gulf of Mexico. The map of Sevilian hydrographer Geronimo Chaves, which appeared in the 1584 edition of Abraham Ortelius's *Theatrum orbis terrarum* is an excellent example of the direct influence of Sevilian hydrography.[29] Though scholars view the work as the best and most influential printed sixteenth-century map for the southern United States, it contains no new information on the Texas coast. For that area, the Chavez map depends on information gleaned from the DeSoto expedition and incorporated into Santa Cruz's map published forty years earlier.[30]

A comparative examination of eleven important printed maps reveals a broad outline of Texas geography in the years before the discoveries of La Salle in 1684–87. These maps are the work of Sancho Gutiérrez (1562),[31] Gerard Mercator (1569),[32] Ortelius-Chaves (1584),[33] Petrus Plancius (1592),[34] Cornelis Wytfliet (1597),[35] Gabriel Tatton (1600),[36] Johannes de Laet (1626),[37] Jan Jansson (1636),[38] Sir Robert Dudley (1646),[39] Nicolas Sanson (1656),[40] and Arent Roggeveen (1675).[41]

Although no two of these maps give exactly the same nomenclature, together they reflect a static geography ultimately derived from Spanish prototypes of the mid-sixteenth century. Piñeda's unnamed bay dominates the Gulf coast on all maps, though the later mapmakers named it variously "Baia del Espiritu Santo," "Mar Pequeno" (the most common) or "Baia de Culata" (once, on Mercator's 1569 map). Certain other names appear regularly for rivers: "R. Escondido" (on four of the maps), "Rio or Medahos de Madalena" (nine maps), "C. de Cruz" (eight maps), "C. or R. Bravo" (seven maps), "c. desierto" (nine maps), "R. montanas (eight maps), "r. de Pescadores" (eight maps), and "r. de Palmas" (seven maps).

The number of place-names given remains constant during the sixteenth century, but tends to proliferate in the seventeenth, with Dudley's map containing over forty names. Internal evidence indicates that this increase in place-names is not the result of an increase in knowledge but is instead caused, in most cases, by the indiscriminate inclusion of all place-names found on earlier maps. For example, Santa Cruz (1544) gives a "R. del Oro" immediately below a "R. de montanas"; Gutiérrez (1562) gives a "R. de Pescadores" in the same position; Sanson (1656) gives "R. de Pescadores"; and Sanson (1656) gives "R. de Pescadores," with "R. de Oro" immediately following. Language barriers and legibility on manuscript maps further contributed to the unreliability of place-names. The fate of Santa Cruz's "c. desierto," which appears just to the west of the Bay of Espíritu Santo, is an example of the corruption caused by continuing transcription. It appears on Gutiérrez's map as "c. de zirto"; on Mercator's map as "C de Cuerto"; as "c. desierto" on the Ortelius-Chavez, Petrus Plancius, Wytfliet, and Tatton maps; as "Diserta" on Dudley's map; "C. de Suerta" on Sanson's; and "Cabo de Zarto" on Roggeveen. The maps contain numerous other errors. Tatton, for example, gives "R. de Palmas" as "R. de Pabnos." Attempts to correct inadequate source maps through the use of inaccurate, contradictory texts further compounded the problems.[42] Thus Ribero, Santa Cruz, and their associates at the Casa de Contratación, most of whose maps are now lost, established a prototype that succeeding cartographers copied in an ever more corrupt form down to the final years of the seventeenth century.

Two modifications to Gulf Coast cartography occurred during the seventeenth century. Piñeda's "Río Espíritu Santo," which flowed into the great bay, became six rivers. Four of these were of considerable and equal magnitude. Johannes de Laet introduced the unfortunate alteration on his map of Florida in 1630, and it had serious consequences for subsequent Gulf Coast cartography.[43] On a more positive note, European cartographers became more knowledgeable about the course of the Rio Grande, and it appeared in a completely recognizable form by 1670. Maps had been locating a "C. Bravo" or "R. Bravo" at the approximate site of the Rio Grande since 1529. By 1600 it was standard practice to locate a "Rio Bravo" just north of "Rio de Palmas" (Sota la Marina, Mexico). On Tatton's map, two place-names (costa de pescadores, "plaia et gada") intervene; on the maps of Jansson and Sanson, only one ("costa de pescadores"). It is possible that the Rio Bravo of these maps is the Rio Grande, but it is on G. B. Nicolosi's map of North America, 1660, that the full course of the river is first identifiable on a printed map.[44] V. M. Coronelli's famous map of North America, 1688, is the first printed map to show the river's entire course and to use the name "Rio Bravo."[45]

In 1674, the Parisian mapmaker Hubert Jaillot published a map of North America by a member of the Sanson family. The map provided interesting insight into the geographical conceptions of the southern United States and the Gulf Coast that were prevalent on the eve of LaSalle's discoveries.[46] The map shows four rivers flowing into the "Bahia del Spiritu Santo," the largest called "Chucagua" and a lesser one called the "Spiritu Santo." Immediately to the north of the "R. de Palmas" is a great unnamed river running due east-west, which is clearly the Rio Grande. A majority tributary is the "Rio Conches," the name of one of the Rio Grande's tributaries since the seventeenth century.[47] The map is of particular interest to Texas cartography as the probable source of many of La Salle's conceptions about the geography of the United States Gulf Coast.[48]

The Cavalier de la Salle's discovery of the mouths of the Mississippi opened a second great period of exploration and cartographic advance for the Texas coast that lasted until the 1720s. This period of roughly forty years can be subdivided into two parts. The first, 1685 to 1699, followed the failure of La Salle's colony on Matagorda Bay. During this period the Spanish conducted an intense investigation of the Gulf Coast, first to locate the French colony and later to ensure there would be no repetition of the French intrusion. William Edward Dunn notes that the Spanish sent no fewer than eleven different expeditions from Mexico and Florida to locate the elusive settlement on Espíritu Santo Bay.[49] The purpose of these expeditions was to rediscover "the coast of the Gulf of Mexico and . . . the greater portion of the vast territory between the Spanish settlement in Florida and those in New Mexico.[50]

It would be a mistake to assume that the Spanish "rediscovery" of the United States Gulf Coast in the late 1680s and the 1690s had an effect on the commercial cartography of the period. It is true that a number of manuscript maps resulted from these expeditions,[51] and that the knowledge of the Gulf Coast increased among Spanish officials.[52] This knowledge, however, was woefully deficient, and the maps generally were filled with ancient errors and rumors of French discoveries.[53] The maps exerted no influence on the great geographers and commercial mapmakers of northern Europe.[54] During the late seventeenth century, French mapmakers were responsible for all the geographical advances for the Gulf Coast.[55]

The cartographic unveiling of the western United States Gulf Coast that occurred during the years 1685–1721 was in all regards a French undertaking. During the first subperiod (1685–1700), the French tried to reconcile the often misleading accounts of La Salle's expeditions with the traditional geography that had descended in an aberrant and mutilated form from the early *Padron*-type maps.

La Salle's primary error was his identification of the Rio Escondido of the old maps as the Mississippi; he thus insisted that the mouth of the Mississippi lay on the Texas coast.[56] Commercial cartographer J. B. L. Franquelin introduced La Salle's geography through various maps dated 1684–97.[57] These maps showed the Mississippi emptying into the Gulf of Mexico just north of the Rio Grande, with the old Spanish bay of Espíritu Santo further to the east. Although many mapmakers (most notably V. M. Coronelli on his 1688 map of North America)[58] accepted the theories and assumptions of Franquelin,[59] there was a great deal of variation in the treatment of individual details.

The second subperiod began with the first expedition of M. P. LeMoyne Iberville, when the French once again took the lead in Gulf coast exploration and cartography. Between early 1699 and the spring of 1700, Iberville, founder of French Louisiana, reconnoitered the coast from Pensacola to the Mississippi, and explored the lower course of the river.[60] Commercial cartographers lost no time incorporating Iberville's discoveries into their works.

The first printed map to present Iberville's discoveries was the second state of Guillaume de L'Isle's 1700 map of North America.[61] For the first time, the Mississippi appeared in the correct position, with a delta.[62] The Bahía del Espíritu Santo had disappeared completely, with only its name preserved and applied to present-day Breton Sound, Louisiana.

The correct positioning of the Mississippi revealed for the first time the true extent of the coast between that river and the Rio Grande. The new information allowed a new, much more accurate geography for Texas to develop, and the years 1700–18 witnessed a dramatic advance in Texas cartography, culminating in the publication in Paris of De L'Isle's *Carte de la Louisiane*.[63] It is the first map to use the name "Texas" in any form ("mission de los Tejas"). The interior courses of the rivers of Texas appear for the first time on a printed map, and with some accuracy. Matagorda Bay, site of La Salle's colony is named "Baye St. Louis ou S. Bernard,"[64] but the coast from Matagorda to Louisiana is little understood.[65] As on all previous maps, Galveston Bay does not appear in an identifiable form. The Trinity River does appear with its present name for the first time on a printed map, however, and there is a small inlet at its mouth. On the east bank of this inlet is the place-name "Judosa." Some of the many mapmakers who copied De L'Isle applied that name to the inlet itself.

The expedition of Bénard de la Harpe to Texas in 1721, prepared the first large-scale map of Galveston Bay.[66] The French government had instructed La Harpe to reestablish the French beachhead in Texas and to build and maintain a fort and trading post at "St. Bernard's Bay," the site of La Salle's colony. Unfortunately, the prevailing ignorance of the geography of the Texas coast led him to land at Galveston Bay, rather than Matagorda Bay. La Harpe did not have the resources to resist the hostile natives, and he retreated. That retreat signaled the temporary cessation of the advance of Texas cartography. Although French cartographers prepared at least two manuscript charts of Galveston Bay from La Harpe's field sketches, his discoveries exerted no real influence on commercial mapmaking.[67] J. B. B. D'Anville's map of *North America,* 1746, bears a notation of the Texas coast concerning a "Port Francois" discovered by the French in 1720. Otherwise, we have not encountered an eighteenth-century map that alludes to La Harpe's expedition.[68]

French interest in Texas was largely dormant after 1721,[69] and ceased altogether with her expulsion from most of her American colonies at the conclusion of the French and Indian War in 1763. Thus, the great commercial mapmakers of Paris and London were once again dependent upon the secretive Spanish for current geographical information about the western part of the Gulf Coast. After 1763 the Spanish Royal Corps of Engineers took an active part in colonizing efforts along the northern frontier of New Spain, the present-day southwestern United States. The engineers prepared a number of manuscript maps during the second half of the eighteenth century, which Fireman calls "the best examples of eighteenth-century cartographic knowledge of the area."[70] For the region as a whole, Fireman is correct, but for the eastern fringes of the northern frontier, including the Texas coast, these maps do not live up to our expectations. The Spanish engineers concentrated their efforts along New Spain's northern frontier in Arizona, New Mexico, and far western and southern Texas. The few intrusions they made into the eastern and coastal regions of Texas invariably came from the interior, and their maps are generally inferior to De L'Isle's *Carte de la Louisiane* of 1718.[71] Even if these maps had been more accurate, they would still have exerted no influence on commercial cartography, as the still prevalent Spanish penchant for secrecy made them unavailable as sources.

Spanish engineer Nicolas de La Fora's map of northern New Spain, 1771, is one of the most important maps constructed by the corps that relate to Texas.[72] On La Fora's map the Texas coast is so confused and schematic, that it is meaningless. He names only two features, a misshapen "Bahía del Espíritu Santo" (Matagorda Bay) and a "R. de S. Antonio" that flows into the bay. The "La Paz" map, ca. 1782,[73] gives the old Spanish name for Galveston island, "Isla de Culebra," but seems to apply it to an island that stretches east from Matagorda Bay to the mouth of an unnamed river that must be the Brazos. There is no bay of any kind at the mouth of the Trinity River.

In 1768 there appeared in Paris one of the few eighteenth-century printed maps that is important to America and based directly on Spanish prototypes.[74] The cartographer Jose Antonio de Alzate y Ramírez, member of the Royal Academy of Paris, seems to have had access to the manuscripts of Don Carlos de Siguenza y Gongora and Royal Engineer Francisco Alvarez y Barreiro.[75] This is most certainly the first printed map to apply the name "Texas" to a geographical region, and the first to use the name in any form with its current spelling ("Provincia de los Texas"). Alzate y Ramírez's configuration for the Texas coast is generally more confused than that published by De L'Isle fifty years earlier. A giant "Bahía de la San. Trinidad" occupies virtually the entire east Texas coast. We cannot identify the body of water conclusively as Galveston Bay, however, as it combines the characteristics of both Galveston Bay and Sabine Lake. A host of rivers empty into the body of water, including the Trinity and the Neches. The Sabine, however, flows far to the east, to disgorge its waters beyond the boundaries of the map.

During the second half of the eighteenth century, when London reigned as the capital of advanced cartography, English mapmakers had to rely on outdated French maps for their geography of the Texas coast. The best English maps of the period for Texas, in fact, were those such as Henry Popple's map, 1733, that most slavishly copied De L'Isle.[76] A case in point is Thomas Jefferys' highly imaginative *The Western Coast of Louisiana and the Coast of New Leon,* 1775.[77] On this sheet, the Texas coast appears on a larger scale than any previous map. Thomas Streeter calls this map "the principal authority for the Texas coast" before the publication of the *Carta Esférica* in 1799.[78] The geography of the Jefferys map is genuinely worthless. He shows an inlet named "Judosa," a corruption of the one De L'Isle included at the mouth of the Trinity on his map of 1718. But here the inlet is wedged between the mouth of a "Río Barroso" (associated with the Trinity on its upper reaches) and an "R. Baty" (the Brazos). An "Isle de St. Louis" stretches from Matagorda Bay to the Brazos. Its eastern tip is labeled Punta de Culegras, an old name for Fort Point, at the east end of Galveston island. Thus in the year preceding the American Revolution, the world's leading commercial cartographer, Thomas Jefferys, was unaware of the existence of Galveston Bay.

The founding of the Deposito Hydrográfico (Dirección Hidrografía) at the Spanish Admiralty in Madrid, in 1797, marks the end of the Spanish government's official policy of secrecy concerning her empire, which had affected the progress of Texas cartography so adversely over the centuries.[79] The admiralty was able to disseminate the information of surveys and manuscripts formerly hidden in Spanish archives. In 1799 the Direccion Hidrografica published a magnificent chart of the Gulf of Mexico, the *Carta Esférica que comprehende las costas del Seno Mexico.*[80] The basis for the chart was the 1783–86 survey conducted by the Spanish navigator Evía (or Hevia) for Bernardo de Galvez, viceroy of New Spain. It is the first chart or map to show Galveston Bay correctly and to apply its modern name.[81] The bay's shape is crude—egglike—with East Bay a distinct appendage protruding from its eastern side. An unnamed Galveston island appears, with its eastern point named "Punta de Culebras." Matagorda Bay—here called "Bahía San Bernard"—also appears near Galveston Bay, and there is no sign of the Brazos River.

The configuration of the *Carta Esférica* represented a tremendous advance over anything previously seen, and the map inaugurated a third period of rapid progress for Texas cartography (1800–30). Leading mapmakers of Europe, most significantly Alexander von Humboldt and Aaron Arrowsmith, copied the chart.[82]

The Louisiana Purchase of 1803 led to increased American interest and activity in Texas. As a result, a number of maps appeared in the United States that would dominate the subsequent evolution of Texas cartography. Humboldt acknowledged, for example, that on his previously mentioned map of New Spain, 1809, he altered the configuration given by the *Carta Esférica* of 1799 in accordance with "a manuscript map which General Wilkinson communicated to me at Washington, on his return from

Louisiana."[83] The 1810 publication of Zebulon Pike's narrative included the first maps significant to Texas cartography that were published in the United States. These maps rivaled the maps of Arrowsmith and Humboldt in influence.[84] John Melish's *Map of the United States with the contiguous British and Spanish Possessions,* Philadelphia, 1816, was the greatest achievement of American commercial cartography to date. It established a new prototype for the depiction of the United States, and it is generally recognized as the first map to show the present-day nation's entire territory as running from the Atlantic to the Pacific.[85] In his *A Geographical Description . . . intended as an accompaniment to Melish's Map,* Philadelphia, 1816, Melish notes, "for the Spanish part, Humboldt's very excellent map was selected as the basis [for the 1816 map], use being made of Pike's Travels, for filling up some of the details."[86] But Melish's map was far from a slavish copy of Humboldt's or Pike's maps; his configuration for the Texas coast is different from either. He informs us that "after work [on the map] was wholly finished, Mr. William Darby, and Mr. Lewis Bringien, arrived in Philadelphia with a MS. map of Louisiana of great value and importance. Mr. Darby's map embraced the whole . . . country west nearly to the Rio Bravo del Norte [Rio Grande]."[87]

Melish's map established a new prototype for Texas that remained very influential until the publication of Stephen F. Austin's map in 1830. It was an improvement on Humboldt because it showed more correctly the relationship between the Texas rivers. The Melish map does show Galveston Bay; however, the map lacks correct proportion and refinement of detail for the Texas coast.

Henry Schenck Tanner, the famous Philadelphia map publisher, included an extremely influential map of North America in *A New American Atlas,* 1823.[88] The coastal configuration of Texas, although similar to that on Melish's map, shows some variation in outline and detail.

The beginning of Anglo-American settlement, 1823, spurred new interest in Texas, both in newly independent Mexico and in the United States. A little-known landmark in the history of Galveston Bay was Alexander Thompson's 1828 reconnaissance for the Mexican navy. Thompson drew a chart that was the most accurate rendering of the bay since La Harpe's chart a century earlier. Unfortunately, Thompson's chart never appeared in print, except as an inset on several of the more general maps of the period.[89]

Contemporary with the visit of Alexander Thompson was the extensive work conducted by Stephen F. Austin for his map of Texas. This map marks the beginning of modern Texas cartography, in that it shows for the first time the result of the initial Anglo settlement in Texas. Austin's map was published by Henry Tanner in Philadelphia in 1830.[90] The Texas coast appears at last with a configuration accurate in all but the smallest of details (Galveston Bay is a bit too large, for example). This configuration would be refined to a high degree of accuracy through the efforts of the United States Coast Survey in the years following the annexation of Texas (1846).

Although Austin's map and the subsequent charts of the Coast Survey brought the cartographic unveiling of the Texas coast to a close, a number of additional maps published during the years 1830–60 are important for their contribution to Texas geography as a whole. They also provide a valuable record of the social and political evolution of the state during the crucial years when much of its territory was first settled by a population of European origin. The most noteworthy of these include David Burr's *Texas*, 1833;[91] John Arrowsmith's *Texas*, 1841;[92] William Emory's *Map of Texas*, 1844;[93] Jacob De Cordova's *Map of Texas*, 1849;[94] and Charles Pressler's *Map of the State of Texas*, 1858.[95]

Place-names associated with Galveston Island first appear on maps in the late eighteenth century. The island's nomenclature has changed continuously, but it has stabilized somewhat since the midnineteenth century. Before 1830 the island was known by various names: "Isla Blanca," "Isla Arnajuez," "Isla San Luis" or "St. Louis," and "Isla Culebra."[96]

The island is roughly cigar-shaped, about twenty-seven miles long and three miles or less wide. Its long axis runs northeast-southwest; the southern side is the Gulf shore, and the northern side is the bay shore. The Gulf shore is generally smooth and without distinguishing natural features, and a number of inlets penetrate the bay shore. The easternmost inlet, and the most significant to the city of Galveston is Offatt's Bayou. This bayou cuts into the island from the west, almost parallel to the long axis, and divides a jutting peninsula from the main part of the island. This peninsula, now known as "Teichman's Point," was sometimes called "Eagle Point" in early accounts, as it was the site of the Eagle Grove so often mentioned by early nineteenth-century navigators and chroniclers.[97] The peninsula is not noted on La Harpe's map, circa 1721,[98] or on the *Carta Esférica*, 1799.[99] Alexander Thompson's map, 1828,[100] is unique in that is shows Offatt's Bayou as a channel and Teichman's Point as an island.

Because of its proximity to the swift waters of the channel connecting Galveston Bay with the Gulf, the eastern tip of the island has been extremely vulnerable to the ravages of nature. On some early nineteenth-century maps, 1816 to 1838, this tip appears completely separated from the main body of Galveston Island by a channel.[101] Its present size and form are totally artificial, the result of the protection offered by the south jetty and seawall.[102] The earliest references to this point usually call it "Punta de Culebra." In the Republic Period and during most of the nineteenth century, it was "Fort Point," the name that we have used throughout this work.[103]

When the city of Galveston was laid out in 1837–38, bayous occupied much of the area south of present-day Broadway. These bayous continue to appear in changing, usually diminishing form on maps until late in the century. The most important were McKinney's and Hitchcock's bayous.

At present, Galveston Harbor is a narrow channel bounded by Galveston and Pelican islands. Pelican Island appears on maps as early as 1721.[104] Originally, it was much smaller;[105] the present-day island is totally artificial, the work of the U.S. Army Corps of Engineers in this century. At some time before 1851 a smaller sandbar appeared above water between Pelican Island and Fort Point. It was called "Pelican Spit," and the channel into Galveston Harbor passed between it and Galveston Island.[106] Pelican Island and Pelican Spit had continually shifting perimeters until after 1900, when the two joined into one enlarged, stabilized Pelican Island created from silt dredged from Galveston Harbor.

Several pre–Civil War surveys or reconnaissances of the Galveston Bay area left tangible proof in the form of maps and documents: Bénard de la Harpe, of Galveston Bay, for France and the Company of the Indies, 1721; Josef Evía, of Galveston Bay, for Bernardo de Galvez, viceroy of New Spain, 1783; Alexander Thompson, of Galveston Bay, for the Mexican navy, 1828; I. N. Moreland, of Galveston Island, at the direction of the Alcalde of the Trinity Jurisdiction of the State of Coahuila and Texas, 1834;[107] the Borden Survey of Galveston Island, 1835;[108] Trimble and Lindsey, of West Galveston Island, for the Republic of Texas, 1837;[109] John Groesbeck, of the site of the city of Galveston, for the Galveston City Company, 1837–38;[110] and the United States Coast Survey for 1849.[111] A number of individuals did additional, but less comprehensive, survey work in the area. The most noteworthy of the surveys are those of Stephen F. Austin for the Mexican government during the 1820s; Levi Jones and Edward Hall of West Galveston Island, 1839;[112] William Bollaert at the request of William Kennedy, British consul in Galveston and the British Admiralty, 1840–44;[113] Commodore Moore for the navy of the Republic of Texas, ca. 1840;[114] and Tipton Walker, ca. 1848.[115] These surveys form the foundation for the cartographic unveiling of Galveston Bay, Island, and City. It should also be pointed out that Piñeda may have reconnoitered the bay in 1519, and Alvar Nuñez Cabeza de Vaca probably landed there in his American journey of 1528–36.[116]

Galveston was founded in 1839. The stories of the early growth of the city and the importance of Galveston in Gulf Coast shipping are well known. After 1900 the city declined, displaced by neighboring Houston, a city with similar goals.

The cartographic history of the city falls into three periods bounded by major historical events. The first (1836–65) begins with the official founding of the city and concludes with the close of the Civil War. These years are the formative years, when the basic outline of the city and the island takes shape. The second period, ending with the hurricane of 1900, is one of rapid development and intense commercial activity. A particularly noteworthy development was the lowering of the bar and the deepening of the harbor by the U.S. Army Corps of Engineers. These events largely transformed the map of the city and its harbor. The third period, beginning in 1900, is a period of relative stability. The map of the city saw few changes, except for some extension westward, the construction of the seawall, and extensive alterations to the Gulf shore and harbor facilities, especially with regard to Pelican Island.

The city was laid out on a grid plan in 1837–38, and there have been relatively few alterations to this original plan. The design method was similar to that of many western cities: an entrepreneur, or in this case, a group of entrepreneurs proposed a scheme that fit their own conception of the plan of an important city. They engaged a professional surveyor to lay out the plan, and he made whatever alterations were necessary to fit the exigencies of the site. Austin is another Texas city laid out in a similar manner, but there Mirabeau B. Lamar, president of the Republic of Texas, acted the role normally played by an entrepreneur.[117] Although Austin has completely outgrown its original limits, Galveston is still largely confined to the original league and labor of land granted to Michael B. Menard in 1836, and laid out by John Groesbeck according to the designs of the trustees of the Galveston City Company.

Galveston was to be a mixture of urban and rural development. According to the plan, a major boulevard (Broadway) bisected the city along its long axis. City blocks, each 260 x 300 feet and divided into ten or fourteen lots, occupied the area north of Broadway. Agricultural outlots, each the size of four regular city blocks, occupied the land south of Broadway.[118] Prosperous settlers, such as the Menards, Bordens, and Williamses, lived on the sparsely populated outlots. By 1838 concentrated settlement began to develop at two different sites within the city. A group of carpenters from Maine located their community, known as "Saccarap," on the harbor front east of Fourteenth Street near the site of Laffite's old fort[119] and the current University of Texas Medical Branch campus. The other settlement was located in the area of Tremont Street and the Strand, near the deepest part of the harbor, and it eventually developed into the original business district of the city. In 1860 the developed portion of the city scarcely extended beyond the bounds of the present-day central business district.

Although most southern cities suffered in the aftermath of the Civil War, Galveston experienced some prosperity. The postwar period saw increased immigration to Texas from the North and from other southern states; and Galveston, as the state's main port of entry, benefited appreciably. The population of the city increased from 7,307 in 1860 to 13,818 in 1870;[120] 152,780 bales of cotton passed through Galveston in 1866, compared with 495,237 in 1877.[121] This rapid increase in population and commerce transformed the city itself. As early as 1869, the city began to resurvey the old outlot system southeast of Broadway into regular blocks and lots to help accommodate a burgeoning population.[122] By 1900 this process was largely complete. Disastrous hurricanes, such as that of 1875, and fires, such as that of 1885, led to the complete rebuilding of the old parts of the city. Galveston not only increased in area, but took on a more substantial, modern, and densely urban look in the late nineteenth century.

Galveston demonstrates how closely history is tied to geography. Early entrepreneurs chose the site because of its valuable harbor and location at the entrance to Galveston Bay. Geography determined its subsequent history, as the city's beneficial position for trade and commerce continually weighed against the barrier island's instability. Quite early, for example, it became apparent that the island was prone to severe erosion.[123] The Gulf shore tended to retreat during the period 1836–1900, and in 1875 the entire eastern end of the island washed away.[124]

Perhaps even more serious was the rapid shoaling of the bars across the entrance to Galveston Harbor, which threatened to strangle the commerce of the city. By 1867 only nine feet of water lay over the bar. Between 1870 and 1890 the United States Army Corps of Engineers tried several unsuccessful techniques to deepen the harbor. Finally, in 1890, Congress passed a river and harbor improvements appropriation to build massive twin stone jetties at the entrance of Galveston harbor.[125] The corps completed the project in 1897, and by 1900 twenty-five feet of water were over the bar.[126] In addition, the south jetty's protective wall allowed the eastern end of Galveston island to reestablish itself.

None of these disasters or problems had the impact of the hurricane of 1900, which still ranks as the greatest natural disaster in this country. More than 6,000 died, and the majority of buildings and residences suffered considerable damage or were totally destroyed. To lessen destruction from future hurricanes, the city built a seventeen-foot seawall along the Gulf shore and raised the grade behind the seawall as much as fifteen feet.

It is the ephemeral quality of the city and its environs in the face of ongoing natural events that makes the study of old maps of Galveston especially rewarding for insight into the important currents of the city's history.

NOTES

1. *Carta da navigar per le Isole nouam tr[ouate] in le parte de l'India: dono Alberto Cantino al S. Duca Hercole*, Manuscript. Discovered in 1859. Original in the Biblioteca Estense, Modena. The chart was completed by the end of 1502. Henry Harrisse speculates that Vespucci had a hand in its construction, although not necessarily in the inclusion of the Florida-type landmass, which "doubtless originated with other maps, and proceeds from a type on which had been grafted data borrowed from fragmentary surveys brought by mariners of different nations . . . who must have visited that coast several times in the course of clandestine expeditions" (*The Discovery of North America, 1892*; reprint, Amsterdam: N. Israel, 1969), p. 425. For the Cantino chart, see pt. 3, "Cartographia Americana Vetustissima," no. 47, (hereafter cited as "Cartographia"). See also Seymour I. Schwartz and Ralph E. Ehrenberg, *The Mapping of America* (New York: Harry N. Abrams, 1980), pp. 20–23, pl. 2; Woodbury Lowery, *The Lowery Collection: A Descriptive List of Maps of the Spanish Possessions within the present limits of the United States, 1502–1820*, (Washington D.C.: U.S. Government Printing Office, 1912), no. 3; Leo Bagrow, *History of Cartography*, trans. D. L. Paisey (Cambridge: Harvard University Press, 1964), pp. 108–109, pl. G; Adrian Johnson, *America Explored: A Cartographical History of the Exploration of North America* (New York: Viking Press, 1974), p. 31, illus.; Lawrence C. Wroth, "The Early Cartography of the Pacific," *Papers of the Bibliographical Society of America* 38, no. 2 (1944): 87–268, map no. 21.

2. [Untitled, undated manuscript chart of the world], signed, "Opus Nocolay de Caneiro [or Caveiro] Januensis." Original in the Archives de Hydrographie de la Marine, Paris. Place-names and legends in Portuguese. This chart can be described as the earliest to show the Texas coast in any form. Near the southern terminus of the extended coast are the mouth and delta of a large river, which is also shown on Waldseemüller's 1513 map, where James P. Bryan and Walter K. Hanak implausibly identify it as the Rio Grande; see their *Texas in Maps* (Austin: University of Texas Press, [1961]), p. 4. The Caneiro chart is thought to have been constructed between 1502 and 1506. Harrisse, "Cartographia," no. 50 (dates it 1502–1504); Lowery, no. 2 (1502–1504); Schwartz and Ehrenberg, pp. 23–24 (probably 1504); John H. Parry, *The Discovery of South America* (New York: Taplinger Publishing Co., 1979), fig. 34 (1502–1506); Wroth, no. 20 (ca. 1502); Edward Luther Stevenson, *Marine World Chart of Nicolo de Caneiro Januensis, 1502 (circa): A Critical Study, with Facsimile . . .* (New York: [American Geographical Society?], 1907–1908).

3. *Universalis Cosmographia. . . .* Strasbourg, 1507. Despite the fact that no

copy was located until 1901, Harrisse ("Cartographia," no. 69) and other nineteenth-century scholars deduced its existence. See also John Boyd Thacher, *The Continent of America* (1896; reprint, Amsterdam: Meridian Publishing Co., 1971), chap. 6, "The Lost Map," pp. 149–57. This famous map gives two separate depictions of the New World, both of the Cantino type. The main map shows the extended western coast of the Florida-type landmass as separated from South America by a sea passage, in the manner of the Caneiro chart. But, in an inset, Waldseemüller shows the extended coast as joined to the South American landmass, thus for the first time showing the American continents as contiguous. Schwartz and Ehrenberg, pp. 24–28, pl. 4; Parry, figs. 35a, 35b; Wroth, no. 24; Bagrow, pl. LXI; Johnson, p. 15, illus.; Emerson D. Fite and Archibald Freeman, comps. and eds., *A Book of Old Maps Delineating American History from the Earliest Days down to the Close of the Revolutionary War,* (1926; reprint, New York: Arno Press, 1969), no. 8.

4. Harrisse, *Discovery*, p. 425. The identity of the Florida-type landmass shown on the Caneiro, Cantino, and other early maps has been in fact one of the most hotly debated questions in the study of American historical cartography. The most forceful and successful analysis of the issue is conducted by Harrisse, (ibid., pp. 77–92), who unflinchingly identifies the landmass as Florida. The arguments of those who think otherwise seem to us to be highly imaginative and dependent upon great leaps of faith. See, for example, George E. Nunn, *The Geographical Conceptions of Columbus,* (1924; reprint, New York: Octagon Books, 1973); and E. Roukema, "A Discovery of Yucatan prior to 1503," *Imago Mundi* 13 (1956): 30–37. Nunn (p. 93, n. 2) is kind enough to furnish us with the names of eight additional distinguished scholars who support the claim for Florida: F. A. de Varnhagen, J. G. Kohl, H. H. Bancroft, John Fiske, C. R. Markham, E. G. Bourne, E. L. Stevenson, and Woodbury Lowery. To this list may be added David O. True, "Some Early Maps Relating to Florida," *Imago Mundi,* 11 (1954): 73–84, who concludes that the early "maps clearly portray Florida from the year 1500 on, either intentionally or inadvertently." The opinions of the early explorers and geographers as to the identity of this landmass are irrelevant to the question at hand, which is whether its inclusion on early maps is the result of an actual discovery or whether it is a fantastic attempt to illustrate some early theory concerning the geography of then still unexplored regions to the north and west of the Antilles. If based on an actual sighting, the landmass in question obviously can only be Florida.

5. For example, the works of Peter Martyr, Bartolomé de las Casas, Francisco López de Gomara, Antonio de Herrera, and Gonzalo Fernández de Oviedo.

6. Louis-André Vigneras in *The Discovery of South America and the Andalusian Voyages* (Chicago: University of Chicago Press for the Newberry Library, 1976), pp. 23–31, gives a detailed account of the tribulations involved in obtaining a *capitulacion*. He notes that Hojeda waited ten months for approval before one of his South American voyages. Furthermore, a *capitulacion* obligated the bearer to forward from one-sixth to one-half of all resulting profit to the Crown.

7. It has been suggested that the Florida-type landmass and the extension to its west coast are based on discoveries made by Vespucci during his doubtful first voyage (1497–99). See, for example, Thacher, pp. 70–78.

8. We refer specifically, first, to Juan de la Cosa's manuscript world map, 1500 (original in the Naval Museum, Madrid). Fite and Freeman, no. 4; Harrisse, "Cartographia," no. 33; Wroth, no. 19; Schwartz and Ehrenberg, pl. 1; Johnson, p. 17, illus.; Tony Campbell, *Early Maps,* ed. Phyllis Benjamin (New York: Abbeville Press, 1981), pl. 3; Justin Winsor, ed., *Narrative and Critical History of America,* 8 vols. (1884–89; reprint, New York: AMS Press, n.d.), 3:8; George E. Nunn, *The Mappemonde of Juan de la Cosa* (Jenkintown, Pa.: George H. Beans Library, 1934). Second, we refer to the Bartholomew Columbus (or Alessandro Zorsi) manuscript maplets, 1503 or later (originals in the Biblioteca Nazionale, Florence); Fite and Freeman, no. 5; [Nils] A. E. Nordenskiöld, *Periplus: An Essay on the Early History of Charts and Sailing-Directions,* trans. Francis A. Bather (New York: Burt Franklin and Co., [1967]), pp. 167–69; George E. Nunn, "The Three Maplets Attributed to Bartholomew Columbus," *Imago Mundi,* 9 (1952): 12–22; Franz R. von Wieser, "Die Karte des Bartolomeo Colombo über die vierte Reise des Admirals," *Ergänzungsband* 4 (Vienna: Universität, Institute für österreichische Gerschichtsforschung, Mitteil, 1893): 488–98; Third, we refer to the printed map inserted in a later issue of the first edition of the works of Peter Martyr, published in Seville in 1511. Lowery, no. 6; Harrisse, "Cartographia," no. 96; Winsor, *America* 2:109–12, 224; [Nils] A. E. Nordenskiöld, *Facsimile-atlas to the early history of cartography,* trans. Johan Adolf Ekelöf and Clements R. Markhan (1889; reprint, New York: Dover Publications, 1973), p. 67, fig. 38; [Duque de Alba et. al., eds.], *Mapas españoles de América, siglos XV–XVII* (Madrid, 1951), pl. V; *The World Encompassed, an Exhibition of the History of Maps . . .* (Baltimore: Trustees of the Walters Art Gallery, 1952), no. 52, pl. XVII; ("the first printed Spanish map of America. It is also one of the earliest maps printed in Spain"). The Columbus-Zorsi maplets are the most puzzling. Cuba is absent, and there is a mainland labeled "Asia" to the west of Jamaica that bears some resemblance to the Florida-type landmass on the Cantino and Caneiro charts and their successors.

9. Juan de Grijalva explored the Mexican coast as far north as the vicinity of the Río Panuco in 1518. See Samuel Eliot Morison, *The European Discovery of America,* 2 vols. (New York; Oxford University Press, 1971–74), 1:514; Winsor, *America* 2:203; Harrisse, *Discovery,* p. 162. Pensacola is generally accepted as the bay visited by Diego Miruelo in 1516. See Morison, *European Discovery,* 1:515; Harrisse, *Discovery,* p. 724; Winsor, *America,* 2:236.

10. [Untitled, undated manuscript sketch map of the Gulf of Mexico, 1519.] Original in the Archivo General de Indias, Seville. Reproduced in Bryan and Hanak, pl. 2; Jean Delanglez, *El Río del Espíritu Santo,* ed. Thomas J. McMahon, Monograph Series, no. 21 (New York: U.S. Catholic Historical Society, 1945), pp. 12–14, pl. 1; Winsor, *America,* 2:218; Schwartz and Ehrenberg, p. 36, pl. 10. See Harrisse, "Cartographia," no. 123; Lowery, no. 15. This is the first map of the Gulf of Mexico.

11. After 1685, the newly discovered, but usually incorrectly located, Mississippi

would overshadow the bay and river of Espíritu Santo. Guillaume de L'Isle abolished them from the second issue of his famous map of North America, 1700, and they ceased to appear except on the most inferior maps.

12. Harrisse, *Discovery*, p. 219; Winsor, *America* 2:219; Morison, *European Discovery*, 1:517.

13. Walter B. Scaife, *America: Its geographical history, 1492–1892* . . . (1892; reprint, New York: AMS Press, n.d.), pp. 139–76; William Edward Dunn, *Spanish and French Rivalry in the Gulf Region of the United States, 1678–1702*, (1917; reprint, New York: Arno Press, n.d.), p. 78; Peter Joseph Hamilton, "Was Mobile Bay the Bay of Spiritu Santo?" *Transactions of the Alabama Historical Society*, 4 (1901): 73–93.

14. Delanglez, *Espíritu Santo* p. 132; Marc de Villiers du Terrage, *L'Expédition de Cavelier de La Salle dans le Golfe du Mexique (1684–1687)* (Paris: A. Maisonneuve, 1931), p. 54.

15. Piñeda's sketch is the only meaningful evidence for the identity, form, or location of the river that is there labeled "Rio de Espiritu Santo." Piñeda left no firsthand written account (see Delanglez, Espíritu Santo, p. 12), although the map, when discovered, accompanied a transcript of "the letters patent granted to Francisco de Garay in 1521" (Harrisse, *Discovery*, p. 152). These letters patent contained a short summary of the discoveries and events of the expedition, including a description of a "large and mighty river," which is often assumed to be the Río del Espíritu Santo of Piñeda's sketch, and also the Mississippi. But nowhere in the description is either "Espíritu Santo" or any other name used in connection with this river, and Delanglez (Espíritu Santo, pp. 12–14) and Timothy Severin (*Exploreres of the Mississippi* [New York: Alfred A. Knopf, 1968], p. 11) argue forcibly that the description does not fit that of the Mississippi. Furthermore, Harrisse (*Discovery*, p. 153 n. 20) argues that the Piñeda sketch was not originally affixed to the letters patent as they bear the title "Real Cedula." The testimony of later explorers with regard to the identity of the Río del Espíritu Santo is worthless, as they were prone to apply Piñeda's nomenclature, which they found in earlier texts and on copies of the *Padrón* and other maps, indiscriminately to any large river they encountered.

16. See Harrisse, *Discovery*, pp. 263–68.

17. [Untitled, undated anonymous manuscript map, ca. 1523], in Harrisse, "Cartographia," no. 148 ("The legends and names are in Spanish and Latin, with a few in the Portuguese language"); Lowery, no. 20.

18. [Untitled map of the Gulf of Mexico.] Printed on one sheet with a plan of Mexico City presumed to be based on that given to Cortés by Montezuma. From the first Latin edition of the Second Letter of Cortés (1520), Nuremberg, 1524. Harrisse, "Cartographia," no. 133; Winsor, *America* 2:404; Lowery, no. 21; Delanglez, *Espíritu Santo*, p. 14; Schwartz and Ehrenberg, p. 36, pl. 11; Parry, fig. 62; *The World Encompassed*, no. 232, pl. XLVIII; *[Catalogue of] The Celebrated Collection of Americana Formed by the Late Thomas Winthrop Streeter . . .*, 7 vols. (New York: Parke-Bernet Galleries, 1966–69) 1:190 (hereafter cited as *Streeter Sale*).

19. Features given along the northwest part of the Gulf Coast for the Turin map

[east to west]: "Rio del Espiritu Santo" flowing into an unnamed bay, "pa. de arricife," the mouth of an unnamed river, "Rio de la Palma," "Rio de montañas altas," an unnamed river, "prouinica amichel," "Laotan," "Rio Panuco," "Tamaho provincia." For the Cortés map [east to west]: "Rio del Spiritu Santo" flowing into an unnamed bay, "Po. de Arrecifos," the mouths of two unnamed rivers, "R. de Arboledas," "R. la Palma," Tamacho puincia," "Colaoton," "Rio Panu," "Provincia Amichel."

20. A possible source for the Texas nomenclature on the 1524 Cortés map and the Turin map is the now-lost map of Cristóbal de Tapia, ca. 1522 (Harrisse, "Cartographia," no. 139). The place-names may also derive from the 1520 Cortés manuscript itself: although Cortés never explored the Texas coast at the Río Panuco, his agents encountered survivors of the Piñeda expedition, who may have supplied these names.

21. [Untitled, undated anonymous manuscript map of the world.] Original in the Medici Library, Florence. In Spanish, but including Portuguese names. There are twelve place-names along the northwest part of the Gulf Coast (east to west): "mar peqna," "R. de Spu. Sonto," "Cabo Deaus," "R. de Palmas," "palmar," "R. de montanas"(?), "Chamozuo," "R. Hermoso," "Arenas," "R. de Sn. Benito," "Canato," "Mararo," "Rio de panulo [Panuco]." The names and positions of the "R. de Palmas" and "R. de montanas" on the Salviati map resemble those on the Turin map, and Harrisse ("Cartographia," no. 163) notes another similarity between the two: "the configuration of the South American continent [on the Salviati map] recall those of the Turin map." The "R. hermozo" and "R. de Sn. Benito" are missing on the Turin map; they appear in approximately the same location on the earliest of the post-1526 *Padrón*-type maps, the anonymous Weimar map of 1527. For Salviati map, see Harrisse, "Cartographia," no. 163 (the "Laurentiana map"); Lowery, no. 24; Bargow, pl. K; Edward Luther Stevenson, *Maps Illustrating Early Exploration and Discovery in America 1502–30 . . .* (New Brunswick, N.J.: E. L. Stevenson, 1903–[1906]), no. 7.

22. "Carta Universel . . . ," manuscript. Bears legend [in Spanish]: "Made by a cosmographer of his majesty, in the year 1527, at Seville." The map gives the following place-names along the northwest part of the Gulf Coast [east to west]: "Mar pequeña," "C. de+," "R. del Oro," "R. scondido," "la madalena," "R. hermosso," "R. de S. Benito," "Ys. de Lobos," "Villa Rica" [Vera Cruz, Mexico]. The map follows the Salviati map (or its prototype) in the use of the names "Hermosso," "San Benito," and "Mar Pequeña." Harrisse, "Cartographia," no. 177; Lowery, nos. 26, 27; Bagrow, pl. LXIV; Johann Georg Kohl, *Die Beiden ältesten General-Karton von Amerika* (Weimar: Geographisches Institut, 1860), no. 1.

23. Alonso de Santa Cruz gives the name "Medano de Madalena" on his 1536 map and "R. de la Madalena" on his 1541 map (See Duque de Alba et al., *Mapas españoles*, pls. VIII, IX). The latter is the earliest name used to designate a Texas river. None of Santa Cruz's maps show a Rio Escondido, however (see Delanglez, *Espíritu Santo*, p. 74, for comments on this point). The rivers to which these names were originally applied are not now identifiable. La Salle associated the Mississippi

with the "Escondido of the Spaniards" (ibid., pp. 111, 137). At least once, on J. B. Nicolosi's 1660 map of North America, the name "Escondido" is used for the Rio Grande (see note 44). That map was revised in 1670, and the name "R. de Norte" replaced "Escondido." For the 1660 map, see Lowery, no. 151a; Carl I. Wheat, *Mapping the Transmississippi West*, 6 vols. (San Francisco: Institute of Historical Cartography, 1957–63), no. 53.

24. By Bagrow (pl. LXIV), for example. See also Lowery, nos. 26, 27. Harrisse ("Cartographia," no. 177) denied the authorship of Ribero, and Kohl (no. 1) ascribed the map to Ferdinand Columbus.

25. "Carta Universel . . . ," manuscript. Signed "Diego Ribero Cosmographo de Su Magestad: Año de 1529." Gives the following place-names along the northwest part of the Gulf Coast (east to west): "mar peqna," "ostial," "R. del espu. sto.," "c. sirro," "trra. de gigates," "R. del Oro," "playa baxa," "anegadas," "R. escondido," "mal abrigo," "c. bravo," "R. de palmas" (as given in Duque de Alba et al., *Mapas españoles*, pl. VI). See Harrisse, "Cartographia," no. 184; Lowery, no. 31; Winsor, *America* 2:221; Delanglez, *Espíritu Santo*, pp. 20–23, pl. 2; Fite and Freeman, no. 14; Parry, fig. 14; Wroth, no. 40; Edward Luther Stevenson, *Early Spanish Cartography of the New World with Special Reference to the Wolfenbüttel-Spanish Map and the Work of Diego Ribero* [Worcester, Mass.?]: N.p., [1909?].

26. Cape Bravo appears on many of Santa Cruz's maps and is altered, for the first time, to Rio Bravo on his 1545 map (Duque de Alba et al., *Mapas españoles*, pl. XI). The earliest occurrence of the "C. Bravo" on a printed map is probably on Diego Gutíerrez's 1562 map (see note 31); of "R. Bravo," on Gabriel Tatton's 1600 map (see note 36).

27. Frederick W. Hodge and Theodore H. Lewis, eds, *Spanish Explorers in the Southern United States, 1528–1543* . . . (1907; reprint, New York: Barnes & Noble, 1977), p. 14n.

28. *[Mapa del Golfo y costa de la Nueva España]*, unsigned, undated manuscript. Original in the Archivo General de Indias, Seville. Gives the following place-names between the Baya del Espíritu Santo-Mar Pequeña and the "R. de Palmas" [east to west]: "R. del espíritu Santo," "C. de reuz"(?), "c. desierto," "R. de motanas," "R del Oro," "c desierto," "podelcopes"(?), "R de la madalena," "R de Palmas." Immediately below the "R. de Palmas" is a Cape Bravo ("C. Bravo").

William P. Cumming, *The Southeast in Early Maps* . . . (Princeton, N.J.: Princeton University Press, 1958) no. 1, pl. 5: "the only extant contemporary map to illustrate the De Soto expedition (1539–43). . . . most of the coastal names are found on earlier or contemporary Spanish world maps. . . . Indian names such as Ays and Guasco are places in Texas through which Moscoso and the remnants of the expedition passed on their march to the Rio Grande after the death of De Soto on May 21, 1542." See also Bryan and Hanak, pl. 3; Lowery, no. 39; Delanglez, *Espíritu Santo*, pp. 27–28, 62; Harrisse, *Discovery*, pp. 643–44, pl. XXIII; Schwartz and Ehrenberg, p. 58, pl. 27; Duque de Alba et al., *Mapas españoles*, pl. IX.

29. See no. 12, this catalog.

30. Lowery, no. 70: "This map follows very closely the description of Florida

given by Oviedo . . . based [in turn] upon a map of Alonso de Chaves. . . . Oviedo's history was written from 1535 to 1555."

31. *Americae sive quartae orbis partis nova et exactissima descriptio,* Diego Gutiérrez. Engraved by Hieronymus Cock, 1562. Cumming, *Southeast,* no. 2, pl. 6: "the largest and most detailed map of the New World to be engraved and published up to the time of its appearance." It gives the following place-names between the Mar Pequeña and the Rio de palmas (east to west): "R. de Spirito Lant"(?), "Cabo de Crux," "c. de zirto," "R. de monta[nas](?)," "R. de pescadores," "Costa Brava," "R. escondido," "La Madalena," "C. Bravo," "c. darboledas," "R. Solo," "Playa del garda." See also Delanglez, *Espíritu Santo,* pp. 41–43; Bagrow, pl. LXIX; Schwartz and Ehrenberg, pl. 29; *The World Encompassed,* no. 229.

32. *Nova et aucta orbis terre descriptio,* Gerard Mercator. Duisburg, 1569. The most famous and influential printed world map of the sixteenth century. It gives the following names between the "Baia de Culata" and the "rio de palmas" (east to west): "r. del espiritu santo," "C. de Cuerto"(?), "Susatas"(?),"Rio de gigantos," "costa de piscatores," "rio de Piscadores," "Malabrigo," "c. bravo," "Plaia," "Arboledas," "Montanas." Schwartz and Ehrenberg, p. 70, pl. 31; Fite and Freeman, no. 22; Delanglez, *Espíritu Santo,* pp. 39–43; Bagrow, pp. 118–19, pl. LXX; *The World Encompassed,* no. 132, pl. XVI; Cumming, *Southeast,* pl. 7.

33. See no. 12, this catalog.

34. Printed world map, Petrus Plancius. Amsterdam, 1592. (Place-names taken from the late issue entitled "Descrittione Universale Della Terra Con L'Uso Del Navigare, Nuovame. Accresciuta," Arnoldo di Arnoldi, Siena, 1600.) The first large world map published in Holland. Delanglez, *Espíritu Santo,* pp. 77–78: "The Southern United States on Plancius' world map of 1592 [is] nothing else than the Chaves [1584 Ortelius] map of Florida superimposed on the southeast section of Mercator's planisphere of 1569." For the Texas coast, however, there are a few features that do not appear on either the Ortelius-Chaves or the Mercator maps—a Costa de Arboledos, for example. It gives the following place-names between the "Mar Pequeno" and the "r. del palmas" [east to west]: "R. d. Spirito Sto." "C. de Cruz," "C. Desierto," "montanas," "r. del oro," "C[os]ta de Arboledos," "R. ____dbo"(?), "R. de la Mahalena," "Costa Bara," "Palmar r.," "Plaias," "Almeria," "montannas."

35. *Florida et Apalache.* From Cornelis Wytfliet's *Descriptionis Ptolemaicae augmentum* . . . , Louvain, 1597. Gives the following place-names between the "Mar Pequeño" and the R. de Palmas (east to west): "R. de S. Spirito," "C. de Cruz," "C. desierto," "R. de Loro," "R. de Gigantes," "R. de piscatores," "Terra Baxo," "Rio Escondido," "Medanos de la Magdale." Cumming, *Southeast,* no. 18, pl. 17; Lowery, no. 83; Delanglez, *Espíritu Santo,* pp. 76, 78.

36. *Nova et rece Terrarum et regnorum Californiae, novae Hispaniae, Mexicanae, et Peruviae . . . delineatio,* Gabriel Tatton. 1600 [city of publication unknown]. Between the "Mar pequonus" and the "R. de Pabnos" (Palmas) are the following place-names (east to west): "R. de Spiritus Santo," "C. de Cruz," "C. Desirto," "C. de montanhas," "R. ett Oro," "R. de Pescadores," "terra de baxos,"

25

"brava costa," "Baixa Costa," "R. Escondido," "dalena de la mag medanos," "lamalanca," "R. Bravo," "Costa de Pescadores," "Plaia et gada." Cumming, *Southeast*, no. 25, pl. 19. See Lowery, nos. 86, 103; *The World Encompassed*, no. 235, pl. LI (1616 issue).

37. *Florida, et Regiones vicinae*. From Johannes de Laet's *Nieuwe Wereldt . . .* , Leiden, 1626. The map gives no place-names for the northwest part of the Gulf, and the scale is so ambiguous that "Bahia de Spiritu Santo" could represent either Mobile or Galveston Bay. The map is an early example showing a new form for the watershed of the bay. Although Piñeda had shown only the mighty Espíritu Santo flowing into it, De Laet indicates six unnamed rivers, most of equal magnitude. A "Rio del Spiritu Santo" enters the Gulf on the Florida coast.

38. *America Septentrionalis*, Jan Jansson. Amsterdam, [1636]. The first printed Dutch map of North America. Like De Laet, Jansson shows four large and two small rivers flowing into the "Baya d Sp Santo"; one of the small rivers bears the name "Rio de Spiritu Santo." Between the bay and the "R. de Palmas" are the following place-names (east to west): "C. de Cruz," "R. de Montanhas," "R. de Lazo," "Costa Baixa," "R. Buelo," "Plaia," "R. la Madalena," "C. Blanco," "Costa de Arboleda," "R. Solo," "R. Bravo," "Costa de Pescadores." John B. Leighly, *California as an Island* (San Francisco: Book Club of California, 1972), no. 13, pl. V.

39. *Carta particolare della Baia de Messico. . .* , Sir Robert Dudley. From the *Arcano del mare*, Florence, 1646. This is the first printed sea chart of the Gulf of Mexico. Dudley includes well over forty place-names for the region. Although many of these names do not appear on any of the other maps discussed here, all the familiar names are present, and the map cannot be viewed except as within current cartographic tradition. Bryan and Hanak, pl. 5. See John Carter and Percy H. Muir, comps. and eds., *Printing and the Mind of Man* (London: Cassell & Co., 1967), no. 134, for the *Arcano del mare*.

40. *Le Nouveau Mexique, et la Floride . . .* , N. Sanson d'Abbeville. Paris, 1656. Sanson also shows two small and four large rivers flowing into "Mar Pequeno" and "Bahia del Spiritu Santo," three of which are named "R. del Spiritu Santo," "Mattas de Salvador," and R. de Canaveral," respectively. Between the bay and the "R. de Palmas" are the following names (east to west): "C. de Cruz," "C. de Suerta," "R. de Montanhas," "R. Laso," "R. de Pescadores," "R. de Oro," "C. d'Arboledo," "R. Bravo," "C. Baixo," "R. Suelo," "R. de la Magdalena," "Costa deserta," "Escondido R.," "C. Blanco," "R. Solo," "R. Bravo," "Costa de Pescadores." Cumming, *Southeast*, no. 49, pl. 31.

41. See no. 55, this catalog.

42. Delanglez, (*Espíritu Santo*, p. 3) demonstrates how Mercator incorporated into his world map of 1569 mistakes that he found in translations of Lopez de Gomara. In a different vein, William F. Ganong (*Crucial Maps in the Early Cartography and Place-Nomenclature of the Atlantic Coast of Canada*, Royal Society of Canada, Special Publications, no. 7 [Toronto: University of Toronto Press, 1964], p. 8) discusses how the great Italian cartographer Giacomo Gastaldi's printed 1548 map of the northeast United States and Canada represents the attempt to lay down

upon an older topography the results of the Verrazano and Cartier voyages from their reports alone, as Gastaldi did not have access to their maps.

43. Delanglez (*Espíritu Santo,* pp. 81–86) discusses the sources for De Laet's geography, which he holds was based primarily on the "romantic and inaccurate narrative of Garcilaso de la Vega" published in part nine of Antonio de Herrera y Tordesillas, *Historia general de los hechos de los castellanos en las islas i tierra firme del mar oceano . . . ,* 4 vols. (Madrid: En la Emplenta [*sic*; Imprenta] Real, 1601–15. See also Winsor, *America* 2:67. But the six rivers are "purely imaginary. . . . There is absolutely no basis either in Herrera or in any of the accounts of the De Soto expedition for this fanciful hydrography."

44. *Mexicum,* G. B. Nicolosi. Rome, 1660. Earlier cartographers had usually associated the upper course of the Rio Grande (the Rio del Norte of New Mexico) with the Rio Colorado, and their maps showed the Rio Grande emptying into the Gulf of California (see, for example, the maps of Nicolas Sanson.) Nicolosi shows the Rio Grande, which he identifies as the Escondido, emptying into the Gulf of Mexico. In 1670, the map was reissued with the name "Escondido" replaced by "R. del Norte." Wheat, *Transmississippi West,* no. 53; Lowery, no. 151a.

45. *America Septentrionale,* V. M. Coronelli. Venice, 1688. Thomas Streeter (*Streeter Sale,* vol. 1, no. 44) incorrectly states that Coronelli's map is "perhaps the first to show the Rio Bravo emptying into the Gulf of Mexico." Wheat, *Transmississippi West,* no. 70 (left-hand section reproduced opposite 1:48); Leighly, no. 88.

46. *Amerique Septentrionale. . . .* "Par le Sr. Sanson . . . Hubert Jaillot [Paris, 1674]." Delanglez (*Espíritu Santo,* pp. 92–95, pl. 8) considers it the "cartographical expression of Garcilaso de la Vega's text as adapted by Richelet."

47. See Dunn, p. 67, for the visit of Captain James Dominguez de Mendoza to the junction of the Rio Conchos and the Rio Grande in 1686. The Rio Conchos is clearly marked on De L'Isle's 1718 map as a tributary of the Rio Grande.

48. Delanglez (*Espíritu Santo,* pp. 96–103) emphasizes the role that all the maps of the Sanson family had in forming the geographical conceptions of the French explorers of the period, and he argues forcibly that La Salle had a copy of the 1674 map during his descent of the Mississippi in 1682.

49. Dunn, p. 105. The Spanish assumed that this bay was the location of La Salle's colony, and indeed, Alonso de León bestowed the name on Matagorda Bay in 1689, when he discovered that bay to be the colony's site.

50. Ibid., p. 58.

51. There survive a number of Spanish manuscript maps prepared during the years 1686 to 1700 that show Texas or the United States Gulf Coast. While many of them do show topographical features that had previously been unrecorded, a comparsion of these maps with substantially more numerous non-Spanish manuscript and printed maps of these years reveals that their cartographers as a whole had little facility for the science of mapmaking and that the maps had absolutely no effect on contemporary or subsequent geographical thought. Generally, the more specific of these maps—those focusing on particular geographical features such as Pensacola Bay or Matagorda Bay—are more worthwhile than those of a general na-

ture. The most important of these maps are those prepared by Echaragay, Sigüenza y Góngora, and Ronquillo.

The geographical conceptions of Martin de Echaragay are preserved on a single schematic, and largely speculative, map of North America, 1686 (manuscript. Original in the Archivo General de Indias, Seville. Reproduced in Dunn, p. 44. See also Lowery, no. 185). The map was prepared by Echaragay, at the request of the Spanish government, to illustrate the explorations and discoveries of La Salle. That the government would rely on such a faulty map, by an adventurer who never visited most of the Gulf Coast, is a good indication of the poor state of geographical knowledge in Spain.

The maps usually attributed to Pedro de Ronquillo were in actuality only tracings of French maps that that illustrious diplomat found in London (see Dunn, p. 157). The true author of Ronquillo's maps was the French engineer Minet (See Lowery, no. 183). Compare, for example, Ronquillo's "Planto del Lago donde dejaron à Mr. La Salle 20 Enero 1687" (manuscript, original in the Archivo General de Indias, Seville, reproduced in Dunn, p. 33; see also Lowery, no. 187) with Minet's "Entrée du lac où on a laissé M. de la Salle" (manuscript, n.d., but ca. 1685, original in the Dépôt de la Marine, Service Hydrographique, Paris). See Lowery, no. 183; Émile Lauvrière, *Histoire de la Louisiane française, 1673–1939*, Romance Language Series, no. 3 (Baton Rouge, La.: Louisiana State University Press, 1940). p. 40, illus. Lowery does not seem to be aware of the relationship between the maps of Minet and Ronquillo. Dunn devotes the third chapter of his book ("Spanish Diplomacy in England, 1685") to this crucial period in Ronquillo's career.

Carlos de Sigüenza y Góngora, who explored the Gulf Coast in 1693 with Admiral Pez, constructed several maps that relate to the United States Gulf Coast. Sigüenza was instructed on this occasion to construct a map of the coastline of the Gulf (see Dunn, p. 159; Delanglez, *Espíritu Santo*, pp. 130–31). In the collection of the Real Academia de la Historia in Madrid (Coleccion Boturini, vol. 8) there is a detailed manuscript map of New Spain that shows the Gulf Coast as far east as Pensacola and bears the name "Dn. Carlos Sigüenza y Góngora" ("Descripcion de esta Parte America Septentrional"; Duque de Alba et al., *Mapas españoles*, pl. LXXV). Robert Weddle is of the opinion that this map must date earlier than the Pez-Sigüenza expedition of 1693 (private correspondence with author); the map is dated 1641, which the editors of *Mapas españoles* take to be in error for 1691. See also the sketch map of the Gulf Coast by Sigüenza that is preserved in the Archivo General de Indias and is reproduced in Dunn (p. 163).

The Real Academia manuscript gives six place-names along the United States Gulf Coast (east to west): "Panzacola," "Lago de Pez," "Ro de la Palisada," "Ba. de Espiritu Sto.," "Lago de Sn. Bernardo," "Rio Bravo." The two most remarkable features of this geography are the presence of the Mississippi ("Ro de la Palisada") in an approximately correct position and the placement of a Bay of Espíritu Santo midway between Matagorda Bay (San Bernardo) and the mouth of the Mississippi. If Sigüenza's Espíritu Santo is to be associated with any existing Gulf Coast bay, it must be either Galveston Bay, Sabine Lake, or Calcasieu Lake. The sketch map does not show Espíritu Santo at all but does locate Mobile Bay, which is absent from the Real Academia manuscript. Neither Dunn (p. 159), Irving A. Leonard (*Spanish Approach to Pensacola, 1689–93* [1939; reprint, (New York: Arni Press, 1967], p. 191, n. 55), nor Delanglez (*Espíritu Santo*, p. 131) was aware of the existence of the Real Academia manuscript. In the case of Delanglez, this is indeed unfortunate, for this map supports his theories with regard to the identity of Espíritu Santo better than any other early map of which we are aware. See Irving A. Leonard, *Don Carlos de Sigüenza y Góngora, a Mexican Savant of the Seventeenth Century*, University of California Publications in History, vol. 18 (Berkeley: University of California Press, 1929); Dunn, pp. 146–69. Sigüenza's excellent chart of Pensacola Bay, 1693, is reproduced in Dunn (p. 160) and in William P. Cumming, *The Exploration of North America, 1630–1776*, (New York: G. P. Putnam's sons, 1974), fig. 228.

Sigüenza also drew a good map of south Texas that shows Alonso de León's route to Matagorda Bay in 1689 ("Mapa del Camino que el año de 1689 hizo el Gobernador Alonso de Leon desde Cuahuila hasta haller cerca del Lago de San Bernardo . . . , Siguenza, 1689," manuscript, original in the Archivo General de Indias, Seville). See Delanglez, *Espíritu Santo*, p. 131, n. 29. Neither Bryan and Hanak (fig. 6) nor Lowery (no. 193) attributes this map to Sigüenza, although his name is clearly inscribed at the lower center. None of these Spanish maps exerted any influence on geographical theorists or cartographic practice.

52. Interesting insights into the geographical ignorance of Spanish officials are provided by Dunn (p. 154, n. 9; p. 155, n. 12; p. 157, n. 13). Evidently it was common practice in Madrid during the early 1690s to make policy based on the assumption that the Bahía del Espíritu Santo lay to the west of the Mississippi, probably as a result of de León's use of that name for Matagorda Bay. Colonial officials, on the other hand, consistently used the name "Bahía del Espíritu Santo" for Mobile Bay, which is to the east of the Mississippi. This made the comprehension of colonial reports potentially difficult for, say, the Junta de Guerra, and vice versa. For example, how does one interpret the Junta's 1692 command to the viceroy of New Spain, to "make a detailed examination of Pensacola Bay, and to explore the Gulf region westward as far as 'Espíritu Santo'" (Ibid., p. 157)?

53. Echaragay's map (see note 51), for example, shows the Mississippi discharging into a "Baya del Esptu Sto." An elaborate system of large rivers connects the bay with the Great Lakes.

54. In the late seventeenth century, Paris, Amsterdam, and Italy, in that order, were the primary centers for both the scientific study of geography and commercial map publishing. Amsterdam was still the largest single center of map publishing, but the center of gravity of geography as an intellectual discipline had shifted to Paris, which would reach its greatest importance in the field during the first half of the eighteenth century. Italy, which had been preeminent in the field of cartography during the early and midsixteenth century, was in relative decline. After the Seven Years' War (1756–63), London replaced Paris as the capital of cartography.

The quantity and quality of a nation's cartographic output are determined by numerous factors. The crucial elements seem to be a government or citizenry actively engaged in overseas commerce, exploration, or conquest, and a relatively well-developed economic and intellectual climate. (For example, the economic advances in postmedieval Europe, which were largely the result of the expansion of international commerce, exploration, and conquest, were undertaken in the hope of establishing a monopoly, or at least primacy, in overseas commerce. The economic advances encouraged the development of freely operating intellectual disciplines, which are generally related to economic prosperity, largely through the resulting expansion in the scale and breadth of urban life.) Not all nations that have nurtured noteworthy schools of commercial cartography have exhibited all these characteristics, but when a nation has ascended to a leading position simultaneously in each, as did France in the late seventeenth century, then its position as a leading cartographic center seems to have been assured.

55. This generalization is true even with regard to place-names of Spanish origin. For example, from about 1716, French cartographers were correctly using the current Spanish nomenclature for the rivers of south Texas. These names had been used by the Spanish since 1689 (see Dunn, p. 102), but it was only after the visits of the French adventurer St. Denis that the locations and names of these rivers were introduced to the geographers of Europe. It is interesting to note that all of the early French maps that show and name accurately the south Texas rivers also show the route of St. Denis. Three examples of these maps are Le Maire's "Carte nouvelle de la Louisiane . . . ," 1716 (manuscript, original in the Bibliothèque Nationale, Paris, reproduced in Lauvrière, p. 143; Raymond Thomassy, *Cartographie de la Louisiane* [New Orleans: R. Thomassy, 1859], p. 210 [separately published extract from *Géologie pratique de la Louisiane*, pp. 205–26]. See Wheat, *Transmississippi West* 1:65; Cumming, *Southeast*, no. 163); Vermale's "Carte Générale de la Louisiane . . . ," 1717 (manuscript, original in the Archives de Hydrographie de la Marine, Paris, reproduced in Wheat, *Transmississippi West*, no. 98. See Thomassy, p. 210; Cumming, *Southeast*, no. 165); and De L'Isle's printed *Carte de la Louisiane . . . ,* 1718 (see no. 108, this catalog).

56. Delanglez reviews La Salle's geographical conceptions in *Espíritu Santo,* pp. 102–105.

57. See Jean Delanglez, "Franquelin, Mapmaker," *Mid-America* 25 (1943): 29–74. See also Winsor, *America,* 4:226–29; Cumming, *North America,* fig. 53; Lowery, nos. 189, 190, and 203; Thomassy, p. 207; Schwartz and Ehrenberg, p. 131, pl. 74; Wheat, *Transmississippi West,* nos. 69, 71, and 176.

58. See note 45.

59. Evidently some skepticism about Franquelin's geography began to be voiced soon after its first appearance. Delanglez (*Espíritu Santo,* pp. 135–36) quotes a letter from Claude de L'Isle to Cassini, published in 1701: "It was a much debated question in the 1680s among those interested [in geography] to know exactly where the Mississippi emptied into the sea."

60. As with the earlier exploits of La Salle, the explorations and discoveries of Iberville are well documented. The most important single source is Pierre Margry,

Découvertes et établissements des Français dans l'ouest et dans le sud le l'Amérique Septentrionale (1614–1754) . . . , 6 vols. (Paris: D. Jouaust, 1876–86). See Benjamin F. French, ed., *Historical collections of Louisiana and Florida . . . ,* new ser. (New York: J. Sabin & Sons, 1869), pp. 19–31, for Iberville's "Narrative of Louisiana and Florida."

61. *L'Amerique Septentrionale.* G. de L'Isle, "Rue des Canettes," Paris, 1700. Until quite recently, this second state was assumed to be the original printing of the map; see Ronald V. Tooley, *French Mapping of the Americas,* Map Collectors' Series, no. 33 (London: Map Collectors' Circle, 1967), no. 28, pl. IX (second state); Wheat, *Transmississippi West,* no. 84. In the summer of 1981, a previously unknown and earlier state exhibiting a Franquelin-type geography was discovered (see Seymour I. Schwartz and Henry Taliaferro, "A Newly Discovered First State of a Foundation Map, *L'Amerique Septentrionale,*" *Map Collector,* no. 26 [March, 1984]: 2–6.) For a late issue of the map, see no. 93, this catalog.

62. Louis Hennepin had previously located the river's mouth correctly, but without delta, on his *Carte de la Nouvelle France et la Louisiane,* from *Description de la Louisiane,* Paris, 1683. That map is generally regarded to have been based on speculation rather than exploration. Hennepin was an associate of La Salle's who claimed that he followed the Mississippi to its mouth in 1683, and on his map he indicates the river's lower course by a broken line that terminates near the actual site of the river's mouth. Most scholars discount Hennepin's claims. See Thomas D. Clark, ed., *Travels in the Old South,* 3 vols. American Exploration and Travel, no. 19 (Norman: University of Oklahoma Press, 1956–59), vol. 1, no. 98; Frank K. Walter and Virginia Doneghy, *Jesuit Relations, and Other Americana in the Library of James F. Bell: A Catalogue* (Minneapolis: University of Minnesota Press, [1950]), p. 255; Wheat, *Transmississippi West,* no. 62; Joseph Sabin, Wilberforce Eames, and R. W. G. Vail, *Bibliotheca Americana,* 29 vols. (1868–1936; reprint, 29 vols. in 2, Metuchen, N.J.: Scarecrow Press, 1966), no. 31347; Brown University, John Carter Brown Library, *Bibliotheca Americana,* 7 vols. (1919–31, 1973; reprint, Millwood, N.Y.: Kraus Reprint Corp., 1975) 7:117; Fite and Freeman, no. 45; *Streeter Sale,* vol. 1, no. 102, illus., p. 93; Schwartz and Ehrenberg, p. 130, pl. 73; Delanglez, *Espíritu Santo,* p. 123; Winsor, *America,* 4:249; Louis C. Karpinski, *Maps of Famous Cartographers Depicting North America,* 2d ed. (1931; reprint, Amsterdam: Meridian Publishing Co., 1977), p. 100, pl. VI.

63. See no. 108, this catalog. Here De L'Isle has supplemented his earlier data with information he found on the manuscripts of Le Maire (1716) and Vermale (1717). See note 55.

64. The Spaniard Alonso de León named Matagorda Bay "Bahía del Espíritu Santo" in 1689. He had been instructed to discover the site of La Salle's fort, which was believed to be the Bahía del Espíritu Santo. It was logical that he should apply the name to the site along this unknown coast, where he found the fort's remains. The name was not commonly used by the French, who preferred "Baye St. Louis." By the eighteenth century, the name "Baye St. Bernard" was most commonly used for Matagorda Bay. See Delanglez (*Espíritu Santo,* pp. 123–25; Dunn, pp. 77, 85.

65. In 1691, Domingo Teran de los Rios, the first provincial governor of Texas, forged the Camino Real or old San Antonio Road from Monclova, Mexico, to the missions in east Texas (Walter Prescott Webb and H. Bailey Carroll, eds., *The Handbook of Texas*, 3 vols. [Austin: Texas State Historical Association, 1952–76], 2:309). Between the Rio Grande and Nacogdoches, the Camino Real crossed eleven major rivers: Neches, Frio, Medina, San Antonio, Guadeloupe, San Marcos, Colorado, Brazos, Navasota, Trinity, and Angelina. The courses of these rivers had generally been explored only a short distance on either side of the Camino Real, which lay approximately 150 miles inland. The landmarks of the Camino Real and the country around Matagorda Bay became known to the French mapmakers through the accounts and exploits of St. Denis. (Pierre Margry gives the text of many documents and letters relating to St. Denis in volume six of his work.) But in 1718, aside from the vicinity of Matagorda Bay, neither the French nor the Spanish had much knowledge about the lower courses of these rivers or the true configuration of the Texas coast. (See Herbert Eugene Bolton, *Texas in the Middle Eighteenth Century* [1915; reprint, Austin: University of Texas Press, 1970], p. 63, n. 18; Robert S. Martin, "Maps of an Empresario: Austin's Contribution to the Cartography of Texas," *Southwestern Historical Quarterly* 85 (1982): 372.

66. [Bénard de la Harpe], *Journal historique de l'établissment des Français à la Louisiane* (New Orleans: A. L. Boimare, 1831), pp. 263–73. An English translation of the *Journal historique* by Virginia Koenig and Joan Cain was published in 1971 (*Historical Journal of the Settlement of the French in Louisiana*, USL History Series, no. 3 [Lafayette: University of Southwestern Louisiana, 1971]. See also Henry Folmer, *Franco-Spanish Rivalry in North America, 1524–1763*, vol. 7 of *Spain in the West* (Glendale, Calif.: Arthur H. Clark Co., 1953) pp. 274–75. Margry (vol. 6) gives several documents and letters relevant to La Harpe's visit to Galveston Bay.

67. Historians have long been confused as to whether La Harpe visited St. Bernard's (Matagorda) Bay or Galveston Bay (see, for example, Bolton, pp. 283–84). An examination of La Harpe's map was virtually unknown in this country until quite recently, although a copy has been in the collection of the Library of Congress since the late nineteenth century. Lowery listed this copy (no. 302 [2]), but as the map identifies the bay only as "Port Francois," he did not recognize the bay as Galveston. A second copy of La Harpe's manuscript was acquired by the Rosenberg Library in the late 1970s (see no. 114, this catalog).

68. *Amérique Septentrionale*, Sr. d'Anville. [Paris], MDCCXLVI [1746]. See Lowery, no. 381. The notation is equally as likely to refer to Jean Beranger's 1720 reconnaissance of the Texas coast as it is to that of La Harpe. (See Koenig and Cain, p. 159.) The University of Texas Archives, Eugene C. Barker Texas History Center, contains a manuscript journal of Beranger's voyage that we have not personally examined.

69. A treaty of alliance was signed between France and Spain at Madrid on March 27, 1721. French merchants continued to visit Galveston Bay, however, in order to trade with the Indians along the lower Trinity. See Bolton, pp. 63–66, 327–39.

70. Janet R. Fireman, *The Spanish Royal Corps of Engineers in the Western Borderlands*, vol. 12 of *Spain in the West* (Glendale, Calif.: Arthur H. Clark Co., 1977), p. 28.

71. Fireman (p. 162), for example, excuses "the many distortions and errors" on Manuel Mascaro's map of east Texas ca. 1779 (manuscript, original in the Bibliothèque Nationale, Paris). The lower Trinity was visited by Spanish expeditions in 1728 (Bolton, p. 328, n. 2) and 1745–46 (ibid., pp. 327–32). Both expeditions approached the region from inland routes, and neither appears to have discovered the existence of Galveston Bay, even though the latter is known to have approached as near as a site just north of the mouth of the San Jacinto. In 1756 the Spanish established a short-lived presidio that Bolton (p. 346) concluded was on the left bank of the Trinity, only two miles above its mouth. Even so, the existence of the bay was not recorded by the Spanish until the reconnaissance of Evía in 1783.

72. "Mapa de la frontera . . . de Nueva Espana," Manuscript signed "Nicolas Lafora." Dated 1771. Original in the Bancroft Library, University of California at Berkeley. The map was prepared in connection with the famous reconnaissance of the Marquis de Rubi. Reproduced in Fireman, p. 85. See Wheat, *Transmississippi West*, no. 151; Bolton, p. 379.

73. Wheat, *Transmississippi West*, no. 195, reproduced opposite 1:120.

74. José Antonio de Alzate y Ramírez, *Nuevo mapa geográfico de la América Septentrional . . .* , Paris, 1768. According to Thomas Streeter (*Streeter Sale*, vol. 1, no. 150), Humboldt considered this map to be "hitherto looked upon as the best map of Mexico." Lowery, no. 515; Wheat, *Transmississippi West*, no. 149, reproduced 1:86.

75. According to Lowery (no. 515). For the Texas coast the Alzate y Ramírez 1768 printed map resembles no Sigüenza map that we have examined (see note 51). Alzate y Ramírez was also responsible for the map of New Spain (*Plano de la Nueva España . . .* , 1769) that appeared in Lorenzana's *Historia de Nueva España, escrita por su Eclarecido Conquistador Hernan Cortés, Augmenta con otros Documentos, y Notas por El Ilustrissimo Señor Don Francisco Antonio Lorensana, Arzobispo de México* (Mexico City, 1770). See Winsor, *America* 2:409; Francisco Vindel, *Mapas de América en los libros españoles de los siglos XVI al XVIII (1503–1798)* (Madrid, 1955), pp. 267–68. This map is superior to the 1768 map, in that it shows the United States Gulf Coast as far east as the vicinity of Pensacola. (The 1769 map could be said to resemble Sigüenza's circa 1693 manuscript map in a few particulars; note some similarities in the depiction of the mouth of the Mississippi, for example.) For Alvarez y Barreiro, see Lowery, no. 318; Bolton, p. 328. Wheat (*Transmississippi West*, no. 115) reproduces one of his manuscripts (ca. 1728) opposite 1:82.

76. Henry Popple, *A Map of the British Empire in America with the French and Spanish Settlements adjacent thereto* [London, 1733]. See Lowery, no. 338; Schwartz and Ehrenberg, p. 151, pl. 90.

77. Lowery, no. 577. See no. 167, this catalog.

78. Thomas Winthrop Streeter, *Bibliography of Texas, 1795–1845*, 5 vols. (Cambridge, Mass.: Harvard University Press, 1955–60) pt. 3, vol. 1, p. [6].

79. The French Admiralty had been publishing charts since the 1720s. The first charts published at the Deposito Hidrográfico by the Spanish Admiralty (Dirección Hidrográfica) were two of Vancouver Island that appeared circa 1798. See Henry Wagner, *The Cartography of the Northwest Coast of America to the Year 1800* (1937; reprint, Amsterdam: N. Israel, 1968), p. 252.

80. Streeter, *Bibliography*, no. 1029; Lowery, no. 721. See no. 197, this catalog.

81. The best source for Evía's reconnaissance is Jack D. L. Holmes' *José de Evía y sus reconocimientos de Golfo de México, 1783–1796*, Colección Chimalistac de libros y documentos acerca la Nueva España, no. 26 (Madrid: Ediciones José Porrua Turanzas, 1968). Holmes reproduces several of Evía's manuscript maps, including one of Galveston Bay (pl. 9). Evía honored Galvez by applying his name to the formerly unknown bay. See also Bolton, p. 133; Charles W. Hayes, *Galveston*, 2 vols. (Austin: Jenkins Garrett Press, 1974), 1:15; Lowery, no. 744; Carlos E. Castaneda, *Our Catholic Heritage in Texas*, 7 vols. (1936–58; reprint, New York: Arno Press, 1976), 5:172.

82. Alexander von Humboldt, *Carte Générale du royaume de la Nouvelle Espagne*, from the *Atlas géographique . . . de la Nouvelle Espagne*, 1811. Lowery, no. 745; Streeter, *Bibliography*, no. 1042; Wheat, *Transmississippi West*, no. 302; Schwartz and Ehrenberg, pp. 226–27, pl. 138 (top half only). Aaron Arrowsmith published two maps of importance to Texas cartography: (1) *Chart of the West Indies and Spanish Dominions in North America*, London, 1803 (only the first issue extends far enough to the west to include Texas) (see Streeter, *Bibliography*, no. 1031) and (2) *A New Map of Mexico and Adjacent Provinces . . . ,* London, 1810 (see Streeter, *Bibliography*, no. 1046; Wheat, *Transmississippi West*, no. 295). For Arrowsmith's maps, see nos. 193 and 202, respectively, this catalog.

83. Alexander von Humboldt, *Political Essay on the Kingdom of New Spain . . . ,* trans. John Black, 4 vols. (1811; reprint, New York: AMS Press, n.d.), p. lxxx. See Streeter, *Bibliography*, pt. 3, vol. 1, p. 19.

84. Zebulon Pike, *An account of expeditions to the sources of the Mississippi . . . And a tour through the interior parts of New Spain . . .* (Philadelphia: C. & A. Conrad, & Co., 1810). The most important map in this book for Texas cartography is *A Map of the Internal Provinces of New Spain*. Streeter, *Bibliography*, no. 1047; Wheat, *Transmississippi West*, no. 229. Pike based much of his information on Humboldt's map of 1809 and was himself in turn used extensively as a source by Arrowsmith for his map of 1810.

85. See *Streeter Sale*, vol. 6, no. 3797; Schwartz and Ehrenberg, p. 238–39, pl. 145; Walter W. Ristow, "John Melish and His Map of the United States," in *À la Carte: Selected Papers on Maps and Atlases*, comp. Walter W. Ristow (Washington, D.C.: U.S. Library of Congress, 1972), pp. 162–82.

86. John Melish, *A geographical description of the United States, with the contiguous British and Spanish possessions, intended as an accompaniment to Melish's map of those countries*, 2d ed. (Philadelphia: John Melish, 1816), p. 13.

87. Ibid., p. 11. Melish separately published a portion of Darby's map as *A Map of the State of Louisiana . . .* , Philadelphia, 1816 (Streeter, *Bibliography,* no. 1057; see Schwartz and Ehrenberg, p. 239). The map extends only a bit farther west than Nacogdoches. Streeter can be judged to have considered it superior to any previous map for the included part of Texas. Darby claimed to have been the first to survey the Sabine River. In 1818 Kirk and Mercein published in New York a more extensive version, *A Map of the United States . . .* , by William Darby. (See Wheat, Transmississippi West, no. 326. See also Schwartz and Ehrenberg, p. 239. That map extends as far west as modern-day Utah.

88. *Streeter Sale,* vol. 1, no. 86; Wheat, *Transmississippi West,* no. 350.

89. See no. 230, this catalog.

90. See no. 236, this catalog.

91. See no. 247, this catalog.

92. John Arrowsmith, *Texas,* first issue, 1841. From the *London Atlas.* See Ronald V. Tooley, *Printed Maps of America,* pt. 2, Map Collectors' Series, no. 69 (London: Map Collectors' Circle, 1971) pp. 261–63 (identifying three issues); Streeter, *Bibliography,* no. 1373 (identifying two issues); Philip Lee Phillips, *A List of Maps of America in the Library of Congress, Preceded by a List of Works Relating to Cartography* (1901; reprint, New York: Burt Franklin & Co., n.d.), p. 843; Wheat, *Transmississippi West,* no. 451; James M. Day, comp., *Maps of Texas, 1527–1900* (Austin: Pemberton Press, 1964), p. 35.

93. William Emory, *Map of Texas and the country adjacent: compiled in the bureau of the Corps of Topographical Engineers from the best authorities. . . .* For the State Department [Washington, D.C.], 1844. Wheat, *Transmississippi West,* no. 478; Day, p. 39.

94. See nos. 295A, 295B, and 295C, this catalog.

95. See no. 317, this catalog.

96. See Hayes, 1:13.

97. Hayes (1:248) gives a description of Eagle Grove, as well as of the "Three Lone Trees." These few trees were the only Galveston Island landmark for navigators on what was otherwise a monotonous landscape of high sedge grass.

98. See no. 114, this catalog.

99. See no. 197, this catalog.

100. See no. 230, this catalog.

101. See, for example, nos. 204, 205, and 259, this catalog.

102. See, for example, nos. 167, 200, and 230, this catalog.

103. See Hayes, 1:249.

104. Koenig and Cain, no. 115.

105. See, for example, Colonel Warren D. C. Hall's description of Pelican Island in 1815 (Hayes, 1:247).

106. The earliest printed map we have examined that shows Pelican Spit is the United States Coast Survey's *Map of Galveston Harbor and City,* 1851 (see no. 298, this catalog). See Lynn M. Alperin, *Custodians of the Coast* (Galveston: U.S. Army Corps of Engineers, 1977), p. 26.

107. See no. 452, this catalog; Hayes, 1:172–73.

108. See no. 452, this catalog.

109. See nos. 255A, 255B, 255C, and 255D, this catalog.

110. See no. 259, this catalog.

111. See nos. 298, 300, and 301, this catalog.

112. See nos. 255A, 255B, 255C, and 255D, this catalog; Hayes, 1:251–52.

113. See no. 272, this catalog.

114. See Webb and Carroll, 2:228.

115. See Hayes, 1:251.

116. Alvar Nuñez Cabeza de Vaca, *La relación y comentarios . . . de la acaescido enlas Indias . . .* (Zamora: Impresso por Augustin de Paz y Juan Picardo . . . , 1542).

117. See no. 259, this catalog; Hayes, 1:260; John W. Reps, *Cities of the American West* (Princeton, N.J.: Princeton University Press, 1979), p. 135.

118. See no. 259, this catalog.

119. Hayes, 1:288.

120. Ibid., 2:794.

121. Ibid., 778.

122. See no. 339, this catalog.

123. See, for example, Alperin, p. 22.

124. See nos. 351, 356A, 356B, and 356C, this catalog; Hayes, 2:730–34.

125. See nos. 338, 429, and 447, this catalog; Alperin, pp. 23–33, 43–55.

126. Alperin, pp. 23, 55.

Cartographic Sources

1. *Orbem terrarum jn planam et maria omnia mappam: A Map of the World.* Designed by Giovanni Matteo Contarini. Engraved by Francesco Roselli. 1506. Reprint, with an introduction by J. A. J. de Villiers. London: British Museum, 1924. Scale indeterminable, 43 × 69 cm. folding map, bound in quarto boards.

This 1924 edition of *Orbem Terrarum . . .* is a facsimile of the earliest extant printed map showing the New World discoveries of Christopher Columbus and his contemporaries. The only surviving copy of the original map was discovered in 1922 and is now in the British Museum.

The map is a more primitive conception of American geography than any of the relevant manuscript maps predating it (La Cosa, 1500; Cantino, 1502; Caneiro, 1502–1506). The West Indies, including Cuba, appear with a well-developed form, but to the west is an open sea that extends to a nearby Japan and beyond to the coasts of Asia. A sizable fragment of the Southern American coast is immediately south of the West Indies; to the north are the lands discovered by the Corte-Reals (Labrador, Newfoundland). An imaginary coast connects the northern lands to the Asian mainland. There is no sign of any part of the temperate mainland of North America.

2. *[New World.]* Martin Waldseemüller. N.p., n.d. Woodcut, scale indeterminable, 29 × 38 cm. From the 1525 edition of Ptolemy's *Geography*, Strasbourg. MMNHMC.

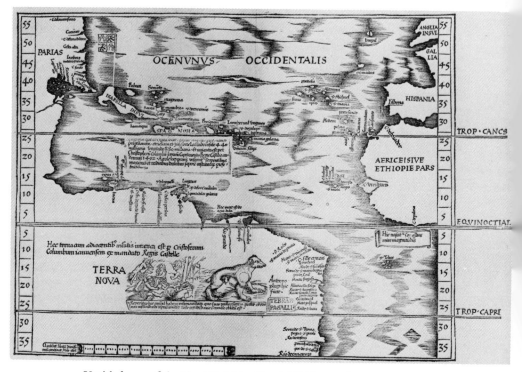

Untitled map of the New World, by Martin Waldseemüller, from Ptolemy's *Geography,* 1525. (See no. 2.) Waldseemüller's work is the first to show the two American continents with a continuous coast. Scholars have variously described the large river flowing into the Gulf of Mexico as the Rio Grande, the Mississippi, and the Ganges.

The map is a reduced, revised version of the *Tabula Terre Nove* that appeared in the 1514 Strasbourg edition of the *Geography* (Phillips, *Atlases,* no. 354). The original 1513 issue is the first printed map devoted specifically to European discoveries in the New World. Waldseemüller compiled information from earlier manuscript maps by Alberto Cantini and Januensis Caneiro.

The Cantino chart (1502) shows an isolated landmass resembling Florida, just north of Cuba. The Caneiro chart (ca. 1504) is the earliest extant map showing the Gulf of Mexico. Caneiro added a lengthy coast to the western end of Cantino's Florida-type landmass. The coast curves south and forms an enclosed gulf to the west of Cuba.

Waldseemüller included Caneiro's information on his 1507 map of the world; however, in an inset of America, he extended Caneiro's coast farther south and connected it to the South American continent. Thus, the two American continents appear with a continuous coast for the first time. Waldseemüller adopted the 1507 inset in an enlarged and more detailed fashion for his 1513 map. This map, like the Caneiro chart and the 1507 world map, shows the mouth and delta of a large river on the extended coast. The 1513 map was reprinted for the 1520 Strasbourg edition of *Geography*. Lorenz Friess reengraved the map on a smaller format for inclusion in the 1522, 1525, and 1535 Strasbourg editions and the 1541 Vienna edition.

The 1525 version reflects minor, but interesting, changes from the 1513 map. South America is "Terre Nova" instead of "Terre Incognita"; the name "Tebrapa Pagalli" is applied to Brazil; and a vignette of Brazilian natives and fauna, after a description given by Vespucci, fills the blank interior of the continent. A Spanish flag now waves over Cuba ("Isabella Insul"), and a lengthy notation on Hispaniola Spagnoha has been added below that island.

See Tooley, "The Strait That Never Was," for a discussion of the mythical isthmian strait.

3. *Charta Cosmographica, cum ventorum propria natura et operatione.* Gemma Frisius. N.p., n.d. Woodcut, scale indeterminable, 19 × 27.5 cm., bound in a copy of the 1551 edition of Petrus Apian's Cosmography, Paris. MMNHMC.

This woodcut map of the world is by Gemma Frisius, teacher of Mercator, and is "his only surviving world map" (Skelton, *Decorative Printed Maps*, p. 133). The map was originally published in 1540. From 1544 onward, it appeared in Peter Apian's *Cosmography*, originally published in 1524 and republished several times during the sixteenth century. (Shirley, Mapping of the World, p. 93). The map is on the cordiform (heart-shaped) projection of Apian (see Nordenskiöld, *Facsimile-atlas*, p. 88) and gives an interesting view of America as perceived in the midsixteenth century. North America, called "Baccalearum," is a slender, trailing appendage attached to the northern tip of South America ("America"). An unnamed strait separates North America from Asia and is completely separated from Asia by an unnamed strait.

4. *Tierra Nova.* Giacomo Gastaldi. N.p., n.d. Scale indeterminable, 13 × 17 cm. From the 1548 edition of Ptolemy's *Geography*, Venice. MMNHMC.

Extracted from a significant edition of Ptolemy's *Geography*, *Tierra Nova* is the earliest separately printed map of South America. Italian cartographer Giacomo Gastaldi constructed all the maps in the 1548 edition of *Geography* near the beginning of his illustrious career.

For a discussion of the significance of the 1548 edition, see Phillips, *Atlases*, no. 369; Nordenskiöld, *Facsimile-atlas*, pp. 25–26; *The World Encompassed*, no. 122; Sabin, Eames, and Vail, no. 66502.

5. *L'Isola Spagnola una delle prime che Colombo tironasse, hogi e detta L'Isola di S. Dominico, el'habitano Spagnoli, percioche pohi Isolani uisono rienasi, Efertilissima di molte cose, come di Corone Mastice.* Fernando Bertelli. Venice, 1566. Scale indeterminable, 18 × 24.5 cm. MMNHMC.

Tooley, "Maps in Italian Atlases," no. 86, lists eleven known copies of this second issue of *L'Isole Spagnola*. The first issue (1564), bearing the imprint of Paolo Forlani, Venice, is more common.

Very few maps of the period depicted American areas, but Hispaniola was of special interest at this early date. Isabella, the site of the first European settlement in the New World, is on the north coast of Hispaniola and was a center of activity throughout the sixteenth century.

6. *Americae Sive Novi Orbis, Nova Descriptio.* Abraham Ortelius. N.p., n.d. Reprint, by (?). N.p., n.d. Facsimile of printed map, color, scale indeterminable, 36.5 x 50 cm. From the first edition of Ortelius's *Theatrum orbis terrarum,* Antwerp, 1570. MMNHMC.

"This delineation of Ortelius, with that of Mercator, may be said to have established a type for the contours of the Americas, which long prevailed" (Kohl, *Die ältesten General-Karten,* no. 72). This is the first state of two; it differs from its successor in some ways, but the Gulf Coast is identical on both states.

Ortelius adopted the geographical information on the Gulf Coast from Mercator's world map of 1569. At the coast's center, a "R. de S. Spirito" flows into a "Baia de culata." Between this point and the "R. Palmar" (Rio de Palmas) to the west are four place-names (east to west): "R. de gigates," "Malab ? o," "C. Bravo," and an interior town, "Gacos."

The *Theatrum* was the first standardized collection of printed maps that showed contemporary rather than classical information. For this reason it is generally acclaimed as the first modern atlas. (See Carter and Muir, no. 91; Phillips, *Atlases,* nos. 374, 400. Skelton gives a full description of the Ortelius atlas in his introduction to the facsimile edition of the *Theatrum.* See also Lowery, no. 56; Koeman, *Atlantes Neerlandici,* 3:25–32.)

7. *Descrittione Dell'Isola Cuba.* Tomaso Porcacchi. N.p., n.d. Scale indeterminable, 10 × 14 cm. From Porcacchi's *L'Isole del Mondo,* Venice, 1572–90. MMNHMC.

This map of Cuba was originally part of an island book, or pocket-size atlas, that preceded the more sophisticated pilot books, or nautical atlases, of the late sixteenth century. The maps lacked depth soundings and usually lacked rhumb lines. Porcacchi's was the most popular of the island books. Its miniature maps are accomplished examples of the Italian style. This map is of Cuba.

8. *Descrittione Dell'Isola Di S. Giovanni.* Tomaso Porcacchi. N.p., n.d. Scale indeterminable, 10 × 14 cm. From Porcacchi's *L'Isole del Mondo,* Venice, 1572–90. MMNHMC.

This is a miniature map of Puerto Rico. (See no. 7 for further information.)

9. [This number is not in use.]

10. *Nova Descriptio Hispaniae.* Pirrho Ligorio. Drafted by Joannes "à deutecum," and Lucas "à deutecum, fecerunt," N.p., n.d. Scale indeterminable, 38 × 51 cm. From the second edition of Cornelis de Jose's *Speculum Orbis Terrarum,* Antwerp, 1593. MMNHMC.

This is a reduced, revised version of Pirrho Ligorio's 1559 map of Spain, which is in turn modeled on Thomas Geminus's map of 1555. This version originally appeared in the first edition of Gerard de Jode's *Speculum* published in Antwerp in 1578. There are no differences between the 1578 version and this 1593 issue of the map.

11. *Portugalliae Quae Olim Lusitania.* Drawn by Fernando Alvarez Seco. Drafted by Joannes "à deutecum," and Lucas "à deutecum, fecurunt." Printed by Gerard de Jode. N.p., n.d. Scale indeterminable, 31 × 52 cm. From the second edition of Cornelis de Jode's *Speculum Orbis Terrarum,* Antwerp, 1593. MMNHMC.

Second issue. This is a reduced, revised version of Seco Fernando Alvarez's map of Portugal, first published in Rome in 1561. Alvarez's map appeared in both editions of the *Speculum* (1578 and 1593). Abraham Ortelius used the map as the basis for his map of Portugal in the first edition of *Theatrum*, published in Antwerp in 1570.

12. *La Florida*. Geronimo de Chaves. N.p., n.d. Color, scale indeterminable, 15 × 22 cm. map on 33 × 47 cm. sheet, with *Guastecan Reg.* and *Peruviae Auriferae Regionis Typus*, by Diego Hurtado de Mendoza, n.p., n.d. From Abraham Ortelius's *Theatrum orbis terrarum*, Antwerp, 1584. MMNHMC.

This important map illustrates the Spanish conception of the Gulf Coast around 1550. It is the first printed map of present-day southern United States and the first to reflect Hernando De Soto's exploration. It is also one of the few maps published in northern Europe in the sixteenth century to show the influence of Sevillian hydrography. Lowery (no. 70) notes that the map closely follows Oviedo's description of the southern United States written between 1535 and 1555. The description appears to be based on a now-lost map by Alonso de Chaves, a relative of Geronimo de Chaves. Both were cosmographers at the Casa de Contratación in Seville.

Between the "Mar Pequeña" (Bahía del Espíritu Santo) and the "Rio de las Palmas" are eight place-names (east to west): "C. de Cruz," "C. Desierto," "Montañas," "Rio del Oro," "Rio de Pescadores," "Costa Bara," "Rio Escondido," "Medanos della Magdalena." This is the first printed map to show a second Bahía del Espíritu Santo on the west coast of Florida (see Delanglez, *Espíritu Santo*, pp. 6–7).

13. *Beschrijuinghe der Zee Custen van Landt vā Argarbe, Eñ ēē deel vande Condada, Soe hem tlandt aldaer verthoont eñ in ghedaent eñ mesen is*. Lucas Janszoon Waghenaer. N.p., n.d. Color, scale indeterminable, 32 × 51 cm. From Waghenaer's *De Spieghel der Zeevaerdt*, Leiden, 1584. MMNHMC.

This chart shows the Algarve region of southern Portugal. (See no. 14 for further information.)

14. *The Mariners Mirrour*. Lucas Janszoon Waghenaer. London, 1588. Reprint, with an introduction by R. A. Skelton. Amsterdam: Theatrum Orbis Terrarum Ltd., 1966. Facsimile of printed atlas, scale varies, forty-five charts bound into folio volume. MMNHMC.

Facsimile of the English edition of Waghenaer's *De Spieghel der Zeevaerdt* (first edition Leiden, 1584), the first systematic collection of navigational charts bound together in book form. For this English edition the printer reengraved the original twenty-three charts and added twenty-two more, for a total of forty-five charts. The Rosenberg's chart of the Algarve region of southern Portugal (see no. 13) is from the 1584 edition of the atlas.

15. *Indiarum Orientalium Occidentaliumque Descriptio.* Petrus Maffei. N.p., n.d. Scale indeterminable, 25.5 × 48.5 cm. From Maffei's *Historiarum Harum Verissimae,* which appeared in three editions, Venice and Cologne, 1588–93.

This world map is based on the map in Abraham Ortelius's *Theatrum orbis terrarum,* Antwerp, 1570. MMNHMC

16. *Americae Pars Magis Cognita.* Theodore de Bry. Copyright by Casearece Matis. N.p., 1592. Scale indeterminable, 36.5 × 44.0 cm. From part four of the Latin edition of De Bry's *Grands et Petits Voyages,* Frankfurt am Main, 1592. MMNHMC.

The first state. The map was included unaltered in all editions of *Grands et Petits Voyages* until 1630, when it was reengraved for the third Latin edition and given a new date (MDCCXXIV [1724]). This important late-sixteenth-century map shows the two American continents as far north as the Carolinas. Garratt points out that the shape of South America is generally quite different from that of other sixteenth-century and early-seventeenth-century maps. The configuration of Florida is based on Jacques le Moyne's map of 1591.

The map gives approximately twenty-five place-names along the U.S. Gulf Coast, including a "R. de S. Spirito," with a "Baia de Culata" at its mouth. Between this point and a river to the west that bears the name "R. Palmar" are five place-names [east to west]: "R. de gigantes," "Tagil," "Malabrigo," "C. Brauo," and "Culias."

The *Church Catalogue* 1:316–20 gives a good account of De Bry's *Grands et Petits Voyages,* including a census of the various editions.

17. *Galliae Amplissimi Regni tabula.* Cornelis de Jode. N.p., n.d. Scale indeterminable, 30.5 × 45 cm. From the second edition of de Jode's *Speculum Orbis Terrarum,* Antwerp, 1593. MMNHMC.

First and only issue. Cornelis de Jode replaced with this example the general map of France that his father, Gerard, had used in the first edition of the *Speculum.* Gerard had pulled his work from Jean Jolivet's map of

1560. Cornelis's map is based, without attribution, on the Plancius map of France, first published in 1593.

18. *Occidentalis Americae partis.* Theodore de Bry, after Girolamo Benzoni. N.p., 1594. Scale indeterminable, 32 × 43.5 cm. From part four of the Latin edition of de Bry's *Grands et Petits Voyages,* Frankfurt am Main, 1594. MMNHMC.

This is a general map of the Gulf of Mexico and the Caribbean Sea. The westernmost part of the Gulf of Mexico is omitted. At the left edge of the map is a "Rio de S. Spirito," with a "C. de Crutz" but with no bay at its mouth. Florida has the wedge shape described by Oviedo and used by Jacques le Moyne on his map, which De Bry published in 1591.

19. *Descriptionis Ptolemaicae augmentum, sive Occidentis notitia brevis commentario.* Cornelis Wytfliet. Louvain, 1597. Reprint, with an introduction by R. A. Skelton. Amsterdam: N. Israel, 1964. Facsimile of printed atlas, scale varies, folio volume. MMNHMC.

Facsimile of the first atlas devoted specifically to America. Wytfliet's intention was to supplement Ptolemy with a series of maps that would comprehensively cover those parts of the globe known to the ancient geographer. Only this American volume with nineteen maps ever appeared. It was an immensely popular and influential work and was reissued at least seven times without geographical revisions (see Skelton's introduction, pp. xi–xii). Several individual maps from the atlas are in the collection of the Rosenberg Library (see nos. 21–23).

20. [This number is not in use.]

21. *Cuba Insula et Jamaica.* Cornelis Wytfliet. N.p., n.d. Scale indeterminable, 23 × 29 cm. From Wytfliet's *Descriptionis Ptolemaicae augmentum,* Louvain, 1597. MMNHMC. (See no. 19 for further information.)

This is one of the earliest printed maps to focus closely on Cuba and Jamaica.

22. *Iucatana Regio et Fondura.* Cornelis Wytfliet. N.p., n.d. Scale indeterminable, 23 × 28 cm. From Wytfliet's *Descriptionis Ptolemaicae augmentum,* Louvain, 1597. MMNHMC. (see no. 19 for further information.)

This is the earliest separate printed map specifically of Central America.

23. *Residuum Continentis cum Adiacentibus Insulis.* Cornelis Wytfliet. N.p., n.d. Scale indeterminable, 23 × 29 cm. From Wytfliet's *Descriptionis Ptolemaicae augmentum,* Louvain 1597. MMNHMC.

The map shows the West Indies islands to the east of Hispaniola and the South American coast from about present-day Puerto Cumarebo, Venezuela, east to "C. de Norte," near the mouth of the Amazon.

24. *Nueva Hispania Tabula Nova.* Anonymous. N.p., n.d. After Giacomo Gastaldi, 1548. Scale indeterminable, 18 × 25.5 cm. From Ptolemy's *Geography,* edited by Giuseppe Rosaccio, Venice, 1599. MMNHMC.

A late reengraved and revised issue of Giacomo Gastaldi's map from the 1548 edition of Ptolemy's *Geography* (see no. 4 for further information). The original issue had the distinction of being the first separate regional printed map of the viceroyalty of New Spain (Mexico and its loosely attached, vaguely known hinterlands in the southwestern United States). The map actually extends from Baja, California, in the west to Florida in the east. It was reengraved on a larger scale in 1561 and reissued with the 1561 format in 1562, 1564, 1574, and 1599.

The most noticeable feature of the north shore of the Gulf of Mexico is the large unnamed bay introduced by Piñeda in 1519, with the words "R[io]. de Spirito Santo" above. No river is actually indicated aside from the appearance of these words, however. To the west of the bay, in the area corresponding roughly to modern-day Texas, are the following place-names (east to west): "C. de+," "R. de Loro," "R. Atlas," "R. de S. Heneto," "Morato." These names are the same on all issues. The main changes effected between 1548 and 1599 are the correction of Yucatan from an island to a peninsula, the addition of a few random place-names outside Texas, and some decorative features.

25. *[West Indies.]* Jodocus Hondius. N.p., n.d. Scale indeterminable, 36 × 48 cm. sheet with five maps: *Cuba Insula* (inset: "Havana"); *Hispaniola Insula; Insula Iamaica; Ins. S. Ioannis* [Puerto Rico]; *I.s. Margareta Cum Confiniis.* From the 1643 edition of the *Mercator-Hondius Atlas,* Amsterdam. MMNHMC.

The *Mercator-Hondius Atlas* was the most important and influential of early-seventeenth-century atlases. Its core was Mercator's *Atlas* (from 1585), which was first republished in 1606 by Hondius, who supplemented it with a host of new maps. This West Indies sheet was one of the new Hondius maps, and it continued to be included, unaltered, in all subsequent editions, down to the last in 1638.

26. *Nova Totius Orbis Mappa, ex Optimis Auctoribus Desumta = The World Map of 1611*. Pieter van den Keere. Amsterdam, 1611. Reprint. Edited by Gunter Schilder and James Welu. Amsterdam; Nico Israel, 1980. Facsimile of printed map, scale indeterminable, twelve sheets, plus thirty-two pages of introductory text, bound in folio volume with stiff paper wrappers; original in the Sutro Library, San Francisco. MMNHMC.

27. *Nova Universi Terrarum Orbis Mappa ex Optimis Quibusque Geographicis Hydrographicisque Tabulis Summa Industria Accuratissime Delineata, et Duobus Planisphaeriis Graphice Depicta Auctore Ludoco Hondio: The World Map of 1624*. Willems Jans Zoon Blaeu and Jodocus Hondius. Amsterdam, 1624, Reprint. Edited by Gunther Schilder. Amsterdam: Nico Israel, 1977. Facsimile of printed map, scale indeterminable, twenty sheets, plus seventeen-page introductory text, bound in folio volume with stiff printed wrappers; original in the Bibliotheque Nationale, Paris. MMNHMC.

28. *Tierra Firma item Nuevo Reyno de Granada atque Popayan*. Joannes de Laet. N.p., n.d. Scale indeterminable, 28.5 × 36.5 cm. From De Laet's *Nieuwe Wereldt ofte Beschrijuinghe van West Indien*, Leiden, 1630.

An important prototype of Panama and Columbia. The map originally appeared with a slightly different title in the 1625 edition of De Laet's work. This is the second issue.

29A. *America noviter delineata*. Jodocus Hondius. Printed by Jan Jansson, Amsterdam. 1632. Scale indeterminable, 41 × 55 cm., flanked by sixteen panels with illustrations of native inhabitants and European settlements. Untitled insets: Greenland; North Pole; South Pole. MMNHMC.

An early state of an influential general map of America. It was originally published as a separate map in 1630 with an additional border of panels along the lower margin. That first oversized version was part of the *Mercator-Hondius Atlas* (see Koeman, *Atlantes Neerlandici*, 2:349), but it proved unwieldy, as it had to be folded down. Subsequent issues came first from the original plate, but with the lower panel removed (as with this example), and later, and more commonly, from new plates, with all the panels removed (see 29B). This is Tooley's third state, but with the verso blank rather than with text in Dutch. Hondius used geographical information from Mercator's 1569 *Planisphere* and Ortelius-Chaves's 1584 *Florida* through Blaeu's 1608 map of America.

B. Another issue: same title, printer, and insets, but revised ca. 1645 and 30 × 58 cm. Hondius's name has been removed. MMNHMC.

All panels have been removed, and the treatment of embellishments (sailing ships, etc.) is quite different. There is some revision to geographical detail, but none in the Gulf Coast region. Most significantly, this issue extends a few degrees farther north to include more of the Arctic regions.

Henricus Hondius reengraved his father's map in 1631. This is a late issue of the reengraving. Tooley identifies this as the tenth state and dates it [1645?]. Copies of this issue were found in some editions of Jan Jansson's *Novus atlas*. Phillips (*Atlases*, no. 459) describes a copy of this atlas, with the four volumes dated 1646–49, containing an issue of the Henricus Hondius map dated 1641.

Tooley, *A Sequence of Maps of America*, gives a census of all states, including foreign examples. See also Delanglez, *Espíritu Santo*, pp. 78–79.

30. *Mappa Aestiuarum Insularum, alias Barmudas dictarum, ad Ostia Mexicani aestuary jacetium. . . .* Henricus Hondius. N.p., n.d. Scale indeterminable, 36 × 51 cm. From the 1634 edition of the *Mercator-Hondius Atlas*, Amsterdam. MMNHMC.

Bermuda was first settled in 1609; this map was added to the atlas in 1663. (See no. 25 for further information.)

31. *Anglia Regnvm.* Jan Jansson. N.p., n.d. Color, scale 1 in. to ca. 24 mi., 38.5 × 50 cm. From volume four of Jansson's *Novus Atlas*, Amsterdam, 1646. MMNHMC.

A general map of England.

32. *Virginiae partis australis, et Floridae partis orientalis, interjacentiumque, regionum Nova Descriptio.* Willem Jans Zoon Blaeu. N.p., n.d. Color, scale indeterminable, 39 × 60 cm. From the Latin edition of Blaeu's *Theatrum*, Amsterdam, 1640. MMNHMC.

The map shows the American Atlantic coast from northern Florida to Chesapeake Bay. This is one of the earliest issues, from the Latin edition of Blaeu's *Theatrum,* 1640. The Blaeus continued to include this map, unrevised, in their various atlases until fire destroyed their printing house in 1672.

33. *Nova Totius Terrarum Orbis Geographica Ac Hydrographica Tabula.*
Henricus Hondius. Printed by Jan Jansson, Amsterdam. 1641. Scale indeterminable, 38 × 54 cm. map surrounded by decorative motifs, including personifications of the elements and portraits of Julius Caesar, Claudius Ptolemy, Jodocus Hondius, and Gerard Mercator. From the Dutch edition of Jansson's *Novus Atlas.* Donated by Harry Bennett.

On the United States Gulf Coast, a large "R. de Cruz" flows into an (unnamed) Bahía del Espíritu Santo. To the west, in the area of present-day Texas, Hondius shows (east to west) a "Breva Costa," a large "R. Secon-dido" (Escondido), and an Indian village named "Cacos."

For the first issue of the *Novus atlas,* see Koeman, *Atlantes Neerlandici,* 2:403. Phillips (*America,* p. 1087) lists an example found in a 1653 Spanish edition of the atlas.

34. *Brasilia Generis nobilitate, armorum et litterarum Scientia prestant.*
Joan Blaeu. N.p., n.d. Color, scale indeterminable, 38 × 49 cm. From volume two of the Latin edition of Blaeu's *Theatrum,* Amsterdam, 1642. MMNHMC.

This general map of Brazil is based on De Laet's map of 1625.

35. *Carta particolare che comincia con il capo S. Andrea è finiscie con il capo Matas d'America.* Robert Dudley. Engraved by Antonio Francesco Lucini. Florence, n.d. Scale indeterminable, 36.5 × 48 cm. Map of America, no. 21, from the first edition of Dudley's *Dell'Arcano del mare,* Florence, 1646. MMNHMC.

This chart shows the coast of Argentina from lat. 36°S to 48°S. Dudley's *Dell'Arcano del mare* was the most important of the seventeenth-century sea atlases. Although published in Italy, it was the first sea atlas by an Englishman. It was also the first to use Mercator's projection for all its charts and the first to contain a selection of charts of American areas. A second edition of the atlas appeared in Florence in 1661. There were no significant changes, as the publisher used the same plates. The only difference was the addition of the cypher "L6" at the end of the imprint on most of the charts in the atlas. The library has examples of charts from both editions.

36. *Carta particolare dell'mare: del'Zur che comincia con il capo Lucar è finisce con Cagidos nella nuoua Spagnia, è la Baia di Honduras.* Robert Dudley. Engraved by Antonio Francesco Lucini. Florence, n.d. Scale indeterminable, 46 × 65.5 cm. Map of America, no. 25, from the second edition of Dudley's *Dell'Arcano del mare*, Florence, 1661. MMNHMC. (See no. 35 for further information.)

A sea chart of the Central American coast from lat. 8°30'N to 17°N.

37. *Carta particolare dell'Isola Ispaniola è S. Giovanni nel'India ocidentale con l'Isole Intorno.* Robert Dudley. Engraved by Antonio Francesco Lucini. Florence, n.d. Scale indeterminable, 48.5 × 75.5 cm. Map of America, no. 6, from the second edition of Dudley's *Dell'Arcano del mare*, Florence, 1661. MMNHMC. (See no. 35 for further information.)

The first printed sea chart of the area of Hispaniola, Puerto Rico, and the Virgin Islands.

38. *Carta particolare della Brasilia, che comincia con il capo S. Antonio et finisce con il Porto del' Spirito Sancto.* Robert Dudley. Engraved by Antonio Francesco Lucini. Florence, n.d. Scale indeterminable, 46 × 74 cm. Map of America, no. 17, from the second edition of Dudley's *Dell'Arcano del mare*, Florence, 1661. MMNHMC. (see no. 35 for further information.)

A sea chart of the Brazilian coast from lat. 10°S to 20°S.

39. *Carta particolare dell'Rio della Plata che comincia con la costa in Gradi 31 di latine Australe, è Finisce con il capo S. Andrea.* Robert Dudley. Engraved by Antonio Francesco Lucini. Florence, n.d. Scale indeterminable, 46 × 76.5 cm. Map of America, no. 20, from the second edition of Dudley's *Dell'Arcano del mare*, Florence, 1661. MMNHMC. (See also no. 35 for further information.)

A sea chart of the Rio de la Plata on the Atlantic South American coast.

40. *Carta particolare della Costa di America Australe che comincia al C. di Matas sin al C. di Galegos.* Robert Dudley. Engraved by Antonio Francesco Lucini. Florence, n.d. Scale indeterminable, 38 × 47.5 cm. Map of America, no. 22, from the first edition of Robert Dudley's *Dell'Arcano del Mare*, Florence, 1646. MMNHMC. (See no. 35 for further information.)

This chart shows the coast of Argentina from lat. 46°S to about the Straits of Magellan.

41. *Carta particolare che comincia con il capo Mogera in Portogallo è Finisce con il capo di Coriano in Ispagna*. Robert Dudley. Engraved by Antonio Francesco Lucini. Florence, n.d. Scale indeterminable, 37.5 × 47.5 cm. Map of Europe, no. 20, from the second edition of Dudley's *Dell'Arcano del mare*, Florence, 1661. MMNHMC. (See no. 35 for further information.)

This chart shows the Atlantic coast of Portugal and Spain from approximately lat. 41°15′ N to 43°30′ N.

42. *Carta particolare del Oceano che comincia con la costa di C. Roxo è Finisce con il capo di Mogera ni Portogallo*. Robert Dudley. Engraved by Antonio Francesco Lucini. Florence, n.d. Scale indeterminable, 35.5 × 46.5 cm. Map of Europe, no. 18, from the second edition of Dudley's *Dell'Arcano del mare*, Florence, 1661. MMNHMC. (See no. 35 for further information.)

This chart shows the north Portuguese coast from lat. 39°N to 41°30′ N.

43. *Orbis Terrarum Veteribus Cogniti Typus Geographicus*. George Hornius. Amsterdam; Jan Jansson, 1652. Scale indeterminable, 40.5 × 51 cm. Appeared first in Hornius's *Accuratissima orbis antiqui delineatio sive geographia vetus, sacra, & profana*, published by Jan Jansson, 1652, and later in volume six of Jansson's *Novus atlas*, Amsterdam, 1658. MMNHMC.

44. *Mexique, ou Nouvelle Espagne, Nouvelle Gallice, Iucatan, &c. et autres Provinces jusques a l'Isthme de Panama; ou sont Les Audiences de Mexico, de Guadalaiara, et de Guatimala*. Nicolas Sanson. Printed by Pierre Mariette. Paris, 1656. Color, scale indeterminable, 37 × 56 cm. MMNHMC.

45. *La Floride*. Nicolas Sanson. Printed by Pierre Mariette. Paris, n.d. Color, 18 × 25.5 cm. From Sanson's *L'Amérique en plusieurs cartes*, Paris, 1657. MMNHMC.

An important map of the southern United States. According to Delanglez, Sanson's interior detail was the first attempt to harmonize the geographical data of two of the most important written accounts of the De Soto expedition, those of Garcilaso de la Vega and the "Gentlemen of Elvas" (*Espíritu Santo,* p. 91).

With regard to its configuration and nomenclature for the Gulf Coast, the map is more important for its influence than its geography. It generally follows current convention, and most of its features appear on contemporary charts, such as those of Dudley, De Laet, and Roggeveen. The ubiquitous Bahía del Espíritu Santo is present in its usual position. Six rivers flow into it, three of which are named, respectively (east to west), "R. del Spiritu Santo," "Matta de Salvador," and "R. de Canaveral." A second "R. del Spiritu Santo" disgorges independently on the Florida coast. A chain of mountains encircles the watershed of the Gulf coast.

Between the Bahía del Espíritu Santo and the "R. de Palmas" (modern-day Soto de Marina, northern Mexico) are the following fourteen place-names (east to west): "C. de Sierta," "R. de Montanhas," "R. Laso," "R. dos Pescadores," "R. de Oro," "C. d'Arboledo," "Rio Bravo," "C. Baixo," "R. Suelo," "C. Blanco," "R. Escondido," "R. Salo," "R. Brava," "Costa de Pescadores." The former Rio Bravo is undoubtedly the same river called the "R. de Baixos o R. Bravo" on Sir Robert Dudley's 1646 sea chart of the Gulf of Mexico. The later Rio Bravo is intended for the present-day Rio Grande and represents an early appearance of that river on a map.

46. *Pas caert van Nieu Nederland, Virginia en Nieu Engelant.* Hendrick Doncker. Amsterdam, n.d. Color, scale indeterminable, 44.5 × 53.5 cm. From the 1670 edition of Pieter Goos's *Zee-Atlas ofte Waterwaereldt,* Amsterdam. MMNHMC.

This is the first of three different charts of New Netherland that Doncker published between 1660 and 1688, and the only chart contemporary with the actual Dutch possession of the New World colony. The chart shows the United States Atlantic coast from Cape Hatteras north to Cape Ann.

The *National Maritime Museum Catalogue* (vol. 3, nos. 84–88) lists several editions of the atlas (1661–76), all of which contain this map.

47. *Extrema Americae versus Boream, ubi Terra Nova, Nova Francia, Adjacentiaque.* Jan Blaeu. Amsterdam: Covens and Mortier, ca. 1737. Color, scale indeterminable, 45 × 56 cm. MMNHMC.

A map of Newfoundland and the Gulf of St. Lawrence. Geographical detail is the same on all issues.

48. *Nova Totius Terrarum Orbis Geographica Ac Hydrographica Tabula.* Jacob Colom. Amsterdam, 1663. After Jodocus Hondius, 1641. Color, scale indeterminable, 39 × 54 cm. map surrounded by decorative motifs, including personifications of the elements and portraits of Julius Caesar, Claudius Ptolemy, Nicolas Copernicus and Tycho Brahe. MMNHMC.

This is a reengraved, revised copy of the Henricus Hondius world map of 1641 (see no. 33). Medallion portraits of Copernicus and Tycho Brahe have replaced portraits of Gerard Mercator and Jodocus Hondius. There are a number of geographical alterations, especially to the American Arctic, Australia, and the Pacific, but the configuration for the Gulf coast is unchanged.

Phillips (*Atlases,* no. 480) lists a 1669 Spanish edition of Colom's atlas (*Atlas Maritimo*) that contains this map.

49. *Pascaerte Van West-Indien de Vaste Kusten en de Eylanden.* Pieter Goos. N.p., n.d. Color, scale 1 in. to approx. 25 mi., 44 × 54 cm. From the first edition of Goos's *Zee Atlas ofte Water-Weereld,* Amsterdam, 1666. Inset: northwest Cuba. MMNHMC.

This Dutch sea chart shows the entire Gulf of Mexico, the Caribbean Sea, and the North American Atlantic coast as far north as New Jersey. The configuration of the Gulf coast is typical for the period before 1684. Just west of the coast's center, the "R. de Spirito Santo" flows into the familiar large bay (here "Mar Pequeno").

Between the "Mar Pequeno" and the Rio Grande ("Rio Bravo") are eleven place-names (east to west): "C. de la Cruz," "C. deserto," "R. de Montanhas," "R. de Laso," "Costa baixa," "R. Suelo," "Plaia," "La Madalena," "C. Blanco," "Costa de areboledas," "R. Solo." The name "Costa de pescadores" appears just below the "Rio Bravo."

50. *Paskaarte van Het Zuydelijckste van America Van Rio de la Plata, tot Caap de Hoorn, ende inde Zuyd Zee, tot B. de Koquimbo.* Pieter Goos. N.p., 1666. Color, scale indeterminable, 46 × 53.5 cm. From the first edition of Goos's *Atlas ofte Water-Weereld,* Amsterdam, 1666. MMNHMC.

A sea chart of all of South America south of the Rio de la Plata.

51. *Novissima Ac Exactissima Totius Orbis Terrarum Descriptio Magna.*
Jodocus Hondius and Nicolas Vissher. Amsterdam, 1669. Reprint. Edited
by Gunter Schilder. Amsterdam: Nico Israel, 1978. Facsimile of printed
map, scale indeterminable, twenty sheets, plus thirty-five page introductory text, bound in folio volume with stiff printed paper wrappers; original in the Bibliothèque Nationale, Paris. MMNHMC.

52. *A mapp or Generall Carte of the World Designed in two Plaine
Hemispheres.* Nicolas Sanson. 1651. Rendered into English and illustrated
by Richard Blome. N.p., n.d. Scale indeterminable, 39 × 52 cm. From
Blome's *A Geographical Description of the Four Parts of the World,* London, 1670. MMNHMC.

This is the lavishly ornamented English issue of Nicolas Sanson's *Mappemonde* of 1651.

53. *A Map of all the Earth and how after the Flood it was Divided among
the Sons of Noah.* Joseph Moxon. N.p., n.d. Scale indeterminable, 31.5 × 44
cm. map surrounded by fourteen panels containing biblical scenes. From
Moxon's *Sacred Geography,* London, 1671. Key identifying seventy-eight
sites. MMNHMC.

54. *L' Amerique Septentrionale divisée en ses principales parties, ou sont
distingués les uns des autres Les Estats suivant qu'ils appartiennent pre-
senteṁet aux François, Castillans, Anglois, Suedois, Danois, Hollandois,
tirée des Relations de toutes ces nations.* Guillaume Sanson. Paris, 1674.
Color, scale indeterminable, 60 × 89 cm. MMNHMC.

According to Jean Delanglez (Espíritu Santo, pp. 92–108), this map was
of utmost importance to Gulf coast cartography. It influenced European
geographers and later explorers of the Mississippi Valley. La Salle, for example, presumably carried a copy of the map with him when he descended
the Mississippi in 1682 (*ibid.,* p. 103).

The map varies from the elder Sanson's maps of America, in that the
largest river shown flowing into the Bahía del Espíritu Santo is Garcilasco
de la Vega's "Chucagua." Between that bay and Rio de Palmas are located
(east to west): a "R. de Montanas," a "C. [for Cape] d'Arboledo" at the
mouth of an unnamed river, a "R. de la Madalena," and a large unnamed
river. This last river is probably the Rio Grande, as a tributary named "Rio

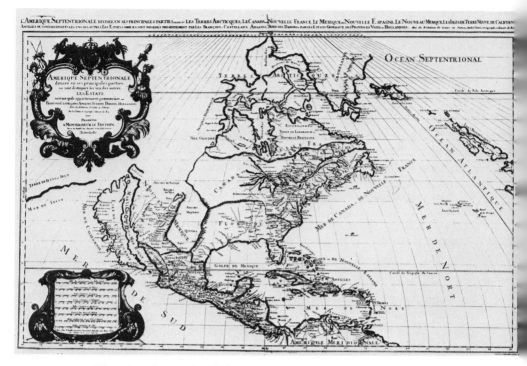

L'Amerique Septentrionale, by Guillaume Sanson, Paris, 1674. (See no. 54.) This map of North America greatly influenced European geographers and explorers of the Mississippi River Valley. According to Jean Delanglez, La Salle carried a copy of the map with him when he descended the Mississippi in 1682.

Conches" flows into it. That name has been in use since the seventeenth century (see, for example, Dunn, p. 67). Sanson probably associated this unnamed river not with the "Rio Bravo," or Rio Grande, but with the Rio Escondido, which La Salle believed to be the Mississippi. The configuration for the river is much more primitive than on Nicolosi's map of 1660–70, and Sanson shows several settlements located along a "R. del Norte" that flows through "Nouveau Mexique" to the "Mer Rouge," or present-day Gulf of California.

55. *De Cust Van Westindien, Van La Desconoscida, tot C. Escondido.* Arent Roggeveen. Amsterdam: Jacobus Robyn, 1675. Color, scale indeterminable, 41 × 50 cm. From Roggeveen's sea atlas, which was published in several languages and is known in English as *The Burning Fen.* MMNHMC.

The large Bahía del Espíritu Santo, so common on maps before the beginning of the eighteenth century, dominates the Gulf coast. The location of the bay near the point where the coast changes its orientation from due east-west to northeast-southwest corresponds closely to that of Galveston Bay. The Rio Grande appears clearly as "Rio Bravo." Eleven place-names are between that river and the Bahía del Espíritu Santo (east to west): "C. de St. Cruys," "Cabo de Zarto," "R. Montanbas," "R. Lasoo," "Costa Baxo," "R. Suela," "Plata," "R. Magdalena," "Cabo Blanco," "R. Descondido," and "R Solo." The coastline north of the Rio Grande is called "Costa de Piscadores."

The editors know of no previous Dutch chart that focuses so closely on the Texas coast. Koeman (*Atlantes Neerlandici*, 4:453) feels that Roggeveen's prototypes were Spanish *portulanos* prepared about 1665 and preserved in the collections of the East and West India companies.

56. *Lighting Colom of the Midland-Sea, Containing a Description of all the Knowne Coasts, Islands, Sands, Depthes and Roads: Beginning from the Narowest of the Streat unto Alexandrette in the Levant.* Jacob and Casparus Lootsman. 1677. Twenty double-page maps of the coasts of the Mediterranean, plus small maps and profiles interspersed with text, in quarto volume, blind-stamped calf covers, partially disbound. Transferred to the Rosenberg Library, 1905, from its predecessor, the Galveston Public Library.

This volume constitutes the third part of Lootsman's *Zeespiegel.* It first appeared, with Dutch text, in 1643. This edition precedes by one year the earliest English version listed by Koeman.

57. *Mappe-Monde ou Carte Generale du Globe Terrestre Representée in deux Plan-Hemispheres.* Nicolas Sanson. Printed by Pierre Mariette. Paris, 1678. Color, scale indeterminable, 43 × 57.5 cm. MMNHMC.

This is an extensively revised version of Sanson's 1651 world map. Particularly noticeable are the changes in the southern hemisphere, where the cartographer has added the discoveries of Dutch navigator Abel Janszoon Tasman.

58. *Orbis Terrarum Tabula Recens Emendata et in Lucem Edita.* Nicolas Visscher. Amsterdam, ca. 1679. Color, scale indeterminable, 30.5 × 48 cm.

map surrounded by decorative personifications of the continents, with two subsidiary hemispheres illustrating the Ptolemaic and Copernican theories. MMNHMC.

59. *Pascaert van Westindien ende Caribise Eylanden.* Frederick de Wit. Amsterdam, ca. 1680. Color, scale 1 in. to about 125 mi. MMNHMC.

This is a general map of the West Indies and the Gulf of Mexico. It is virtually identical in all respects to Peter Goos's map of 1666 (see no. 49) and gives the same eleven place-names for the area corresponding roughly to Texas.

The *National Maritime Museum Catalogue* (vol. 3, no. 191) lists a De Wit atlas (dated ca. 1675) in which this is map 96.

60. *Nova Totius Terrarum Orbis Tabula.* Justus Danckerts. Amsterdam, ca. 1680. Color, scale indeterminable, 49 × 58 cm. map surrounded by decorative personifications of the elements, with two subsidiary polar hemispheres. MMNHMC.

61. *Nova Totius Terrarum Orbis Geographica Ac Hydrographica Tabula.* Moses Pitt. N.p., n.d. Color, scale indeterminable, Mercator projection, 40 × 53 cm. map surrounded by twenty-one panels containing personifications of the seasons, the elements, the planets, and the seven wonders of the world. Untitled insets: North Pole; South Pole. MMNHMC.

This map, like many in the *English Atlas,* was based on an example found in Jansson's *Atlas contractus,* Amsterdam, 1666. Pitt's rendition of the Gulf Coast does not reflect La Salle's discoveries of 1682.

62. *Les Isles Britanniques qui contiennent les Royaumes d'Angleterre, Escosse, et Irlande distingués en leurs principales Provinces subdivisées en leurs Shireries ou Comtés.* Hubert Jaillot, 1681. Printed by Reinier and Josua Ottens. Amsterdam, ca. 1750. Color, scale indeterminable, 47 × 60 cm. Untitled inset: Orkney, Shetland, and Faroe islands. MMNHMC.

Jaillot first published this map in Paris ca. 1681. It was based on the Sanson map, ca. 1650. This is a late issue published by R. & J. Ottens in Amsterdam ca. 1750.

See *National Maritime Museum Catalogue,* vol. 3, p. 240, no. 77, for an example of this map with Jaillot's imprint alone and dated 1719.

63. *Carolina Newly Described.* John Seller. London, 1682. Scale indeterminable, 11 × 14 cm. MMNHMC.

Seller included this map of North and South Carolina in several of his miniature atlases. (See, for example, Phillips, *Atlases,* no. 505; Cumming, *Southeast,* no. 93).

64. *Planisphere, ou Carte Generale du Monde.* Pierre Du Val. Printed by Mademoiselle Du Val. 1684. Color, scale indeterminable, 34 × 58.5 cm. map, with two wind charts and a subsidiary hemisphere illustrating the Ptolemaic theory. MMNHMC.

65A. *Pas Kaart Van de Boght van Florida Met de Canaal Tusschen Florida en Cuba.* Johannes van Keulen. Amsterdam, 1684. Scale indeterminable, 51 × 58.5 cm. From part four of the 1684 edition of Van Keulen's *Zee Fakkel,* Amsterdam. Insets: "Bahia de Matanças"; "Havana"; "Baja Hondo." MMNHMC.

First published in 1684, part four of *Zee Fakkel* contained all the charts in the atlas that were devoted to the Americas. This chart is from an early edition and is the first state (1684). It reflects a pre–La Salle geography and gives relatively few place-names. The Gulf Coast is shown as far west as a "Cabo Escondido." This is probably the same "C. Escondido" that is the eastern terminus of the coastline on Roggeveen's map (see no. 55).

B. Second state: same title and insets, Gerard van Keulen, 1717. Scale indeterminable, 51 × 58 cm. From the 1717 French editions of part four of *Zee Fakkel,* Amsterdam. MMNHMC.

Gerard van Keulen extensively revised his father's map to include information gleaned from La Salle's discoveries and from French and Spanish settlement that followed exploration. The "Cabo Escondido" of the first state has disappeared, and "Rio Perdido" has taken its place. An important new feature, Pensacola Bay, appears just to the east. A "Fort Anconbaxo" is located near present-day Pensacola. The Florida peninsula has changed, and many new place-names appear. (See Koeman, *Atlantes Neerlandici,* 4:380.

The Rosenberg's collection contains an additional ten charts from the 1717 French edition of part four of the *Zee Fakkel* (see nos. 66–75).

66. *Pas Kaart Van de Zuyd Kust van Cuba en Van Geheel Yamaica en and're bygeleegen plaatsen.* Drawn by Claes Jansz Vooght. Amsterdam: Johannes van Keulen, n.d. Scale indeterminable, 51 × 59 cm. From part four of the 1717 French edition of van Keulen's *Zee Fakkel,* Amsterdam. Insets: "Baya Oristan in Yamaica"; "Baya Yamaica." MMNHMC.

The second state of a chart of Jamaica, the adjoining coast of southern Cuba, and a portion of the Honduran coast. (See no. 65 for further information.)

67. *Pas Kaart Van de Noord Kust van Espaniola met d Eylanden daar Benoorden.* Claes Jansz Vooght. Amsterdam: Johannes van Keulen, n.d. Scale indeterminable, 51 × 59 cm. From part four of the 1717 French edition of van Keulen's *Zee Fakkel,* Amsterdam. Insets: "T Eyland Turtuga"; "Porto de Guanives." MMNHMC.

The second state of a chart of the north coast of Hispaniola, the eastern tip of Cuba, and the lower Bahamas. (See no. 65 for further information.)

68. *Pas-Kaart Van de Zuyd-Kust van Espanjola met de Zee Kust van Nuevo Reyne de Granada.* Claes Jansz Vooght. Amsterdam: Johannes van Keulen, n.d. Scale indeterminable, 51 × 59 cm. From part four of the 1717 French edition of van Keulen's *Zee Fakkel,* Amsterdam. Inset: "Baya de Tiburaon." MMNHMC.

The first and only state of a chart that shows the southern coast of Hispaniola and the opposing Venezuelan and Colombian coast. (See no. 65 for further information.)

69. *Pas Kaart Van de Caribes Tusschen I. Barbados en I.S. Martin.* Claes Jansz Vooght. Amsterdam: Johannes van Keulen, n.d. Scale indeterminable, 51 × 59 cm. From part four of the 1717 French edition of van Keulen's *Zee Fakkel,* Amsterdam. Insets: "De Westkust van Guardalupa"; "de Rondom Bay van S Luzia"; "De Santos." MMNHMC.

The second state of a general chart of the Lesser Antilles: Barbados to St. Martin's, Virgin Islands. (See no. 65 for further information.)

70. *Pas-Kaart van de Golff de Guanaios Met' T Canaal Tusschen Yucatan en I. Cuba.* Claes Jansz Vooght. Amsterdam: Johannes van Keulen, n.d.

Scale indeterminable, 51 × 59 cm. From part four of the 1717 French edition of van Keulen's *Zee Fakkel,* Amsterdam. MMNHMC.

The second state of a chart showing the Yucatan and the western tip of Cuba. (See no. 65 for further information.)

71. *Pas-Kaart Vande Zee Kusten van Carthagena, Tierra Firma, Costa Rica ende Honduras. Tusschen Rio Grande de S. Martha en Cabo de Gratias Dios.* Claes Jansz Vooght. Amsterdam: Johannes van Keulen, n.d. Scale indeterminable, 51 × 59 cm. From part four of the 1717 French edition of van Keulen's *Zee Fakkel,* Amsterdam. Insets: "de Haaven van Carthagena"; "d Ithas de S. Barnardo"; "de Haavenen van nombre de Dios en Porta Bella"; "Escuda de Veragua." MMNHMC.

The first and only state of a chart showing the Caribbean coast from Santa Marta, Colombia, to the Honduras-Nicaragua border. (See no. 65 for further information.)

72. *Pas kaart Vande Kust van Guiana Tusschen R. Courantin en R. Oronoque Synde de Diepten van dese Rivieren in Vaademen, maar de diepten van R. Barbice, R. Demerary R., Esequeba, en R. Poumaron.* Claes Jansz Vooght. Amsterdam: Johannes van Keulen, n.d. Scale indeterminable, 51 × 59 cm. From part four of the 1717 French edition of van Keulen's *Zee Fakkel,* Amsterdam. Insets: "het Inkoomen van de Rivier Barbice"; "de Rivier van Esequebe." MMNHMC.

The third state of a chart of the South American Atlantic coast from the Orinoco River to the Courantyne River in the modern nation of Guyana. (See no. 65 for further information.)

73. *Pas-Kaart Van de Zee-kusten van Guiana Tusschen Cabo Noord en Rio Amano.* Claes Jansz Vooght. Amsterdam: Johannes van Keulen, n.d. Scale indeterminable, 51 × 59 cm. From part four of the 1717 French edition of van Kuelen's *Zee Fakkel,* Amsterdam. Insets: "t Fort van Cajana by de Inwoonders genaemt Sobarbiob"; "I Cayana." MMNHMC.

The second state of a chart showing part of the coasts of French Guiana and Brazil. (See no. 65 for further information.)

74. *Pas-kaart Vande Rivieren Commewini Suriname Suramaca Cupanama en Courantin.* Gerard van Keulen. N.p., n.d. Scale indeterminable, 51 × 59 cm. From part four of the 1717 French edition of van Keulen's *Zee Fakkel*, Amsterdam. Inset: "Asteekening van't Inkomen van de Rivier van Suriname." MMNHMC.

The first and only state of a chart of the coast of Surinam. (See no. 65 for further information.)

75. *Pas-Kaart Vande Zee Kusten inde Boght van Niew Engeland Tusschen de Staaten Hoek en C. de Sable.* Claes Jansz Vooght. Amsterdam: Johannes van Keulen, n.d. Scale indeterminable, 51 × 59 cm. From part four of the 1717 French edition of van Keulen's *Zee Fakkel*, Amsterdam. MMNHMC.

The second state of a chart of the American coast from Martha's Vineyard to Cape Sable, Nova Scotia. (See n. 65 for further information.)

76. *A Chart of the Sea Coasts Europe, Africa, and America, From the North Parts of Scotland, to Cape Bona Esperanca, and From Hudsons Straits to ye Maggellan Straits.* John Thornton. London, ca. 1685. Color, scale indeterminable, Mercator projection, 43 × 53 cm. From book three of Thornton's *Atlas Maritimus*, London, 1690–1703. MMNHMC.

77. *Carte Universelle du Commerce, c'est à dire Carte Hidrographique, où sont exactement décrites, Les Costes, des 4 Parties du Monde, Avecque les Routes pour la Navigation des Indes, Occidentales et Orientales.* Pierre Du Val. Paris, 1686. Color, scale indeterminable, Mercator projection, 37 × 53 cm. MMNHMC.

This is one of the earliest maps specifically designed to show major commercial sea routes. Carefully laid down are the two major world trade routes of the time: the route to and from the West Indies and that to and from the East Indies. Subsidiary routes (to India, the Congo, Mexico, the Rio de la Plata, Japan also appear. The discoveries of La Salle on the Gulf Coast (1682–85) do not appear.

78. *Carte Van Westindien, Soo Vaste Landen, als Eylanden, Nieuwelyckx Met Veele Perfexien Gecorigeert Ende Verbeetert, ende alle Clippen, Droochteen, Ree:en, Haavens, Rivieren, steeden, eñ Bergen, et. daar in genoteert soo die ghelege zyn.* Gerard Valk and Pieter Schenk. Amsterdam, ca. 1690. Color, scale indeterminable, 51.5 × 70.5 cm. MMNHMC.

A general map of the Gulf of Mexico and the Caribbean Sea. The Gulf Coast has the typical misconceptions current before La Salle's discovery of the mouth of the Mississippi in 1682. A giant Bahía del Spíritu Santo, with six rivers flowing into it, dominates the coast. The "R. Escondido" is shown as the boundary between Florida and New Spain (Mexico).

79. *Virginia and Maryland.* John Seller. London, ca. 1690. Scale indeterminable, 12 × 14.5 cm. MMNHMC.

This map appeared in various miniature atlases published by Seller. (See, for example, Phillips, *Atlases,* nos. 505, 529.)

80. *L'Amerique Meridionale Divisée en Ses Principales Parties.* Hubert Jaillot. Printed by Reinier & Josua Ottens. Amsterdam, ca. 1750. Color, scale 1 in. to approx. 200 mi., 48 × 60 cm. MMNHMC.

This is a general map of South America.

81. *A Mapp of the North Pole.* John Seller. N.p., n.d. Scale indeterminable, 12 × 14.5 cm. From Seller's *Hydrographia universalis,* London, ca. 1690. MMNHMC.

See Phillips, *Atlases,* no. 505.

82. *L'Espagne Divisée en tous ses Royaumes, Principautés, &c.* Hubert Jaillot. Printed by Reinier & Joshua Ottens. Amsterdam, ca. 1750. Color, scale indeterminable, 48 × 60 cm. MMNHMC.

83. *Aevi Veteris Usque ad Annum Salutis Nonagesimum Supra Milles Quadringentos Cogniti Tantum, Typus Geographic.* Vicenzo Maria Coronelli. Venice, 1691. Scale indeterminable, 44 × 66 cm. map surrounded by signs of the zodiac and descriptive text. MMNHMC.

This historical map shows a conception of the world of the classical period.

84. *Hos Globos Terracqueum, ac Caelestem dicat.* Vicenzo Maria Coronelli. Venice, n.d. Scale indeterminable, 24.5 × 47 cm. sheet containing twelve gores intended to be assembled into a small globe. The sheet was often bound into copies of Coronelli's *Atlante Veneto,* Venice, 1690–96. MMNHMC.

Coronelli follows Franquelin (1684) and places the mouth of the Mississippi too far to the west.

85. *Ocean Atlantique, ou Mer du Nord, Ou sont Exactement observée, le Route d'Europe aux Indes Occidentales, et des Indes Occidentales en Europe.* Pierre Mortier. Amsterdam, ca. 1696–1708. Color, scale indeterminable, 47 × 60.5 cm. MMNHMC.

86. *Planisphaerium Terrestre, Sive Terrarum Orbis, planisphaericē constructi repraesentatio quintuplex.* Carel Allard. Amsterdam, 1697. Color, scale indeterminable, 52 × 61 cm. map surrounded by twelve subsidiary hemispheres, showing the earth from different perspectives. Found in various atlases published by the Allard firm. MMNHMC.

Allard follows Franquelin (1684) and shows the Mississippi River too far to the west, near the mouth of the Rio Grande ("R. Magdelaine").

87. *Insulae Americanae in Oceano Septentrionali ac Regiones Adjacentes.* Nicolas Visscher. Amsterdam, 1698. Color, scale 1 in. to ca. 125 mi., 46 × 56 cm. MMNHMC.

This is a general map of the West Indies and the Gulf of Mexico. Koeman assigns a date of [1698] to this map (see *Atlantes Neerlandici*, vol. 5, *Index*, p. 279). It has the same basic configuration as the earlier charts of Goos (no. 49) and De Wit (no. 59), but it adds extensive interior detail and its treatment of coastal place-names is much fuller. Visscher gives seventeen place-names between a "Bahia del Spiritu Santo" and the "Rio Bravo" (east to west): "C. de Cruz," "C. Deserto," "Rio da Montanhas," "R. de Laso," "R. de Pescadores," "Rio de Oro," "C. de Arboledo," "R. Bravo," "Costa Baixa," "R. Suelo," "Plaia," "R. de Magdalena," "Costa deserta," "R. Escondido," "C. Blano, " "Costa de Arboledas," "R. Solo." The "R. Escondido" is the river that La Salle identified with the Mississippi. It appears as a large stream that forms the boundary between "Florida" and New Spain (Mexico).

By 1698 this configuration was out of date. There is no sign yet of an identifiable Mississippi River or of any French activities along the coast.

88. *Tabula Nova complectens Praefecturas Normanniae, et Britanniae, una cum Angliae parte et Manica.* Nicolas Visscher. Amsterdam, ca. 1698. Color, scale indeterminable, 47 × 56 cm. MMNHMC.

This map focuses on the English Channel.

89. *A Draft of the Golden & Adjacent Islands, with part of ye Isthmus of Darien as it was taken by Capt. Jenefer, Where ye Scots West-India Company were settled,* together with *A New Map of Ye Isthmus of Darien in America, the Bay of Panama, The Gulph of Vallona, or St. Michael, with its Islands & Countries Adjacent.* William Hacke. 1699. London: John Senex, 1721. Color, scale indeterminable, 48.5 × 59 cm. sheet. From Senex's *New General Atlas.* MMNHMC.

Hermann Moll originally published these maps in 1699. Senex pulled this 1721 issue from the original plate, but he removed the names of Moll and Hacke and added a new dedication, to John Holdans of Gleneagles. See Phillips, *Atlases,* no. 563.

90. *Archipelague du Mexique ou sont les Isles de Cuba, Espagnole, Jamaïque, &c.* [above upper neat line]: *Téâtre de la Guerre en Amérique telle qu'elle est à present possedée par les Espagnols, Anglois, François, et Hollandois, &c.* Pierre Mortier. Amsterdam, n.d. Color, scale 1 in. to approx. 70 mi., 60 × 100 cm. From volume two of Mortier's *Atlas Nouveau,* Amsterdam, 1702. MMNHMC.

Mortier based this work on La Salle's erroneous reports of Gulf Coast geography. The map shows the mouth of the Mississippi, discovered in 1682, but incorrectly places it on the Texas coast. To the east, at its traditional location near the center of the coast, is the Bahía del Espíritu Santo. Between the mouth of the Mississippi and the Rio Grande are two coastal place names: "Riv. aux vaches" and a point on the Gulf, "Caye de St. Louis," into which the former flows. J. B. L. Franquelin had introduced La Salle's geography on the *Carte de la Louisiane ou des voyages du Sr. de la Salle,* 1684. Franquelin's map remained the standard reference for Gulf Coast geography until the appearance of the maps of Guillaume de L'Isle (from 1700). Coronelli (1688), Hennepin (1697), and others, including Pieter Mortier, copied the misinformation from Franquelin's map to this general map of the Gulf of Mexico and the West Indies.

Koeman mentions Mortier's map only in connection with its inclusion in volume two of the *Atlas nouveau,* published in 1702. The map may have appeared some years earlier for sale as a separate sheet (see Koeman, *Atlantes Neerlandici,* 3:9, for a reference to such a precedent in the maps of Mortier).

91. *Le Golfe de Mexique, et les Isles Voisine=Archipelague du Mexique, ou sont les Isles de Cuba, Espagnola, Jamaica, &c.* Pierre Mortier. Amsterdam, n.d. Color, scale 1 in. to approx. 100 mi., 59 × 85 cm. From part G of Mortier's *Neptune Français,* Amsterdam, 1700 MMNHMC.

This chart is similar to no. 90, with a transitional geography consisting of a "B. de Spirito Sancto" and a misplaced Mississippi River to the west. It is, however, much richer in coastal place-names. Generally these agree with those on the Dutch charts of the late seventeenth century.

92. *Carte Particulière de Isthmus ou Darien, Qui comprend le Golfe de Panama &c.* Pierre Mortier. Amsterdam, n.d. Color, scale 1 in. to approx. 8 English leagues. From part G of Mortier's *Neptune Français,* Amsterdam, 1700. Insets: "Rade de Darien et les Isles aux Environs"; "Carte de la rade de Cartagène et des Environs &c." MMNHMC.

93. *L' Amerique Septentrionale.* Guillaume de L'Isle. Printed by Covens & Mortier. Amsterdam, n.d. Color, scale indeterminable, 45 × 58 cm. From Covens and Mortier's *Atlas Nouveau,* Amsterdam, 1700–30.

A late issue of a foundation map of North America. De L'Isle was the most illustrious and privileged French cartographer during the age when that nation's explorers led all others in contributing to the geographical knowledge of North America. As a result, virtually all of his maps of America were innovative and influential.

This was De L'Isle's first map relating to North America, and it has been widely acclaimed as the earliest map to show the results of Iberville's discoveries and explorations. This state previously was assumed to be the original printing, but in mid–1981 there was discovered a formerly unknown state of the map, which exhibits a more primitive, pre-Iberville geography identical to that on De L'Isle's globe of 1700 (see Stevenson, *Terrestrial and Celestial Globes,* vol. 2, fig. 118; Delanglez, "Documents," pp. 278–79). The plate from which this newly recognized first state was printed was revised shortly after Iberville's return from America in the summer of 1700, so that the second state (Tooley's first issue) shows the results of Iberville's first and second voyages. Both the first state and the second state bear De L'Isle's "Rue des Canettes" address, and all issues preserve the date 1700.

The familiar second state is the earliest map to abandon the old Franquelin-type geography, which had located the mouth of the Mississippi on the south Texas coast. Thus, Texas geography begins to assume a comprehensible form for the first time. There is no sign of Galveston Bay, but a number of Texas rivers, including the Brazos ("La Maligne R."), are identifiable.

This late issue, published in Amsterdam about 1730, preserves the geography of the revised second state, but the publishers have rearranged the map's decorative elements.

94. *Carte Particuliere de la Caroline Dresse sur les Memoires le Plus Nouveaux.* Pierre Mortier. Amsterdam, n.d. Color, scale 1 in. to ca. 1 French league., 48 × 59.5 cm. From part G of Covens and Mortier's *Neptune Français,* Amsterdam, 1700. MMNHMC.

95. *Mappe-Monde.* Guillaume de L'Isle. Paris, 1700. Color, scale indeterminable, 43 × 65.6 cm. MMNHMC.

The delineation of the Mississippi River and Ohio River valleys is quite advanced, except that the lower course of the former river veers too much to the northeast. The Mississippi River Delta still appears in a schematic fashion.

96. *A New Map of the Terraqueous Globe according to the latest Discoveries and most general Divisions of it into Continents and Oceans.* Edward Wells. Engraved by Michael Burghers. Oxford, n.d. Color, scale indeterminable, 37 × 50.5 cm. From Wells's *A New Set of Maps both of Ancient and present Geography,* Oxford, 1700. MMNHMC.

This historical map shows a conception of the world in the classical period.

97. *A New Map of the Tarraqueous Globe according to the Ancient Discoveries and most general Divisions of it into Continents and Oceans.* Edward Wells. Engraved by Michael Burghers. Oxford, n.d. Scale indeterminable, 37 × 50.5 cm. From Wells's *A New Set of Maps both of Ancient and present Geography,* Oxford, 1700. MMNHMC.

98. *Planisphaerium Coeleste.* Peter Schenk. Amsterdam, ca. 1700. Color, scale indeterminable, 48 × 55.5 cm. chart surrounded by six hemispheres illustrating various astronomical theories. MMNHMC.

99. *Carte du Mexique et de la Florida des Terres Angloises et des Isles Antilles du Cours et des Environs de la Riviere de Mississippi. Dressée sur un grand nombre de memoires principalement sur ceux de Mrs. d'Iber-*

ville et le Sueur. Guillaume de L'Isle. Engraved by Charles Simonneau. Paris, 1703. Color, scale indeterminable, 47 × 65 cm.

First issue, with the "Rue des Canettes" address. This is an important map in the evolution of knowledge of Texas, the Mississippi Valley, and the United States Gulf Coast. It is quite similar to De L'Isle's 1702 manuscript map, now preserved in the French Bureau of Foreign Affairs (see Wheat, *Transmississippi West,* no. 82), and is the first detailed printed cartographic record of the discoveries and foundations of Iberville. It represents a significant advance over the geographer's map of North America of 1700 (see no. 93), as it is much richer in detail and generally presents land masses more accurately than any previous map. The map was highly influential, went through several issues, and was avidly copied by other cartographers. One measure of the prestige of this map is that it was re-issued for nearly a century.

Galveston Bay is still absent, but Matagorda Bay ("Baye St. Louis nommée par les Espagnols St. Bernard") is prominent. The Texas river system is improved and more detailed. The Colorado River is named "R. aux Cannes," the Brazos is "La Maligne," and the Trinity, which flows directly into the Gulf, is "R. de Sworas." To the east of the Trinity, a "R. Boho," probably the Sabine, flows into a large bay (Sabine Lake?). Bryan and Hanak (p. 7) identified these rivers as follows: "R. Boho," the Trinity; "La Maligne," the Colorado; "R. aux Cannes," the Guadalupe; and "R. de Sivoras," the Navasota. A number of additional streams are located and named.

100. *A Map of the West-Indies or the Islands of America in the North Sea; with ye adjacent Countries; explaining what belongs to Spain, England, France, Holland, &c. also ye Trade Winds, and ye several Tracts made by ye Galeons and Flota from place to place.* Herman Moll. London, ca. 1710. Color, scale indeterminable, 58 × 100.5 cm. Insets: "La Vera Cruz"; "A Draught of St. Augustin and its Harbour"; "A Draught of ye Citty of Cartagena its Harbour & Forts"; "A Draught of ye bay & Citty of Havana"; "The Bay of Porto Bella." Vignette: "The city of Mexico in New Spain," with key identifying sites. MMNHMC.

A general chart of the Gulf of Mexico and the Caribbean Sea. The mouth of the Mississippi is correctly positioned, with a delta, at the midpoint of the coast. New Orleans, not founded until 1718, is absent, but a number of French and Spanish settlements in the region (Pensacola, Mobile, Fort St. Pierre) and a host of Indian villages appear. The geography of the Texas coast is dominated by "St. Bernard or St. Louis Bay" (Matagorda) and is otherwise confused. A number of rivers appear, but they are not identifiable. Moll shows Florida as English and Texas as French.

101. *A View of ye General & Coasting Trade-Winds, Monsoons or ye Shifting Trade Winds through ye World, Variations &c.* Herman Moll. London, ca. 1710. Scale indeterminable, Mercator projection, 19 × 52.5 cm. MMNHMC.

102. *Nova Delineatio Totius Orbis Terrarum.* Pieter van der Aa. Leiden, ca., 1713. Color, scale indeterminable, 26 × 34.5 cm. map surrounded by decorative personifications of the four elements and of day and night. MMNHMC.

103. *Mappe-Monde ou Carte Universelle.* Nicolas de Fer. Engraved by Charles Inselin. Paris, 1714. Scale indeterminable, Mercator projection, 23 × 34 cm. MMNHMC.

104. *Virginia Marylandia et Carolina in America Septenrionali Britannorum industria excultae repraesentatae.* Johann Baptista Homann. Nuremberg, 1714. Color, scale indeterminable, 48.5 × 58.5 cm. MMNHMC.

This map shows the American coast from South Carolina north to Connecticut. A few depth soundings and anchorages are given for coastal areas.

105. *A Chart of Ye West Indies or the Islands of America in the North Sea &c. being ye Present seat of War.* Herman Moll. Printed by Thomas and John Bowles. London, ca. 1715. Color, scale indeterminable, 27.5 × 35.5 cm. Inset: "La Vera Cruz." MMNHMC.

106. *Le Golfe de Mexique, Et les Provinces et Isles qui l'Environe comme sont La Floride Au Nord, Le Mexique ou Nouvelle Espagne A l'Ouest La Terre-Ferme Au Sud, Les Is. Antilles, Lucayes, St. Domingue et Jamaique A l'Est.* Nicolas de Fer. Paris, 1717. Color, scale indeterminable, 46.5 × 60.5 cm. MMNHMC.

A general map of the Gulf of Mexico and the West Indies, showing a well-formed Mississippi Delta and Gulf Coast and locating La Salle's fort ("Fort de Francois") on Matagorda Bay, Texas ("Baye de St. Louis et de St.

Bernard"). Unlike most maps of the period, including De L'Isle's famous *Carte de la Louisiane* (1718), De Fer's displays Florida correctly as a peninsula rather than as the broken archipelago introduced by Thomas Nairne in 1711.

107. *Mappe-Monde ou Carte Generale de la Terre.* Nicolas de Fer. Paris, 1717. Scale indeterminable, 23 × 34 cm. map surrounded by nine portraits of early explorers. MMNHMC.

108. *Carte de la Louisiane et du Cours du Mississippi.* Guillaume de L'Isle. 1718. Revised by Philippe Buache. Paris, 1745. Color, scale indeterminable, 48 × 65 cm. Inset: "Carte Particulière des Embouchures de la Rivie. S. Louis et de la Mobile."

This is the fourth state of the five identified by Tooley, who cites the work as "the first detailed map of the Gulf region and the Mississippi" (*French Mapping of the Americas,* no. 46).

Texas is named for the first time ("Mission de los Teijas etablie en 1716") and includes a wealth of human detail (missions, settlements, Indian villages, mines). Other features include Natchitoches (France's most westerly permanent outpost, established 1717), Adaïe (Adaes), Ainaïs, Les Cenis, and Naouadiches (Nacogdoches). The routes of La Salle, De Soto, and St. Denis appear; and De L'Isle shows La Salle's fort ("Fort Francois") on Matagorda Bay and identifies the site of his death on a tributary of the Trinity. De L'Isle drew many of his details from the manuscripts of Le Maire (1716) and Vermale (1717) (see introduction, note 55).

Eleven rivers enter the Gulf of Mexico between Nachitoches and the Rio Grande (east to west). First are "Petite R. de la Madelene," "R. de Flores," "R. de Se. Susanne," "Bocachica," and "R. de la Trinite." The last-named river is of course the present-day Trinity, which flows into Galveston Bay. De L'Isle shows a very small bay, really no more than a widening of the river's mouth. On the east bank of this inlet is a site labeled "Judosa." (The Vermale manuscript shows the inlet, but it applies the name "Judosa" to a stream just east of the Trinity that De L'Isle has omitted.) This small inlet is the first definitely identifiable bay at the site of Galveston Bay. Next is a "la Dure R.," followed by "la Maline R." (the modern-day Brazos), "la Sablonniere R.," "R. aux Cannes" (the Colorado), "Rio Guadalupe ou de la Madelaine," and "Rio Hondo."

For more information on this foundation map, see Fite and Freeman, no. 46; Lowery, no. 288; Karpinski, p. 133; Cumming, *Southeast,* no. 170;

Thomassy, p. 211; *Streeter Sale*, vol. 1, no. 113; Wheat, *Transmississippi West*, no. 99.

109. *Partie la Plus Meridionale de L'Amerique, ou se Trouve Le Chili, Le Paraguay, et les Terres Magellaniques avec Les Fameux Detroits de Magellan et de le Maire Dressée Sur divers Memoires et Relations des Flibustiers et Fameux Voyageurs.* Nicolas de Fer. 1720. Revised by Guillaume Danet. Paris, 1737. Color, scale indeterminable, 49 × 62.5 cm. Key locating ten sites.

This is a general map of the southern part of South America.

110. *Carte Generale de la Terre ou Mappe Monde.* A. Danet. Printed by Guillaume Danet. Paris, 1720. Color, scale indeterminable, 49 × 72.5 cm. Map surrounded by text and astronomical diagrams. MMNHMC.

111. *A New map of the English Empire in the Ocean of America or West Indies.* Christopher Brown. 1700. Revised by John Senex. London, 1721. Color, scale indeterminable, 51 × 60 cm. From Senex's *A New General Atlas,* London, 1721. MMNHMC.

The sheet contains a small general map of the West Indies plus six individual maps of British colonial islands: Jamaica, Bermuda, Barbados, Antigua, Tobago, and St. Christopher.

112. *Introduction a la Geographie de la Correspondance du Globe Terrestre ou Mappe Monde avec la Sphere Celeste par les Cercles, les Lignes, et les Points qui sont Imaginés dans celle cy, et ceux qui se decrivent sur l'Autre.* Nicolas de Fer. Printed by A. Danet. Paris, 1722. Color, scale indeterminable, 45 × 68 cm. map surrounded by text. MMNHMC.

This map illustrates the various divisions that man makes of the globe: meridians, parallels, climatic zones.

113. *Hemisphere Occidental,* accompanied by *Hemisphere Oriental.* Guillaume de L'Isle. Engraved by Jean Baptiste Delahaye. Paris, 1724. Color, scale indeterminable, two sheets forming 51 × 102 cm. map. MMNHMC.

See Wagner, no. 527. The *British Museum Catalogue* (15:544) lists an issue of this map published by Covens and Mortier in Amsterdam. See

Tooley, *French Mapping of the Americas,* no. 22, for the left-hand (American) sheet.

114. *Plan du Port decouvert dans le Golfe du Mexique le 21. d'Aoust 1721. par mr. Benard de la Harpe l'un des commandants a la Louisianne il est sçitué par les 29 degrez 15. minuttes de Lattitude a 100. lieües a l'Ouest de l'Embouchure du Mississipi.* France. Navy. Paris, 1725. After Bénard de la Harpe, 1721. Ink and watercolor on paper, scale indeterminable, 49.5 × 74 cm. MMNHMC.

The French hydrographic office prepared this highly finished manuscript map of Galveston Bay from field sketches made during La Harpe's 1721 expedition. It is both the earliest known map specifically of Galveston Bay and the earliest of any kind to show this major feature of the Texas coast. A variant of this manuscript is in the collection of the Library of Congress (see Lowery, no. 302 [2]).

Bénard de la Harpe was one of the most memorable of the French explorer-adventurers who figured prominently in the early history of Louisiana and Texas. On December 19, 1720, he was appointed commander of an expedition that was organized to reestablish a French beachhead on the western Gulf Coast. His instructions were to erect a trading post and fort at the "Bay of St. Bernard" (Matagorda Bay), the site of La Salle's fort in 1685. La Harpe entered a large body of water, which he quickly realized was not St. Bernard's Bay, but an unknown one. The French force was too small and poorly supplied, however, to establish a foothold against strong opposition from the local Indians, and the project was abandoned.

This important episode in Texas history, the first European attempt to plant a colony at Galveston Bay, went largely unnoticed in contemporary Europe and has been the source of considerable confusion among modern historians. J. B. B. Anville's great map of North America, Paris, 1746, contains a notation concerning a "Baye des Français" discovered by the French in 1720 [sic]. "Port des Français" is the name given to the bay discovered by La Harpe on the Library of Congress copy of La Harpe's manuscript (see below), but Anville associates La Harpe's bay with modern-day San Antonio Bay rather than with Galveston Bay. Apart from this ill-informed reference, commercial cartographers completely overlooked La Harpe's discovery, and they continued to omit Galveston Bay from printed maps until the publication of the *Carta Esférica* in 1799. La Harpe's own written account of the expedition remained unpublished until 1831.

Modern historians have been uncertain whether La Harpe landed at St.

Bernard's Bay, as instructed, or at Galveston Bay (see, for example, Bolton, pp. 283–84). La Harpe's manuscript map proves conclusively that the bay he entered in August, 1721, was Galveston, and it is puzzling that the map has so long remained in obscurity, especially since the Library of Congress copy has been in that collection since at least the turn of the century. Cartographic scholar Woodbury Lowery examined the map, but he did not recognize its configuration as that of Galveston Bay.

The map in fact shows Galveston Bay in an accurate and easily recognizable form. It is far superior to the Evía-type maps that were published from 1799. Galveston Island is unnamed, but bears the legend "Isle de nuiron vingt lieues de long." On the northeastern shore of the bay, in the vicinity of the present-day town of Anahuac, are two notations: "Etangs d'eau douce" and "dans ce lieu Mr. de la Harpe a trouvé une nation errante et Antropophages composeé de 200 personnes." The latter reference is to the Indians, who, La Harpe notes in the *Journal historique*, refused to allow the French to establish their settlement. Pelican Island appears but is unnamed. The main channel into the bay passes between Pelican and Galveston islands, the site of present-day Galveston Harbor. West Bay is labeled "Chenal qui conduit aux environs de la Baye St. Bernard," which completely refutes Folmer's Contention (p. 274) that the bay designated St. Bernard's Bay in La Harpe's instructions was not Matagorda Bay but Galveston Bay. La Harpe clearly distinguishes between St. Bernard's Bay and this bay, discovered August 21, 1721. Hanna's Reef and Red Fish Bar are crudely noted and labeled "batture remplie d'Hots de Sable." Half Moon Shoal and Dollar Point Shoal are "Hots de Sable." Fort Point is a fragmented archipelago marked with a flag; evidently this was the site where La Harpe landed and laid claim to the country for France.

The Library of Congress copy, which is found in an eighteenth-century manuscript copy of La Harpe's *Journal historique,* is generally sketchier, with fewer depth soundings, and gives the bay the name "Port des Français," as already noted. Galveston Island is named "Isle de la Harpe." This copy bears the additional notation "Il peut avoir dans cette ouverture de Baye quelques Enfoncements où Rivieres dont on n'a pu prendre connaissance" along the bay's west bank. The date of discovery is mistakenly given as "27 aoust."

[Bénard de la Harpe], *Journal historique* . . . (see Streeter, *Bibliography,* no. 1126, about the questionable authorship of this work); Margry, 6:319–54; Bolton, pp. 283–84; Folmer, pp. 319–54; Wedel, "J. B. Benard, Sieur de la Harpe: Visitor to the Wichitas in 1719." See also Lowery, no. 302 [2].

115. *Atlas Coelestis.* John Flamsteed. 1729. Printed by C. Nourse. London, 1781. Scale varies, twenty-seven double-folio plates bound in folio volume, contemporary marbled boards, modern calf backstrip with original spine label. MMNHMC.

The *Atlas coelestis* is generally recognized as one of the great printed works to issue from British astronomy. Flamsteed prepared twenty-five of the plates, celestial charts focusing on major constellations visible from Greenwich. He used an innovative projection now known as the Sanson-Flamsteed Sinusoidal Projection. Abraham Sharp prepared the two remaining plates, which are equatorial planispheres.

Preparation of the plates began as early as 1696, but the first edition did not appear until 1729.

116. *Plan de la Baye de Riosanerio située a la Coste du Bresil.* France. Navy. Drawn by P. Capassi. Paris, 1730. Ink and watercolor on paper, scale indeterminable, 50 × 72.5 cm. MMNHMC.

Official scientific cartography in Brazil can be said to begin with the royal charter that Joao V extended in November, 1729, to P. Doningos Capaci, or Capassi, and his companion Diego Soares. Baron Homem de Melo places this charter (*alvara*) immediately after his preface to *Atlas do Brazil.*

117. *Typus Orbis Terrarum.* Phillip Cluver. Amsterdam, 1729. Scale indeterminable, 16 × 30.5 cm. map surrounded by decorative personifications of the elements and of day and night. MMNHMC.

118A. *Carte de la Terre Ferme du Perou, du Bresil et du Pays des Amazones, Dressée sur les Descriptions de Herrera, de Laet, et des P. P. d'Acuña, et M. Rodriguez, et sur plusieurs Relations et Observations posterieures.* Guillaume de L'Isle. Printed by Covens and Mortier. Amsterdam, 1730. Color, scale indeterminable, 47.5 × 57 cm. MMNHMC.

B. Another issue: same title (with slight variations), cartographer, and color, but revised by Philippe Buache, 1745, and revised and augmented by J. A. Dezauche, Paris, 1782. 47.5 × 65 cm. MMNHMC.

These are two late, revised issues of Guillaume de L'Isle's landmark map of the northern part of South America, first published in 1703. Tooley identifies them as the fifth and seventh issues, respectively (*French Mapping of the Americas*, nos. 74, 76). The 1782 issue is the last issue and is a revision of Buache's issue of 1745 (ibid., no. 75). Tooley reproduces the imprints of the first and third issues of the map (ibid., pl. XVI).

119. *Mappe-Monde.* Guillaume de L'Isle. 1700. Printed by Covens and Mortier. Amsterdam, 1730. Color, scale indeterminable, 50 × 63.5 cm. map, with subsidiary hemispheres showing the world from different angles. MMNHMC.

This is the revised Dutch issue of Guillaume de L'Isle's world map of 1700.

120. *Nova Designatio Insulae Jamaicae ex Antillanis Americae Septentrion.* George Matthaus Seutter. Printed by Johann Michael Probst. Augsburg, 1730. Color, scale indeterminable, 48.5 × 56 cm. Descriptive text. MMNHMC.

121. *Atlas historique.* Henri Abraham Chatelain. Paris, 1732–39. A collection of five maps from this atlas: (1) *Nouveaux Mappemonde ou Globe Terrestre avec des Tables et des remarques pour conduire a la connoissance de la Geographie et de l'Histoire.* Scale indeterminable, 48 × 67.0 cm. map surrounded by geographical tables and text. (2) *Mappe-Monde pour connoitre les progres & les conquestes les plus Remarquables des Provinces-Unies, Ainsy que celles des Campagnies d'Orient et d'Occident, Et les Païs qu'elles possèdent dans l'un et dans l'autre Hemisphere.* Scale indeterminable, 33.5 × 45 cm. map surrounded by text illustrating the rise of the Dutch empire. (3) *Nouvelle Carte pour conduire a l'Astronomie et à la Geographie et pour faire connoitre les differens Sistemes du Monde, avec diverses Observations.* Scale indeterminable, 51 × 60.5 cm. sheet containing the map, a celestial chart, several diagrams of astronomical theories, etc. (4) *MappeMonde ou Description Generale du Globe Terrestre.* Scale indeterminable, 34.5 × 45 cm. map with geographical text and tables, including a dictionary of thirty-three terms. (5) *Plan de l'Histoire universelle, où l'on voit les quatre Monarchies du Monde, et tous les Anciens Etats aussi bien que ceux qui subsistent aujourdhuy.* Scale indeterminable, 34 × 44.5 cm. MMNHMC.

122. *A Map of the British Empire in America with the French and Spanish Settlements adjacent thereto.* Henry Popple. London: William Henry

Thoms and R. W. Searle, 1733. Color, scale indeterminable, two untitled 50 × 67 cm. sheets, nos. 9 and 13, from a twenty-sheet set of the given title. MMNHMC.

Henry Popple's *Map of the British Empire . . .* was the most important English depiction of North America published to date. It is especially remarkable for its grand scale ("the first large-scale printed map of North America," according to Schwartz and Ehrenberg). These two continuous sheets show the western half of the Gulf of Mexico. They include all of the Gulf coast from Pensacola west to the Spanish settlements on the upper Rio Grande and inland to the southern parallel of Kansas. Most of Popple's information for the Gulf Coast came from De L'Isle's *Carte de la Louisiane . . .* , 1718, but there are a number of curious differences, such as the form given to the river system that drains into Mobile Bay.

123. *Les principales Fortresses Ports &c. de L'Amérique Septentrionale.* Henry Popple. N.p., n.d. Color, scale indeterminable, 54 × 60 cm. Originally published in the French edition of Popple's *Map of the British Empire in America,* London, 1733, this version is from the 1741 edition of De L'Isle's *Atlas Nouveau,* Covens and Mortier, Amsterdam. MMNHMC. (See no. 122 for further information.)

Covens and Mortier gathered together the insets on each of the twenty sheets of the 1733 English issue of Popple's map and published them on one sheet. There are eighteen different maps—almost all with individual titles—of important American ports or islands: *The Harbour of Placentia, The Town and Harbour of Charles Town in South Carolina, Fort Royal in Martinica, Curacao, Cartagene on the Coast of New Spain, Harbour of Porto Bello, Bermuda or Summer Islands, Kingston Harbour in Jamaica, Antigua, The Island of Barbadoes, The Harbour of Providence [Bahamas], Harbour of St Augustine, The Havana, Bay of St. Iago in Cuba, A Plan of the Harbour of Port Antonio in Jamaica, New York and Perthamboy Harbours, Boston Harbour,* and *The Harbour of Anapolis Royal.*

124. *Le Globe Terrestre Representé en Deux Plans-Hemispheres, et en Diverses autres figures.* Vicenzo Maria Coronelli. Revised by Jean Nicolas du Trallage. Printed by Jean Baptiste Nolin. Paris, 1740. Color, scale indeterminable, 45.5 × 60 cm. map surrounded by ten maps showing the world in various projections. MMNHMC.

125. *Mappa Geographica, complectens: I. Indiae Occidentalis Partem Mediam Circum Isthmum Panamensem. II. Ipsumque Isthmum. III. Ichnographiam praecipuorum locorum & portuum ad has terras pertinentium.* Nuremberg: Homann Heirs, 1740. Color, scale indeterminable, 48 × 58 cm. sheet with five maps and one view: (1) *Cartes des Isles de l'Amérique et deplusieurs Pays de Terre ferme situés au devant de ces Isles & autour du Golfe de Mexique,* Jean Baptiste Bourguignon d'Anville, Paris, 1731 (map of the Gulf and the Caribbean, color-coded to show the various European possessions). (2) *Delineatio munim enti et Portus S. Augustini* (plan of St. Augustine, Florida, with key locating eight sites). (3) *Delineatio Portus Mexicani Vera Cruz,* from V. S. Crucis, *Hist. de S. Domingue,* vol. 12, p. 505 (plan of Vera Cruz, Mexico, with key locating sixteen sites). (4) *Ichnographia Urbis San-Domingo* (plan of Santo Domingo, Dominican Republic). (5) Untitled map of Panama. (6) *Urbs capitalis Regni Mexicani dicta Mexico* (bird's-eye view of Mexico City). MMNHMC.

126. *Plan de la Ville, Rade et Forts de Porto Bello, Pris par le Vice Amiral Edouard Vernon. Esqr. Avec Six Vaisseaux de Guerre, le 22 Novembre 1739.* Drawn by Philip Durell. Printed by Pierre Mortier. Amsterdam, 1740. Scale indeterminable, 42 × 57 cm. Key locating sixteen sites. MMNHMC.

This is Pierre Mortier's continental issue of Philip Durell's map, which was originally published in the same year (1740). It shows the attack of Admiral Edward Vernon on Portobello during the War of Jenkins' Ear.

127. *Nova Anglia Septentrionali Americae implantata Anglorumque coloniis florentissima Geographice exhibita.* Johann Baptista Homann. Nuremberg, ca. 1740. Color, scale indeterminable, 49 × 59 cm. MMNHMC.

This map shows New England, New York, and New Jersey, and gives depth soundings, shoals, etc., for coastal waters.

128. *Tabula Anemographica seu Pyxis Nautica, vulgo Compass. Charte qua Ventorum Noïa septem linguis graeca fcil. latina, italica, hispanica, gallica, hollandica et germanica repraesentantur succincte elaborata.* George Matthaus Seutter. Augsburg, ca. 1740. Color, scale indeterminable, 49.5 × 57.5 cm. MMNHMC.

This hemispheric wind chart identifies thirty-two winds used by mariners and gives the name of each in six languages.

129. *Plan du Port de la Ville et des Fortresses de Carthagène, représentant exactemant la Vue de la Flotte Angloise, le long de la Côte, dans la Baye proche la Ville &c.* William Laws. Printed by Covens and Mortier. Amsterdam, 1741. Scale indeterminable, 33.5 × 57 cm. map on 50 by 57 cm. sheet. Key locating forty-eight sites. MMNHMC.

This plan illustrates the unsuccessful attack of Admiral Edward Vernon on the Spanish colonial port of Cartagena, Colombia, during the War of Jenkins' Ear.

130. *Cartes des Côtes Meridionales de L'Isle de Terre Neuve Comprenant les Isles Royale et de Sable Avec la partie du Grand Banc, où se fait le pêche de la Morue.* Drawn by Philipe Buache. Engraved by F. Desbruslins. Printed by J. A. Dezuache. Paris, 1741. Color, scale indeterminable, 25 × 33 cm. Map no. 4 from an unidentified book or atlas. MMNHMC.

Harrisse describes a similar Buache map that must be from the same source (*Decouverte*, pl. 26).

131. *Wereld-Kaart.* Isaak Tirion. Drawn and engraved by C. Segp. Amsterdam, 1744. Color, scale indeterminable, 33 × 42 cm. map with two subsidiary polar hemispheres. MMNHMC.

132. *Nova Isthmi Americani, qui et Panamiensis item Dariensis, Tabula, in qua Urbes Porto Bello, Panama et Carthagena.* Reinier and Josua Ottens. Amsterdam, ca. 1745. Color, scale indeterminable, 44 × 54 cm. MMNHMC.

The map shows much of Central America, the Colombian coast, Jamaica, and southern Hispaniola. The routes of the Spanish galleons are noted.

133. *Le Neptune Oriental, ou Routier Général des Côtes des Indes Orientales et de la Chine, Enrichi de Cartes Hydrographiques tant Génerales que Particulieres, pour servir d'Instruction à la Navigation de ces differentes Mers.* Jean Baptiste Nicolas Denis Après de Mannevillette. Engraved by Guillaume Dheulland. Printed by Jean-François Robustel. Paris, 1745. Twenty-five charts, with eleven supplemental charts, bound in folio volume, board covers with vellum backstrip. MMNHMC.

A specially prepared copy of the first edition of Après de Mannevillette's *Le Neptune Oriental.* In most particulars, this volume agrees with the copy in the Library of Congress (Phillips, *Atlases,* no. 3163), with twenty-five charts, all devoted to the coasts of Asia. It lacks, however, the engraved frontispiece (and evidently never contained it) and has special manuscript ornamentation and hydrographic detail (rhumb lines, etc.) added in manuscript to virtually every chart. In addition, the volume has eleven additional maps or fragments of maps bound in at the end, some of great interest: (1) *Carte Réduite de l'Océan Occidental . . .* [Paris.] Par ordre de Mgr. le Comte de Maurepas, 1742. Fragment only— 35 × 51.5 cm. (2) [Cartouche on right-hand side reads]: "West-Indische Paskaert waer in de graden der breedde over weder. . . ." [Cartouche on left-hand side reads]: "Gedruckt t'Amsterdam Bij Pieter Goos Op't Water inde Vergulde Zee-Speigel. Seyn no te Bekkoomen By Johannes van Keulen." [N.d., but ca. 1658– ca. 1700?] Oversized map, trimmed on left-hand and right-hand sides and folded at top and bottom to fit into atlas 90 × 90 cm. (3) *Carte Réduite de l'Océan Méridional Compris Entre Afrique et l'Amérique Méridionale depuis le 7 Degré de Latitude Nord jusqu'au 57 Degré Sud. . . . Dressée au Dépost des Cartes Plans et Journaux de la Marine. . . .* [Paris], 1739. 62 × 78.5 cm. (4) *Oost Indien* [Cartouche on far left reads]: "t'Amsterdam. Bij Pieter Goos op het water inde Vergulde Zee Spiegel. Seyn nu te Bekkoomen by Johannes van Keulen." [N.d., but ca. 1658–ca. 1700.] Heavily trimmed at top and bottom. 63 × 86 cm. First issued by Pieter Goos, probably in 1658; reissued by Johannes van Keulen before 1704. See Campbell, pl. 65, where a copy of this issue printed on vellum is given a color reproduction: "This may well be the first newly engraved map to name all the Dutch discoveries in Australia which culminated in Tasman's two voyages during the period 1642–44." For the first issue, see Schilder, pl. XLIV. (5) *Carte Réduite de l'Ocean où Mers Indes. . . . Dressée au Dépost des Cartes Plans et Journaux de la Marine.* [Paris], 1740. [Lower left]: "Dheulland Sculp." 60.5 × 79 cm. The tracks of several anonymous navigators added in manuscript. (6) *Carte Réduite de l'Océan Oriental qui Contient la Côte D'Afrique depuis le 9e Degré de latitude méridionale, jusqu'au 30e Avec L'Isle Madagascar. . . .* [Paris]: Par Mr d'Apres de Mannevillette, [n.d.]. 56.5 × 80 cm. The track of an anonymous navigator added in manuscript. (7) *Carte Particulière de la Côte d'Afrique depuis le Cap des Courans, jusqu'à la Baye de Ste. Hélène.* [Paris.] [In manuscript]: "en 1753." [As this manuscript notation is the latest date that appears in the atlas and was obviously added at the same time as the numerous other manuscript additions, perhaps it represents the date that this special copy ("Collection Cazeneuve") was prepared.] Trimmed. 44 × 64 cm. (8) *Plan de la Partie Orientale de Madagascar.* . . . [N.p., n.d.]. [Lower left]: "Guill [sic] de la Haye." 33 × 50 cm. (9) *Carte Reduite de l'Isle de Saint Domingue et des ses Débouchements.* . . . *Dressée au Dépost des Cartes Plans et Journaux de la Marine.* . . . *1750.* . . . A Paris chez Mr Bellin Ing *r.* Ord *re.* de la Marine Rue Dauphine pes la Rue Christine. Rhumb lines added in manuscript. 55.5 × 87.5 cm. (10) *Carte Reduite du Golphe du Mexique.* . . . *1749.* . . . Mr. Bellin. . . . 53 × 87.5 cm. (See no. 139 for a full description of this map.) (11) *Carte Particulière de la Coste D'Or.* . . . 1750. A Paris Chez Mr. Bellin. . . . 42 × 59.5 cm.

134. *Amérique Septentrionale.* Jean Baptiste Bourguignon Anville under the auspices of the Duke of Orléans. Engraved by Guillaume Nicolas Delahaye. Printed by Anville and the Louvre Galleries. Paris, 1746. Color, scale 1 in. to 100 mi., four sheets joined to form 82.5 × 96.5 cm. map. Untitled inset: Hudson and Baffin bays. MMNHMC.

Second issue (Tooley, *Printed Maps of America,* pt. 1, no. 104). Karpinski (p. 138) comments: "D'Anville's maps were largely issued as separates, being combined in made-up atlases without consistent sequence. This famous and popular map of North America was found in virtually all issues of the *Atlas général;* its depiction of the U.S. Gulf Coast was among the most influential of the century. Of particular interest is the following legend for 'Lago de San Joseph' (San Antonio Bay): 'Baye que les Francais prirent en 1720 voir celle d. S. Bernard,' which to my knowledge is the only reference on an eighteenth-century printed map to the La Harpe expedition." (See no. 114 for further information.)

Along the Texas coast are the following place-names (east to west): "R. Mexicano" (Sabine?), a small unnamed stream; "R. de Flores," "R. Dulce," "B. de S. Bernard nommee St. Louis par les Francais" (Matagorda Bay). A presidio is shown at Matagorda Bay. The following rivers flow into Matagorda Bay (east to west): "R. Trinidad" (Trinity River); "la Maligne R." (Brazos River), with two tributaries; "la Dure R." (San Jacinto River); "Sablonnière R." (San Bernard River); "R. Colorado" or the "R. aux Cannes"; "Petite R. aux Cannes" (Lavaca River). A short distance down the coast is a "Lago de San Joseph" (San Antonio Bay). The following rivers flow into San Antonio Bay (east to west): "R. de Guadeloupe," "R. de Leon," "R. de Medina." Farther down the coast are "R. de Vino," flowing into "R. Hondo"; "R. de Sarco," flowing into "R. de Nueces"; and "R. de Ramos," flowing into "R. del Norte autrement to Rio Bravo ou Riv. Sauvage" (Rio Grande). Northeast Texas is "Tecas." The following settlements or Indian villages are located in east Texas: "Adayes," "Ayches," "Naouediches" (Nacogdoches), "Nadaco," "Cenis," "Quiches." The *National Maritime Museum Catalogue* (vol. 3, no. 200) lists an edition of D'Anville's *Atlas general* (Paris, ca. 1780) in which a copy of this map (probably the second issue) is no. 68–69.

135. *Mappe-Monde, qui représente les deux Hémisphères, savoir celui de l'Orient et celui de l'Occident tirée des quatre Cartes générales de feu M. le Professeur Hasius.* Homann Heirs. Drawn by George Moritz Lowitz. Nuremberg, 1746. Color, scale indeterminable, 46.5 × 55 cm. map surrounded by subsidiary hemispheres showing the globe from different angles and by two celestial charts. MMNHMC.

136. *Mapa de la Sierra Gorda, y Costa de el Seno Mexiano, desde la Cuidad de Quereláro situada, cerca de los 21g hasta los 28½ en que esta, la Bahia del Espiritu Santo, sus Rios, Ensenadas, y Provincias, que circumbalan la Costa del Seno Mexiano, reconocida, Pacificada, y Poblada en la Mayor parte.* Jose de Escandon. N.p., ca. 1747. Photostat of manuscript map, scale indeterminable, 37.5 × 50.5 cm.; original in the Mexican National Archives. Donated by E. G. Littlejohn, 1930.

The Library of Congress has photostats of two other copies of this manuscript map, which are in the British Library in London and the Direccion Hidrografica in Madrid, respectively. (See Lowery, nos. 385, 386). The titles of the British and Spanish copies vary slightly from this example. This map shows a portion of present-day Texas.

137. *A New & Accurate Map of Mexico or New Spain together with California New Mexico &c.* Emanuel Bowen. London, 1747. Scale 1 degree to 20 mi., 35 × 42 cm. Inset: "The Gallipago Islands Discovered & Described by Capt. Cowley in 1684." MMNHMC.

138. *[Neu Ebenezer.]* Augsburg; George Mattaus Seutter, 1747. Color, scale indeterminable, 49.5 × 57 cm. sheet with three maps: (1) *Plan von Neu Ebenezer.* George Mattaus Seutter. Augsburg, n.d. Key identifying twenty-six sites, (2) Untitled map of the coast from St. Augustine, Florida, to Charleston, South Carolina. Engraved by Tobias Conrad Lotter. Inset: "Great St. Simon's Isle." (3) Untitled map of a section of the Savannah River, showing the location of three mills. MMNHMC.

This plan also appeared in Samule Urlsperger's *Der dreizehnte Continuation der ausfuhrlichen Nachrichten*, Halle, Germany, 1747.

139. *Carte Reduite du Golphe du Mexique et des Isles de l'Amerique Pour servir aux Vaisseaux du Roy.* France. Navy. Jacques Nicolas Bellin. Paris, 1749. Color, scale indeterminable, 55.5 × 87.5 cm. Additional rhumb lines added in manuscript. MMNHMC.

This map is bound into a copy of the first edition of Après de Mannevillette's *Le Neptune Oriental*, Paris, 1745, in the Rosenberg Library's rare-book collection (see no. 133 for further information). A general chart of the Gulf of Mexico and the Caribbean, it shows the small "Baye Judosa" at the mouth of the Trinity River depicted by De L'Isle in 1718. Near the entrance to the bay is a symbol, identified by key as the site of "Observ. de latitute faites a la mer." Possessions of the various European nations are identified by color, with the French shown in possession of the central Gulf Coast from Matagorda Bay to Mobile Bay.

140. *Insulae Americanae Nempe: Cuba, Hispaniola, Jamaica, Pto. Rico, Lucania, Antillae, vulgo Caribae, Barlo-et Sotto-vento, etc.* Renier and Josua Ottens. Amsterdam, ca. 1750, Color, scale indeterminable, 50 × 58 cm. MMNHMC.

This general map of the Gulf and the Caribbean is derived from French models.

141. *Carte de la Louisiane.* Jean Baptiste Bourguignon d'Anville. Paris, drawn 1732, published 1752. Scale 1 in. to approx. 15 French leagues, 52 × 93 cm. Inset: "Partie Superieure de la Louisiane." MMNHMC.

This detailed contemporary map of the French colony of Louisiana focuses more closely on the core of the colony than virtually any other eighteenth-century map of the area. (See no. 108 for a more general map that bears the name of the colony.) D'Anville shows the U.S. Gulf Coast from the Apalachicola River in Florida west to approximately the present Texas-Louisiana border. He locates numerous French settlements, including many now abandoned, and a few rival Spanish settlements. At the left-hand margin is "Adayes," the Spanish presidio that marked the eastern boundary of Texas before 1765. The inset shows the Illinois country and a large part of the central Mississippi Valley.

142A. *Mappemonde ou Description du Globe Terrestre.* Didier Robert de Vaugondy, Paris, 1752. Color, scale indeterminable, 46.5 × 71 cm. MMNHMC.

B. Another issue: same title, cartographer, color, and size, but revised 1776. MMNHMC.

143. *Carte Réduite de L'Ocean Meridionale Contenant toutes les Costes de l'Amerique Meridionale depuis l'Equateur jusqu'au 57 Degré de Latitude Et les Costes d'Afrique qui leur sont opposées.* France. Navy. Jacques Nicolas Bellin. Paris, 1753. Scale indeterminable, 54.5 × 87 cm. From Bellin's *Hydrographie française,* first published Paris, 1756–65. MMNHMC.

A sea chart of the South Atlantic. The contents of the *Hydrographie française* vary greatly for each edition and copy.

144. *Carte Reduite des parties connues Du Globe Terrestre.* France. Navy. Jacques Nicolas Bellin. Paris, 1755. Scale indeterminable, Mercator projection, 54 × 82 cm. From Bellin's *Hydrographie française,* first published Paris, 1756–65. Descriptive text. MMNHMC.

The contents of the *Hydrographie française* vary greatly for each edition and copy. Phillips (*Atlases,* no. 587) lists a copy, which he dates [1737–72], that contains this map.

145. *L'Amerique Meridionale, Dressée sur les Mémoires le plus récens des Meilleurs Geographes.* Amsterdam: Covens and Mortier, 1757. Color, scale indeterminable, 54 × 58 cm. MMNHMC.

This is a general map of the South American continent based largely on J. B. B. D'Anville's large two-sheet map of 1748.

146. *Carte particuliere de L'Isle de la Jamaique.* France. Navy. Jacques Nicolas Bellin. Paris, 1758. Color, scale indeterminable, 56 × 89 cm. Separately issued, but also included in French Admiralty atlases of the period. Descriptive text and key. MMNHMC.

Printed navigational chart giving coastal depth soundings and good interior detail. This chart was separately issued and also included in the French Admiralty atlases of the period.

147. *A Draught of Virginia from the Capes to York in York River to Kui-quotan or Hamton in James River.* Mark Tiddeman. N.p., n.d. Scale indeterminable, 46 × 58.5 cm. From book four of William Mount's *English Pilot,* London, 1758. MMNHMC.

148. *Regni Mexicani Seu Novae Hispaniae. Ludovicianae, N. Angliae, Carolinae, Virginae et Pensylvaniae necnon Insularum Archipelagi Mexicani in America Septentrionali accurata Tabula exhibita.* Johann Baptista Homann. N.p., n.d. From Homann's *Atlas Geographicus Maior,* Nuremberg, 1759. Color, scale indeterminable, 48 × 56.5 cm. MMNHMC.

A German issue of De L'Isle's map of 1703 (see no. 99).

149. *An Accurate Map of the Caribby Islands, with the Crowns, &c. to which they severally belong.* Thomas Kitchin. London, 1759. Scale indeterminable, 18 × 24 cm., folding. Together with *A map of Guadeloupe one of the Caribby Islands in the West Indies Subject to France.* Thomas Kitchin(?). London, ca. 1759. Scale indeterminable, 11.5 × 18 cm. Both maps bound into a complete copy of *The London Magazine: Or Gentlemen's Monthly Intelligencer.* March, 1759. Published by Richard Baldwin, London. MMNHMC.

Carriby Islands shows the Lesser Antilles.

150. *An Accurate Map of the World: upon the Globular Projection, Drawn from the Best Authorities, including the late Discover.* Emanuel Bowen. N.p., 1759. Scale indeterminable, 15 × 28 cm. From the *General Magazine of Arts and Sciences,* London, 1759. MMNHMC.

151. *Carte de la Coste du Nord de Lisle: et du vieux canal y joint partie de lisle de St. Domingue Avec les De Bouquements de Krookeland & Des Kaiques.* Manuscript. Color, scale indeterminable, 61 × 65 cm. Descriptive text. MMNHMC.

This chart, dated by the watermark circa 1760, shows a large section of the northern coast of Cuba, the southern tip of Florida, and a part of the Bahamas and Hispaniola.

152. *La Luisiana cedida al Rei N.S. Por S. M. Christianisiama, con la Nueva Orleans; è Isla en que se halla esta Ciudad.* Tomas Lopez. Madrid, 1762.

After Jean Baptiste Bourguignon d'Anville. Scale indeterminable, 39 × 26 cm. map in 39 × 50 cm. sheet. Insets: "Plano de la Neuva Orleans," by Jacques Nicolas Bellin; "Suplemento del Rio Misissipi, hasta donde se conoce su curso." MMNHMC.

This map of French Louisiana, based on the work of French cartographer Anville, extends westward to include the present Texas coast. Matagorda Bay is called "B. de S. Bernardo." The Brazos is "La Maligna R." Directly to the east of the river is "R. Flores," the Trinity, which flows directly into the Gulf. Galveston Bay is completely absent.

153. *A Description of the Spanish Islands and Settlements On the Coast of the West Indies.* Thomas Jefferys. London, 1762. Scale varies, size varies, thirty-two folding maps and plans bound in quarto volume, gilt-stamped contemporary calf, red morocco spine label. MMNHMC.

The thirty-two plans are [titles given as in table of contents]: (1) *A Chart of the West-Indies to front the Title;* (2) *Puerto de La Guaira;* (3) *Puerto de Cavello;* (4) *Santa Martha;* (5) *Harbour of Carthagena;* (6) *City of Carthagena;* (7) *Bay Zisapata;* (8) *Porto Belo or Puerto Velo;* (9) *The Town of Chagre;* (10) *The Isthmus of Panama;* (11) *The San Fernando de Omoa;* (12) *Port Royal Laguna;* (13) *The Road of Vera Cruz;* (14) *City of La Vera Cruz;* (15) *Pensacola;* (16) *Sant Agustine;* (17) *The Island of Cuba;* (18) *The City of Havana;* (19) *Bahia de Matanzas;* (20) *Bahia de Nipe;* (21) *Puerto de Baracoa;* (22) *Guantanimo;* (23) *Santiago de Cuba;* (24) *Bahia de Xagua;* (25) *The Colorados;* (26) *Bahia Honda;* (27) *Puerto de Cavanas;* (28) *Puerto de Mariel;* (29) *Map of San Domingo;* (30) *City of San Domingo;* (31) *San Juan de Puerto Rico;* (32) *Aguada Nueva.*

154. *Il Gazzattiere Americano Contenente un Distinto Ragguaglio di Tutte le Parti del Nuovo Mond della Loro Situazione, Clima, Terreno, Prodotti, Stato Antico e Moderno, Merci, Manifatture, e Commercio Con una esatta descrizione delle Città, Piazze, Porti, Baje, Fiumi, Laghi, Montagne, Passi, e Fortificazioni.* Mareo Coltellini. Leghorn, Italy, 1763. Scale varies, seventy-eight plates, including thirty-eight folding and single-paged maps and plans, bound in three quarto volumes, contemporary vellum. MMNHMC.

This is the second edition of the first topographical dictionary of the New World. The original edition, published in England in 1762, had a smaller format and contained only six maps. (See Sabin, Eames, and Vail, no. 1090.) Forty of the plates included in this Italian edition depict natural history, views of American cities, historical and allegorical scenes.

The maps and plans are as follows. Vol. 1: (1) a general map of America; (2) Acapulco; (3) St. Augustine, Florida; (4) the course of the Amazon; (5) Barbados; (6) the vicinity of Boston; (7) Yucatan; (8) Cartagena, Colombia; (9) Chagre, Panama; (10) Cuba; (11) Guantanamo Bay, Cuba; (12) Cusco, Peru; (13) Panama; (14) Santo Domingo; (15) Florida. Vol. 2: (16) a general map of the Gulf of Mexico and the West Indies; (17) the island of Granada; (18) Guadeloupe; (19) Havana; (20) Hispaniola; (21) Hudson's Bay; (22) Santiago, Chile; (23) Jamaica; (24) Northeast United States; (25) Lima, Peru; (26) Martinique; (27) the Great Lakes. Vol. 3: (28) South America; (29) Gulf of St. Lawrence; (30) Paraguay; (31) Pensacola, Florida; (32) Porto Bello; (33) Quito, Ecuador; (34) San Salvador, Brazil; (35) Newfoundland; (36) the Caribbean coast of Colombia and Venezuela; (37) Veracruz, Mexico; (38) New York Harbor.

155. *Le petite atlas maritime recueil de cartes et des plans de quatre parties du monde,* 5 vols. Jacques Nicolas Bellin. Paris, 1764. Scale varies, 16.5 × 20.5 cm. unless otherwise noted. A collection of thirteen charts from volume two: (9) *Carte des Provinces de Nicaragua et Costa Rica;* (17) *Carte des Provinces de Cartagene, St. Marthe et Venezuela;* (47) *Carte du Bresil. Prem. Partie . . . ,* 22 × 30 cm.; (48) *Suite du Bresil Depuis la Baye de Tous les Saints jusq'à St. Paul . . . ;* (49) *Suite du Bresil;* (50) *Plan de Fernambouc à la Coste de Bresil;* (51) *Entree de la Riviere de St. François a la Coste de Brésil;* (52) *Carte de la Baye de Tous les Saints à la Coste du Bresil;* (53) *Ville de Saint Salvador Capitale du Bresil,* 16 × 31.5 cm.; (54) *Plan de la Baye de Rio-Janeiro,* 21.5 × 31.5 cm.; (55) *Isle de Saint Sebastien à la Coste du Bresil;* (56) *Carte de l'Isle-Grande et Coste de Bresil aux environs;* (57) *Carte de l'Isle de Ste. Catharine Situee a la Coste du Bresil.* MMNHMC.

156. *Carte des Variations de la Boussole et des Vents généraux que l'on Trouve dans les Mers les plus frequentées.* France. Navy. Jacques Nicolas Bellin. Paris, 1765. Scale indeterminable, Mercator projection, 54.5 × 87 cm. From Bellin's *Hydrographie francaise,* first published Paris, 1756–65. MMNHMC.

157. *Carte D'Amerique.* Guillaume de L'Isle. Amsterdam; Covens and Mortier, ca. 1765. Color, scale indeterminable, 48 × 60 cm. Descriptive text. MMNHMC.

This map first appeared in 1722 and was republished with alterations or improvements until 1790. This edition is a later version of Covens and Mortier's issue of 1755 (Tooley, *French Mapping of the Americas*, no. 6), altered to show the results of the Treaty of 1763. The possessions of various European powers are identified (not always correctly) by color.

Six sites are identified in Texas (east to west): "Cenis ou Texas," "Maligne" (Brazos River), "R. aux Caunes" (Colorado River), "B. St. Bernard" (Matagorda Bay), "Ft. des Francais," and "Rio Bravo" (Rio Grande). There is no Galveston Bay.

158. *South America From the latest Discoveries, Shewing the Spanish & Portuguese Settlements according to Mr. D'Anville.* Louis Stanislas d'Arcy Delarochette. London: John and Carington Bowles, 1765–70. Color, scale 1 in. to approx. 290 mi., 47 × 57.5 cm. MMNHMC.

159. *Kaart van de Aller-Heiligen Baay waar aan de Hoofdstad legt van Brazil.* Isaak Tirion. Amsterdam, ca. 1770. Color, scale indeterminable, 34 × 40 cm. Inset: "Grondtekening van de Stad San Salvador." MMNHMC.

This chart shows All Saints Bay in Brazil.

160. *Plano de la Plaza de Snt. Phelipe de Montevideo, en el Rio de la Plata con sus fortificaciones ejecutadas, y por ejecutar.* Francisco Rodriquez y Cardosa. Montevideo, 1770. Watercolor wash, scale indeterminable, 46 × 96.5 cm. Key identifying thirty-three sites. MMNHMC.

Francisco Rodriguez y Cardoso was a leading Spanish official—probably chief surveyor or engineer—in charge of urban planning at Montevideo. As early as 1753, he submitted proposals to Spain to fortify the South American city. In 1770 he prepared this manuscript illustrating a new, more sophisticated proposal for the city's defense.

Chueca Goitia and Torres Balbas list five plans of Montevideo, preserved in the Archives de Indias, that were prepared about the same time as this example (1769–71; nos. 332–36). Only one plan shows a system of fortifications comparable to that shown on this plan of November, 1770 (no. 334, prepared in Barcelona in 1771); no. 336 is a 1771 copy, made in Barcelona, of Rodriguez y Cardoso's 1753 proposal.

161. *Mappas Das Provincias de Portugal.* João Silverio Carpinetti. Lisbon; Francisco Manoel Pires, [1762]. Scale varies, *portulano* with seven maps on twelve leaves, plus text, bound in oblong octavo volume, gilt-stamped calf.

162. *Dévelopement de la Route faite Autour du Monde.* Louis Antoine de Bougainville. N.p., n.d. From Bougainville's *Voyage autour du Monde 1766–69*, Paris, 1771–72. Color, scale indeterminable, 21 × 52.5 cm.

163. *America Meridionalis Conciñata juxta Observations Dñn Acad: Regalis Scientiarum et nonnullorum aliorum, et juxta annotationes recentissimas.* Guillaume de L'Isle. 1700. Engraved by Gustav Conrad Lotter. Augsburg: Tobias Conrad Lotter, 1772. Color, scale indeterminable, 45 × 58 cm. MMNHMC.

This is a heavily revised German reengraving of Guillaume de L'Isle's 1700 map of South America. (For an illustration of the original 1700 issue, see Tooley's *French Mapping of the Americas,* no. 63, pl. XIV.)

164. *A Plan of Port Royal in South Carolina.* Surveyed by John Gascoigne. Engraved by Jefferys and Faden. London, ca. 1773. Scale 1 in. to 1 mi., 58.5 × 71 cm. Key locating twenty-eight sites. MMNHMC.

Captain John Gascoigne's 1738 survey was the most important of Port Royal to date. Gascoigne's manuscript map, 1729, and the later, more elaborate version drawn by Francis Swain (both in the Public Records Office, London) remained the primary sources for geographical information throughout most of the eighteenth century.

This is the first issue of Thomas Jefferys' printed version of the Gascoigne-Swain map.

The *British Museum Catalogue* (2:774) incorrectly dates this issue 1760. For more information, see also Cumming, *Southeast,* p. 51; Stevens and Tree, no. 71a.

165. *The World Agreable to the latest Discoveries.* Thomas Jefferys. London, ca. 1773. Scale indeterminable, 19.5 × 38 cm. MMNHMC.

166. *Jamaica.* Thomas Jefferys. London, ca. 1774. Scale 1 in. to approx. 6.25 mi. MMNHMC.

"An unfinished map—probably a proof copy of Jefferys' (*Jamaica* issued in the *West India Atlas,* 1775" (Kapp, *Jamaica,* no. 97). On this preliminary version the scale of miles and the compass rose are in the top rather than bottom right-hand and left-hand corners, respectively. The two insets, all depth soundings, and much topographical detail have yet to be added.

167. *Compleat Chart of the West Indies.* Thomas Jefferys. Printed by Robert Sayer. London, 1775. Scale 1 in. to approx. 25 mi., seventeen 47.5 × 63 cm. sheets. From Jeffery's *West India Atlas,* London, 1775. MMNHMC.

First issue (an unaltered reissue appeared in 1794). This map is remarkable both for its large scale and for the poor state of its geography. No previous printed map had focused so closely on the Texas coast, which makes the depiction's jumbled nature even more striking. Here, the main bays and rivers of the coast are like suits in a deck of cards that has been repeatedly shuffled: each contains characteristics of the others; none is pure enough to identify specifically.

Jefferys was probably the world's leading, most respected cartographer in 1775, and his ignorance of the coast's geography is testimony to the obscurity of eighteenth-century Texas. He shows a small inlet, "Judosa," located between the mouths of a "Rio Barroso" (a name associated with the Trinity on its upper reaches) and the Brazos, which appears on the map with the text "R. Baty named by the Spaniards Ro. de Sta. Theresa & by the French la Maligne." "Judosa" is the name that De L'Isle in 1718 had applied to a rudimentary Galveston Bay (see no. 108). At the mouth of the Brazos a "Pta. de Colubras" forms the eastern tip of an "Isle de St Louis," undoubtedly to be identified with Galveston Island. The western tip of the island forms the eastern edge of the entrance to a large bay, which Jefferys considers Matagorda Bay ("Bahia de Sn. Bernardo named by the French Baye de St. Louis"). A "Rio Colorado," which turns into a "Rio de Flores," runs into the bay, and a "Presidio Nuevo" and a "Presidio Viejo" are located on its shores. Two interesting anomalies cloud the purity of an identification of this bay with Matagorda. First, its shape more clearly resembles that of Galveston Bay than that of Matagorda Bay. Second, Cavallo Pass, the actual entrance to Matagorda Bay, appears farther down the coast, as the entrance to a "Lago de San Josef," and is labeled "Mistaken for the Entrance of St. Bernard's Bay." This map received wide circulation and according to Streeter was "the principal authority for the Texas coast" until the appearance of the *Carta Esférica* (Streeter, *Bibliography,* no. 1029) a quarter of a century later.

The additional sixteen sheets in the *West India Atlas* are (1) *An Index map to the following sixteen sheets, being a Compleat Chart of the West*

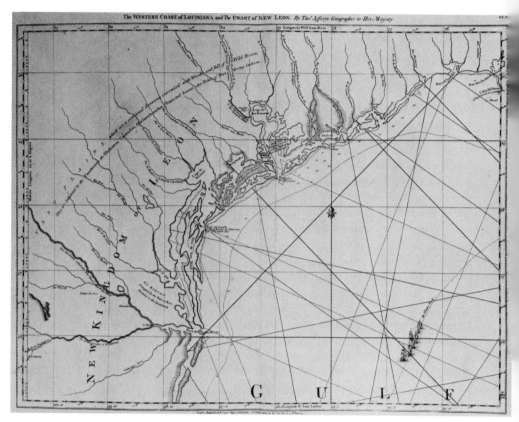

The Western Coast of Louisiana and the Coast of New Leon, by Thomas Jefferys, 1775, from Jefferys' *West India Atlas.* (See no. 167.) Jefferys was a leading cartographer in 1775, but he had little knowledge of Texas geography. A rudimentary Galveston Bay appears as "Judosa," the name that De L'Isle applied to the area in 1718. Rivers trail off into the interior, which is described as "vast plains which are a continual Savanna intermixed with Woods and full of Wild Beeves. They are Inhabited by the Canokosses, the Ebahamas, Caouaches, Quelameloueches, Teaos and several other Tribes of Wandering Indians."

Indies . . . ; (2) The Western Coast of Louisiana and the Coast of New Leon; (3) The Coast of West Florida and Louisiana; (4) The Peninsula and Gulf of Florida or Channel of Bahama with the Bahama Islands; (5) The Coast of Mexico from Laguna de Esmotes to Punta Brava; (6) The Coast of Yucatan . . . ; (7) The Island of Cuba . . . ; (8) The Windward Passage . . . ; (9) The Coast of New Spain from Neuva Vera Cruz to Triste Island; (10)

The Bay of Honduras; (11) *The Island of Jamaica . . . ;* (12) *South Part of St Domingo, or Hispaniola;* (13) *The Caribbee Islands, The Virgin Islands, and the Isle of Porto Rico;* (14) *Part of the Provinces of Costa Rica and Nicaragua . . . ;* (15) *The Isthmus of Panama . . . ;* (16) *The Coast of Tierra Firme . . . ;* (17) *The Coast of Caracas, Cumana. . . .*

168. *Course of the River Mississippi from the Balise to Fort Chartres; Taken on an Expedition to the Illinois, in the latter end of the Year 1765. By Lieut. Ross of the 34th Regiment: Improved from the Surveys of that River made by the French.* Robert Sayer. London, 1775. Color, scale indeterminable, 34 × 133. cm. From Thomas Jeffery's *American Atlas,* London, 1775. MMNHMC.

This is the first map to show the English occupation of the Illinois country, acquired from France under the Treaty of 1763.

169. *A Map of the Province of New-York, Reduc'd from the large Drawing of that Province . . . by Claude Joseph Sauthier; to which is added New-Jersey, from the Topographical Observations of C. J. Sauthier & B. Ratzer.* Claude Joseph Sauthier and Bernard Ratzer. Engraved and published by William Faden. London, 1776. Color, scale indeterminable, 57 × 71.5 cm. Map no. 12 from Faden's *North American Atlas,* London, 1777. MMNHMC.

170. *Nouvelle Carte des Côtes des Carolines Septentrionales et Meridionales du Cap Fear a Sud Edisto Levées et Sondées.* Nathaniel Pocock. 1770. Paris: George Louis Le Rouge, 1777. Scale indeterminable, 16 × 20.5 cm. From Le Rouge's *Atlas Ameriquain Septentrionale,* Paris, 1777. Seven profiles of the Carolina coast. MMNHMC.

This chart is found in both the 1778 and the 1792 editions of the atlas (see Phillips, *Atlases,* no. 1212).

171. *Carte Reduite des Côtes Orientales de L'Amérique Septentrionale contenant Partie du Nouveau Jersey, la Pen-sylvanie, le Mary-land, la Virginie, la Caroline Septentrionale, la Caroline Méridionale et la Georgie, Assujette aux Observations les plus récentes et aux Cartes de détail les plus estimées.* France. Navy. Paris, 1778. Color, scale indeterminable, 58 × 86 cm. From the *Neptune-Americo-Septentrionale,* Paris, 1778. Text giving details of seven areas along the coast: Charleston Harbor, Chesapeake Bay, etc. MMNHMC.

A general chart of the southern American coast, prepared by the French Admiralty for use during the American Revolution.

172. *A New and Accurate Chart of the West-Indies Islands and Coast on a large scale: Together with Forty New Plans, Accurately Surveyed, of the Chief Ports, Bays, Roads, and Harbours on the Spanish Main, the Floridas, Jamaica, Hispaniola or St. Domingo, the Island of Cuba and Porto Rico.* Robert Sayer and John Bennett. 1779. Scale varies, thirty 18 × 25 cm. charts, printed two to a page, disbound. MMNHMC.

This collection includes thirty of the forty charts. Three of the seven small plans from the work that relate to the United States are present: (14) *A Draught of the Entrance of Mobile. Taken in the King's ship "Nautilus" in the year 1764*; (15) *A Plan of Mobile Bar, surveyed by B. Romans, 1771* (first appeared in Romans's *A Concise Natural History of East and West Florida*, New York, 1775); (16) *Plan of the Harbour of Pensacola by B. Romans, 1771* (first appeared in Romans's *A Concise Natural History . . .*).

173. *Carte du Golphe du Mexique et des Isles Antilles.* Henry Popple. 1733. Revised by Philippe Buache, 1740. Corrected and augmented by Jean Nicolas Buache. Printed by J. A. Dezauche. Paris, 1780. Color, scale indeterminable, 19.5 × 93.5 cm. From Jean N. Buache's *Atlas géographique, J. A. Dezuache, Paris*, 1781–84. Text on "measures." Key identifying European possessions. MMNHMC.

This is a general map of the Gulf of Mexico and the Caribbean Sea. When first published in 1740, it bore only the title that appears above the upper neat line, "Carte d'une Partie de l'Amérique pour la Navigation des Isles et du Golfe du Mexique avec L'Intérieure des Terres . . ." and was based on Henry Popple's map of 1733. Buache revised and reissued the map in 1780 and added a new title in the lower left-hand corner. The detail for Texas is the same as on Popple's map. Popple had in turn based his depiction of the western U.S. Gulf Coast on De L'Isle's map of 1718.

174. *Carte Générale des Colonies Angloises dans l'Amérique Septentrionale.* Rene Phelippeaux. Paris, 1781. Color, scale indeterminable, 52 × 75 cm. Untitled inset: Florida and the West Indies. MMNHMC.

175. *A New and Accurate Map of the World, comprehending all the New Discoveries in Both Hemispheres, carefully brought down to the Pres-*

ent Year. Anonymous. N.p., 1782. Scale indeterminable, 30 × 47.5 cm. From Millar's *New and Universal System of Geography,* London, 1782. MMNHMC.

176. *The Coast of Guyana From the Oroonoko to the River of Amazons and the Inland Parts as far as they have been Explored by the French & Dutch Engineers with the Islands of Barbadoes Tabago & ca. from the Observations of Captain Edward Thompson made in the Hyaena, in the Year 1781.* Louis Stanslas d'Arcy Delarochette. Engraved and published by William Faden. London, 1783. Color, scale indeterminable, 51 × 68.5 cm. Insets: "Entrance of River Berbice," by William Thompson; "Surinam River from the Dutch"; "Port of Cayenne from the French"; and "The Entrances of the Rivers Essequebo and Demerari," by William Thompson. Table: "Astronomical Observations." Descriptive text. Two profiles of the Guyanan coast. MMNHMC.

177. *A Draught of South Carolina and Georgia from Sewee to St. Estaca.* Andrew Hughes. N.p., n.d. Sold by William Mount and Thomas Page. Scale indeterminable, 46 × 84 cm. From the 1783 edition of Mount and Page's *English Pilot: West India Navigation,* London. Descriptive text. MMNHMC.

178. *Typus Geographicus Chili Paraguay Freti Magellanici &c.* Homann Heirs. Nuremberg, 1783. Color, scale indeterminable, 48 × 57 cm. Inset: "Plan de la Ville de Santiago," with key locating twenty-eight sites. MMNHMC.

This map shows South America south of the Río de la Plata.

179. *Bowles' New and Accurate Map of North America and the West Indies.* Carington Bowles. London, 1784. Color, scale 1 degree to 69 mi., 111 × 115 cm., cloth-backed; poor condition. Inset: "Environs of Baffin's and Hudson's Bays, being a Supplement to the Map of North America." Table showing the division of North America to the Treaty of Versailles (1783). MMNHMC.

Bowles constructed this map to show the British, French, and Spanish possessions in North America at the end of the American Revolution (see also no. 185).

This is the fourth issue of at least seven, and the second issue to show the results of the Treaty of 1783. Carington Bowles first issued this map in 1768 to illustrate the territorial changes in America resulting from the treaty ending the French and Indian War (1763). In February, 1783, he re-issued the map (third issue) to show the sweeping changes resulting from the American Revolution. In the 1783 issue and in this issue of the following year, the new nation of the United States includes all present U.S. territory east of the Mississippi River except east and west Florida.

180. *Nova Mappa Geographica Americae Septentrionalis in suas praecipuas Partes divisa.* Henry Popple. Revised by Johann Michael Probst. Engraved by Jean George Probst. Augsburg, 1782. Color, scale indeterminable, 44 × 50 cm. Insets: "Plaisance"; "Boston"; "Nouvelle York"; "Charles Town"; "Bermude"; "S. Augustine"; "Providence"; "Havane"; "S. Iago"; "Kingston Pt."; "Lynches I."; "Port s Antoine"; "Port Royal de la Martinique"; "Barbade"; "Antiga"; "Cartagene"; "Porto Bello."

181. *Plano de la Ciudad y Puerto de la Havana.* Tomas Lopez. Madrid, 1785. Color, scale 1 in. to approx. 400 varas, 35 × 37.5 cm. Key identifying forty-three sites. MMNHMC.

182. *Plano de la Ciudad de Cartagena de Indias.* Tomas Lopez. Madrid, ca. 1790. Color, scale 1 in. to approx. 250 varas, 24 × 37 cm. Key identifying fifty-one features. Together with *Plano de la Bahía de Cartagena.* Color, scale 1 in. to approx. 1,500 varas, 19 × 37 cm. MMNHMC.

183. *Mapa de la parte Sur de la América Meridional con la Tierra del Fuego.* (?) de Ibáñez. N.p., ca. 1790–95. Grey wash and black ink on paper, two sheets, one 55.5 × 64 cm., the other 50.5 × 70 cm.. The latter sheet has been trimmed along one edge, then cloth-backed. Text on geographical discoveries, including the Malaspina expedition (1794) and the Cordoba expedition (1789). MMNHMC.

Guillén y Tato lists and illustrates several Ibáñez manuscript maps preserved in various Spanish archives. Two of these (nos. 11.095 and 11.195) are virtually identical to these sheets. Guillén y Tato dates these sheets [1795] (upper) and [1790] (lower). He also notes a large manuscript map of the South American continent (no. 10.024), which he dates [1800]. These sheets and the corresponding examples that he notes (nos. 11.095 and 11.195), may be preliminary working models for the 1800 manuscript map.

The two sheets exhibit the most advanced geographical information then available for the southernmost parts of South America in 1790. The new geographical findings of the Malaspina expedition did not appear on any printed map until 1798 (*Carta Esférica de las Costas de la América Meridional,* Dirección Hidrográfica, Madrid, 1798). See Guillén y Tato, no. 11.099; Phillips, *Atlases,* no. 4155.

184. *Mappe Monde ou Description du Globe Terrestre & Aquatique suivant les Dernieres & Meilleures.* Jan Barend Elwe. Amsterdam, 1792. Color, scale indeterminable, 47.5 × 61 cm. map surrounded by decorative personifications of the continents and mythological figures. MMNHMC.

185. *A New Map of North America with the West India Islands.* Thomas Pownall. London: Laurie and Whittle, 1794. Color, scale 1 in. to approx. 88 mi., four sheets joined to form one 100 × 115 cm. map. Insets: "A Particular map of Baffin and Hudson's Bay"; "The Passage by land to California Discovered by Father Eusebius Francis Kino." Text of article III of the Treaty of Versailles (1783) relating to fishing rights in the Grand Banks.

Like Bowles (see no. 179), Pownall compiled this map to show the division of North America according to the Treaty of Versailles.

Pownall corrected and improved Lewis Evans's map of 1755 and first published it in his *A Topographical Description. . .* , London, 1776. The depiction of Texas comes from Anville's map of North America, 1746 (see no. 134), with some changes and additions. Pownall added Assinais, Aynais, Nacanne, Nondaque, and some "lead mines" east of the Trinity; La Salle's fort on Matagorda Bay; and the site of La Salle's death. Anville's "Lago de San Josef" is now "Bay St. Josef," with an "L. S. Josef" farther south. Pownall omitted Nacogdoches ("Naouediches" on Anville's map).

186. *The United States of America with the British Possessions of Canada, Nova Scotia, New Brunswick and Newfoundland.* London; Laurie and Whittle, 1794. Color, scale indeterminable, 45.5 × 51 cm. Text: article III of the Treaty of Versailles (1783). MMNHMC.

This is the second issue of what may be the first printed map to show the new United States. The preliminary articles of peace were signed on January 20, 1783; and the first issue (Stevens and Tree, no. 51d) was published on February 9, with the imprint of R. Sayer and J. Bennett. This Laurie and Whittle 1794 issue has a few minor revisions. Both issues came from Thomas Jefferys' map of North America, 1755 (Stevens and Tree, no. 51e).

187. *A Map of South America Containing Tierra-Firma, Guayana, New Granada, Amazonia, Brasil, Peru, Paraguay, Chaco, Tucuman, Chili and Patagona.* Jean Baptiste Bourguignon d'Anville. Revised and published by Laurie and Whittle. London, 1794. Color, scale 1 in. to 125 mi., four sheets joined to form one 98 × 118.5 cm. map. Inset: "A Chart of Folkland's Islands named by the French Malouine Islands, and Discovered by Hawkins in the Year 1593." Text: "Division of South America with a Summary Account of its Trade."

See Phillips, *America*, p. 799, for the original French version of 1748.

188. *West Indies from the Best Authorities.* Engraved by Amos Doolittle. Boston: Thomas and Andrews, n.d. Scale indeterminable, 18 × 30.5 cm. From Jedediah Morse's *The American Universal Geography*, Boston, 1796. Key identifying European possessions. MMNHMC.

189. *Georgia, from the latest Authorities.* Engraved by Benjamin Tanner. New York: John Reid, n.d. Scale indeterminable, 22 × 39 cm. From Reid's *American Atlas*, New York, 1796. MMNHMC.

This is the second state.

190. *Cary's New and Improved Celestial globe on which is carefully laid down the whole of the Stars and Nebula, contained in the Astronomical Cataloge of the Revd. Mr. Wollaston.* John & William Cary. London, 1799. Papier-mâché globe, 54 cm. diameter, covered with a celestial chart on eighteen gores, mounted on a contemporary stand. MMNHMC.

This is the earliest of six celestial globes produced by J. & W. Cary between 1799 and 1826. Yonge (pp. 16–19) and Stevenson (*Terrestrial and Celestial Globes*, 2:255, also 2:194) locate a total of eight additional examples, three in the United States (Birmingham Public Library, Birmingham, Alabama; Redwood Library and Athenaeum, Newport, Rhode Island; and Western Reserve Historical Society, Cleveland, Ohio).

191. *Plan of the Isle of Trinidad, from actual Surveys made in the year 1797.* Engraved by Laurie and Whittle. London, 1800. Color, scale 1 in.

94

to approx. 3 mi., 49.5 × 64.5 cm. Tables: the island's population and sections. MMNHMC.

192. *Carta General del Oceano Atlantico ú Ocidental desde 52' de Latitud Norte hasta el Equador.* Spain. Navy. Madrid, 1800. Scale indeterminable, 58 × 92 cm. MMNHMC.

This is a general chart of the central Atlantic.

193. *Chart of the West Indies and Spanish Dominions in North America.* Aaron Arrowsmith. Engraved by Jones, Smith & Co. London, 1803. Color, scale 1 in. to approx. 40 mi., four sheets joined to form 120 × 289.5 cm. chart. Texts on winds, proposed isthmian canal, etc. MMNHMC.

The first issue; the only issue to show Texas (later issues do not extend so far west). This is the first major map in the English language to follow the *Carta Esférica*, 1799, and therefore the first such to give Galveston Bay its present name.

194. *The American Coast Pilot.* Lawrence Furlong. Fourth edition. Printed by Edmund M. Blunt. Newburyport, Massachusetts, 1804. Eleven charts, two folding, with accompanying text, bound in octavo volume, contemporary calf. MMNHMC.

This is the best edition of the first book of sailing directions compiled and printed in the United States. It is the first edition to contain charts and specific sailing directions for Newfoundland and Labrador. The first 116 pages are entirely new (see p. vii). Pages 201–302 are devoted to the Gulf of Mexico and the Caribbean Sea. Each chart bears the imprint (below lower neat line): "Newburyport Published by E. M. Blunt 1804. A. M. Peasley, Sc." The charts are (1) *Portland Harbour* [Maine]; (2) *Portsmouth Harbour* [New Hampshire]; (3) *Newburyport Harbour* [Mass.]; (4) *Annis Squam Harbour* [Mass.]; (5) *The Isle of Sable;* (6) *Boston Harbour;* (7) *Newport Harbour;* (8) *New York Harbour;* (9) *The Bay and River Delaware;* (10) *The Bay of Chesapeake, from its Entrance to Baltimore;* (11) *Charleston Harbour.*

195. *[Chart of the North Atlantic Ocean].* Aaron Arrowsmith. London, 1805. Scale indeterminable, four sheets forming 125 × 185 cm. map. Together with the *[Chart of South America]*. Aaron Arrowsmith, London,

1805. Scale indeterminable, four sheets forming 125 × 185 cm. map. MMNHMC.

196. *A Map of Part of the Viceroyalty of Buenos Ayres.* Aaron Arrowsmith. London, 1806. Color, scale indeterminable, 51 × 95 cm. MMNHMC.

197. *Carta particular de las Cóstas Setentrionales del Seno Mexicano que comprehende las de la Florída Ocidental las Margenes de la Luisiana y toda la rivera que sigue por la Bahia de S. Bernardo y el Rio Bravo del Norte hasta la Laguna Madre.* Spain. Navy. Madrid. 1807. Survey by José de Evía, 1783–86. Color, scale indeterminable, 59 × 89 cm. MMNHMC.

According to Streeter, *Bibliography,* no. 1041: "This chart, showing the northern coast line of the Gulf of Mexico beginning at Cape San Blas on the Gulf Coast of Florida and extending as far as 24° 15′ on the Mexican coast, follows with slight changes and on a larger scale the *Carta Esférica of 1799*" (Streeter, *Bibliography,* no. 1029; Lowery, no. 721).

The *Carta Esférica* was the most advanced depiction of the Texas coast, when it appeared in 1799, and it remained the foundation map for the region until the beginning of the Anglo-American settlement in the 1820s. It shows a crudely conceived Galveston Bay, based on the survey conducted by the Spanish navigator José de Evía from 1783 to 1786. Bernardo de Galvez, viceroy of New Spain, ordered the survey, and the bay was named in his honor. No contemporary printed chart showing the results of Evía's reconnaissance exists, as the Direccion Hidrografica (Spanish Admiralty) began issuing charts only in 1797 or 1798.

From the Texas point of view, this *Carta particular* of 1807 is an improvement in one respect over the *Carta Esférica*. As it omits the easternmost ten degrees of longitude of the latter map, the *Carta particular* shows Texas on a larger scale. In addition, the Trinity River is correctly named on this map, whereas it is called "Archisas" on the *Carta Esférica*. The Brazos is absent from both maps.

198. *Carte Politique, Physique, Hydrographique et Itinéraire, d'une grande parte De L'Europe donnant dans leur Etat actuel et d'après les meilleures Sources et Autorités les Pays suivans; L'Empire Français, La Hollande, La Suisse, L'Allemagne, L'Empire Autrichien, La Prusse, L'Italie, La Dalmatie, avec les Bouches du Cattaro et une grande partie de la Turquie.* Drawn by Jean Baptiste Poirson. Printed by Hyacinthe Longlois. Paris, ca. 1807.

Color, scale 1 degree to approx. 69.5 mi., 119 × 149 cm., cloth-backed and folding into marbled slipcase. Inset: Greece.

This map shows Napoleon's reorganization of Europe.

199. *[American Pilot.]* Penelope Steele. London, ca. 1808. Scale varies, eight charts, each about 90 × 175 cm., bound into folio volume. MMNHMC.

This made-up atlas contains eight charts by various authors, all published at Steel's Navigation Warehouse between 1803 and 1807. The *National Maritime Museum Catalogue* lists three made-up atlases attributed to "P. Steele" (nos. 445–47), but none is similar to this example, and only three of these charts are listed in the contents of any of those atlases.

The atlas is especially designed to aid in navigation from London to the American Atlantic coasts. The maps are: (1) *East Coast of England.* . . . *John Knight, Tho. Fotheringham.* David Steel. London: P. Steel, May 30, 1803. (2) *A Chart of the British Channel,* John Knight. London: P. Steele, Jan. 12, 1806. (3) *Harbors and Islands in the British Channel.* London: P. Mason at Steel's Navigation Warehouse, March 25, 1806. (4) *A General Chart of the Atlantic or Western Ocean.* . . . David Steel. London: P. Steel, March 1, 1804. (5) *A New and Correct Chart of the Coast . . . from Boston and Cape Cod to Cape Hatteras.* London: P. Mason at Steel's Navigation Warehouse, Oct. 5, 1807. (7) *Steele's New and Correct Chart of the Coast . . . from Cape Canaveral to Cape Hatteras.* . . . P. Mason at Steel's Navigation Warehouse, April 23, 1808. (8) *An Accurate Chart of the Gulf Passage or New Bahama Channel.* P. Steel, June 1, 1804.

200. *Bahia de Galvez-Towm.* Spain. Navy. Madrid, 1809–19. Survey by José de Evía, 1783–86. Scale 1 in. to approx. 3.5 mi., 18 × 36 cm. Map no. 34 from the *Portulano de America Septentrionale,* Madrid, 1809–18. MMNHMC.

This is the first printed map devoted specifically to Galveston Bay. It is derived from the 1783–86 survey of the Spanish navigator José de Evía (or Hevía). The Eugene C. Barker Texas History Center at the University of Texas at Austin has a hand-drawn copy of a manuscript map of the Texas coast from Matagorda Bay to Galveston Bay that shows exactly this configuration for the vicinity of Galveston. It bears the notation "Joseph Evia. Copied at Direccion Hidrografica Madrid 1875." It is, however, miscatalogued under the year 1690. (For the original manuscript, see Holmes, pl. 9.)

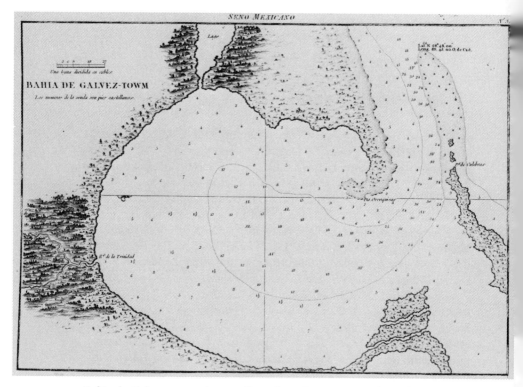

Bahia de Galvez-towm, 1809–19, from the 1783–86 survey of Spanish navigator
José de Evía. (See no. 200.) This is the first printed map of Galveston Bay.

Charles W. Hayes (1:15) calls Evía's survey the "only historically notable
event relating to Galveston Island of the eighteenth century." (Hayes was
evidently unaware of the 1721 visit of Bénard de la Harpe and makes no
mention of it.) It was upon the occasion of this survey that the bay received
its present name, in honor of Bernardo de Galvez, viceroy of New Spain.
Evía's information made its first appearance on a printed map with the
celebrated *Carta Esférica* of 1799 (see no. 197 for further information). This
was, in fact, the first appearance of Galveston Bay in unmistakable form,
with its present name, on any printed map.

Evía's form for Galveston Bay is actually quite crudely conceived, rather
egglike, with East Bay reduced to a small lagoon ("Lago") halfway up its
eastern shore. The "Ro. de la Trinidad" is the only river or stream shown
entering the bay. Galveston Island is unnamed (on the University of Texas
manuscript it is "I. de San Luis"), but Fort Point is called "Pd. de Cule-

98

bras." Two small islands lie due east. Only one channel enters the bay; it sweeps across the site of the absent Pelican Island. Depth soundings are given in "pies castellanos," and Hayes interprets Evía's numbers to indicate twelve and one-half feet of water over the outer bar.

201. *[Portulano de la America Setentrional.]* Spain. Admiralty. Direccion Hidrografica. Revised. Madrid, 1818. Scale indeterminable, 18 × 23 cm. MMNHMC.

A collection of 93 of the *Portulano's* 121 maps. Complete, the *Portulano* has four parts: (1) Puerto Rico and the Lesser Antilles; (2) the continental coast of the Caribbean and the Gulf of Mexico; (3) Cuba; and (4) Hispaniola and Jamaica. Present here are 13 maps from part one, all of parts two and three, and none of part four. Part two (46 maps) is bound in stiff paper wrappers, front wrapper mislabeled "Atlas de America Ano 1768." The remaining 47 maps are disbound.

This is the first comprehensive Spanish printed *portulano* devoted to the Gulf and the Caribbean. It is made up of detailed charts, of varying quality, of all important harbors and bays in the region. All maps in the *Portulano* that show the United States coast are present in this collection, including the first printed charts of Matagorda and Galveston bays (see no. 200). These charts are (33) *Bahia de S. Bernardo* [Matagorda Bay]; (34) *Bahia de Galvez-towm;* (35) *Puerto de Panzacola;* (36) *Bahia de Tampa;* (37) *Boca y puerto de Sn. Agustin;* (38) *Boca y barra del rio Sn. Juan;* (39) *Boca y barra del rio nasau;* (40) *Boca y barra del rio Sta. Maria.*

202. *A New Map of Mexico and Adjacent Provinces compiled from Original Documents.* Aaron Arrowsmith. London, 1810. Color, scale 1 in. to approx. 38 mi., two folding sheets forming one 128 × 158 cm. map. Insets: "Valley of Mexico, from Mr. Humboldt's map"; "Veracruz"; "Acapulco." MMNHMC.

This general map of Mexico shows the southwestern United States north to the forty-second parallel and the Gulf Coast east to the Pascagula River in Mississippi. Drawing on Humboldt's *Carte Generale du Royaume de la Nouvelle Espagne,* 1809, Arrowsmith recorded significant advances in Texas geography over his earlier *Chart of the West Indies,* 1803.

In coastal detail, Arrowsmith's maps are very similar and show little or no advance over the *Carta Esférica,* 1799, which they generally follow, independently or through Humboldt. In interior detail, however, the Arrowsmith maps are quite distinct, with *Mexico* being far superior. Most noticeably, Arrowsmith added the Brazos River, which he had omitted entirely on the 1803 map, and he correctly named the Trinity River, which he had previously called the "Rio Arrokisos."

203. *Portulano de las Côstas de la Península de España, Islas adyacentes y parte de la Costa de Africa.* Spain. Admiralty. Direccion Hidrografica. Cadiz, 1813. Scale varies, seventy maps, four folio volumes bound as one, in contemporary gold-stamped calf. MMNHMC.

The four parts of the *portulano* are Catalonia, sixteen maps; Valencia and Murcia, twenty maps; Granada and Seville, twenty-four maps; Portugal, ten maps. There is one general title page, but each part has a separate table of contents. The maps in the last part, plus the first map in part one, entitled "Puerto de Provendre," are unnumbered. The seventy maps include all the important harbors and cities on the Spanish and Portuguese coasts.

204. *[Galveston Bay.]* N.p., 1816. Photostat of a Spanish manuscript map in the National Archives in Mexico City, scale indeterminable, 49 × 53 cm. Donated by Regan Brown.

The photostat is accompanied by a modern manuscript map, in which all place-names and notations are translated into English. The original was probably produced ca. 1816, when Louis Aury and Henry Perry occupied Galveston Island. The cartographer described Bolivar Point as "flat land 3 feet above sea level where Gnl. Humbert was camped with his troops" and referred to the area as "Humbert Point." Jean Joseph Humbert was associated with Jose Alvarez de Toledo and Perry in filibustering efforts against Mexico. Aury probably named the area "Bolivar Point" in honor of Simon Bolivar, from whom he held a commission.

The most interesting feature of the map, which shows the east end of Galveston Island, is a channel that cuts through the island at about present-day Sixth Street. According to Warren D. C. Hall, who accompanied Perry to Galveston in 1815, Fort Point "was a little island lying to the eastward of Galveston, then being separated from the main island by a pass from the gulf to the bay, which pass is now closed up." The pass was five to six feet deep and was frequently used by small vessels. Hall claimed that it was this island that was named "Little Campeachy," not Laffite's town, which was located west of the channel. A Kentuckian who visited Galveston in 1827 reported that "Jim Campbell and Roach, two of Laffite's captains, assert that the best entrance to Galveston Bay in their time was through the island, east of the city proper." (Hayes, 1:35, 128). Remnants of this channel are shown as late as Groesbeck's map of 1838. On the island's Gulf shore is the notation, "vessel aground." "Houses and little trees" mark Aury's encampment, the site that Jean Lafitte took over when he came to the island. Galveston Island is labeled "Isla de Culebras" (Snake Island); Pelican Island is unnamed and marked "easily flooded." The map shows only the eastern part of Galveston Island.

205. *Entrada de la Bahía de Galvestown.* Photostat of manuscript map. Scale indeterminable, 29 × 29 cm. Map was copied from uncited volume in Bogota, Colombia, by Carlos Fallon. Donated by Carlos Fallon, 1954.

The source of Fallon's sketch is unknown. Whether it is a historical map, whether it reflects contemporary information, and whether the original was printed or a manuscript is uncertain.

The island is named "Isla Serpiente" and has the familiar hooked eastern tip. This tip is separated from the main body of the island by a channel with a depth of "13-½ feet," the same channel that appears on other early maps (see nos. 204 and 259). Bolivar Point is so named and is the site of the "Campamento del Coronel Perry." There is a "Bateria" on Fort Point, a "fuerte" on high ground at about Fifteenth Street and the Strand, and a "vigia" on the Gulf shore.

206. *Spanish North America.* John Thompson. London, 1814. Color, scale indeterminable, two 51 × 62 cm. sheets. The first sheet, with the given title, was drawn and engraved for Thompson's *New General Atlas,* London, 1814. The second sheet, *Spanish North America Southern Part* (showing only Central America), bears the same statement of responsibility but is dated 1816.

207. *Cary's New Celestial Globe on which are correctly laid down upwards of 3500 Stars Selected from the most accurate observations and calculated for the Year 1800. With the extent of each Constellation precisely defined.* (?) Gilpin. Produced by J. & W. Cary. London, 1816. Papier-mâché globe covered with a celestial chart printed on twelve gores, scale indeterminable, 31.5 cm. diameter, mounted on a contemporary wooden stand. MMNHMC. (See also nos. 190 and 271.)

208. *United States of America Corrected and Improved from the best Authorities.* Engraved by Hugh Anderson. Philadelphia; B. Warner, 1820.

Color, scale indeterminable, 42 × 64 cm. From the *General Atlas for Guthrie's Geography,* Philadelphia, 1820. Donated by the Friends of the Rosenberg Library.

This is a reduced version of the 1816 map of John Melish. The geography of the Texas coastline is confused: all important topographical features are present and with the correct relationship, but their forms are distorted. Galveztown, Louisiana, appears on the west bank of the "Attoyaque River," just above Sabine Lake.

209. *America.* Drawn by Johann Marias Friedrich Schmidt. Berlin: Simon Schropp & Co., 1820. Color, scale indeterminable, 45.5 × 59.5 cm. Key identifying the possessions of the European nations by color. MMNHMC.

210. *Amerique Septentrionale Dressee.* N. Lorrain. Paris, ca. 1820. Color, scale indeterminable, 26.5 × 37.5 cm. MMNHMC.

211. *Map of Arkansas and other Territories of the United States.* S. H. Long. N.p., n.d. Color, scale indeterminable, 38 × 38 cm. map surrounded by a descriptive text about the Arkansas Territory on a 44 × 56 cm. sheet. From the 1827 edition of Carey and Lea's *American Atlas,* Philadelphia.

Long, a major in the Army Corps of Topographical Engineers, inscribed the map to John C. Calhoun, then secretary of war. Long's reconnaissance of 1819–20 established the true relationship between the river systems of Oklahoma and for the first time correctly mapped the eastern wall of the Rockies from Spanish Peaks to Long's Peak. Long's map also incorrectly labeled the Great Plains as the "Great American Desert." This designation was commonly accepted and caused apprehension for years. The map was printed without revisions in all three editions of Carey and Lea's atlas (1822, 1823, and 1827) and also appeared in several later printed forms.

212. *Geographical, Statistical, and Historical Map of Maryland.* Drawn by Fielding Lucas. Engraved by Boyd(?). N.p., n.d. Color, scale 1 in. to approx. 25 mi., 28 × 48 cm. map on a 42 × 52 cm. sheet. Descriptive text on lower panel. Map no. 20 from Carey and Lea's *American Atlas,* Philadelphia, 1822. MMNHMC.

213. *Geographical, Statistical, and Historical Map of Alabama.* Drawn by Fielding Lucas. Engraved by B. Tanner. N.p., n.d. Color, scale 1 in. to approx. 25 mi., 23.5 × 30 cm. map on 42 × 53 cm. sheet. Descriptive text on lower panel. Map no. 30 from Carey and Lea's *American Atlas*, Philadelphia, 1822. MMNHMC.

214. *Geographical, Statistical, and Historical Map of Mississippi.* Drawn by Fielding Lucas. Engraved by Young & Delleker. N.p., n.d. Color, scale 1 in. to 20 mi., 22.5 × 30 cm. map on a 42 × 53 cm. sheet. Descriptive text on lower panel. Map no. 29 from Carey and Lea's *American Atlas*, Philadelphia, 1822. MMNHMC.

215. *Geographical, Statistical, and Historical Map of South Carolina.* Reduced by J. Drayton from the map by John Wilson. Engraved by Samuel Hufty. N.p.: W. Kness, n.d. Color, scale 1 in. to approx. 10 mi., 32.5 × 37.5 cm. map on a 42 × 53 cm. sheet. Descriptive text on lower panel. Map no. 24 from Carey and Lea's *American Atlas*, Philadelphia, 1822. MMNHMC.

216. *A New and Accurate Chart (From Captain Holland's Surveys) of the North American Coast, for the Navigation Between Cape Cod, in Massachusetts, and the River Mississippi.* Revised edition. London: Richard H. Laurie, 1824. Scale indeterminable, 80 × 312 cm. Insets: "Supplement. The Coasts from Havanna to the River Mississippi"; "Entrance of the Havanna"; "Plan of the Entrance and Harbor de St. Augustin"; "Plan of the Mouth of Nassau River"; "The Inlet of St. Mary River"; "Plan of the Harbor of Port Royal"; "Plan of the Bar and Harbour of Charleston"; "Plan of Delaware Bay and River"; "Chart of New York Harbour"; "The Harbour of Newport in Rhode Isld."; "Sketch of the Entrance to Long Island Sound." Text: "Remarks on the Light Houses, Ec." MMNHMC.

Laurie lists himself as "chartseller to the Admiralty" but inscribes this map to James Monroe. This is an update of the 1821 edition.

217. *Map of Massachusetts, Connecticut and Rhode Island Constructed from the Latest Authorities.* Drawn by D. H. Vance. Engraved by James H. Young. Philadelphia: Anthony Finley, 1825. Color, scale 1 in. to approx. 11 mi., 43.5 × 55 cm. From Finley's *New American Atlas*, Philadelphia, 1826. Table: population. MMNHMC.

218. *Hooker's New Pocket Plan of the City of New York.* William Hooker. New York, 1826. Color, scale indeterminable, 31 × 38 cm., folding into stiff paper covers. From the John Grant Tod papers.

219. *Amér. Sep. Partie du Mexique.* Philippe Marie Vandermaelen. N.p., n.d. Color, scale 1:1,600,000, 45.5 × 50.5 cm. Sheet no. 60 from volume four of Vandermaelen's *Atlas Universelle*, Brussels, 1827 (Koe Vdm 1). Text on Mexico after Humboldt. MMNHMC.

This is one of five sheets from Vandermaelen's atlas that depict Texas, and it is the only printed map from the colonial period devoted specifically to the Texas coast. Although the atlas was innovative, this particular map displays a confused geography. Streeter *Bibliography,* no. 1095) points out that Vandermaelen failed to consult either the *Carta Esférica,* 1799, or Humboldt's map of 1809, despite the use of Humboldt's text. Instead, his configuration strongly resembles the Texas coast on Henry Tanner's *Map of North America,* 1822, and on John Melish's *Map of the United States,* 1816. Yet Vandermaelen so carelessly adapted the detail that he must have taken it indirectly from one or both of the American maps through some inferior intermediary. The shape of Galveston Bay, for example, is quite different on all three maps. Vandermaelen calls it "Baie Trinidad," and, curiously, he locates a town of Galveston on an unnamed river whose position corresponds to the Brazos. But, to the east of the bay, he shows a "R. Magdale ou Bororos," which is possibly intended as the Brazos. Like both Tanner and Melish, Vandermaelen shows the Nueces as the southern boundary of Texas. The coastal region below the border is labeled "Nouveau Santander," with Texas and Nouveau Santander as subdivisions of "[San Luis] Potosi." There is no sign yet of Austin's colony or any other Anglo settlement.

220. *The Mexican and Central States of America. Together with the Southern Part of the United States of North America.* London: Richard H. Laurie, 1827. Color, scale 1 in. to approx. 75 mi., 63.5 × 95 cm., folding into octavo black leather covers with brass clasps. Front cover: "Mexico." Inset: "Mexico and the Adjacent States." MMNHMC.

Shown in Texas are three Indian villages ("Coshattee," "Bedi," and "Naddeo") and the settlements of "Bedies," "La Trinidad," and Nacagdoches. On the upper Brazos are "Guardia Barca" and a "Toucani" Indian village. Near the Guadeloupe is "Guardia de Cabello." San Antonio is prominently marked, with an "El Bexar" to the northeast. Four place-names ("S. Antonio Valero," "Espada," "Atascoso," and "Lagunilla") are located between

San Antonio and the Rio Grande. "Pres. del Esp. Santo" appears on the lower reaches of the San Antonio River. Galveston Bay is well formed. Galveston Island is "Ia. de S. Luis"; Pelican Island appears with an anchorage indicated nearby—the only anchorage indicated along the entire United States Gulf Coast. "Austin's Grant, Nth. Amern. Settlers" appears between the Brazos and the Colorado, with San Felipe de Austin shown twice: once as "Sn. Felipe" and once as "Austin's Town." Bastrop (El Mina) is shown but not named.

221. *Carte d'Assemblage de l'Amérique septentle.* Philippe Marie Vandermaelen. N.p., n.d. Color, scale 1:1,600,000. Index sheet to volume four of Vandermaelen's *Atlas Universelle,* Brussels, 1827 (Koe Vdm 1). Inset: "Amerique Russe." MMNHMC. (See no. 219 for further information.)

222. *Amer. Sep. Partie des États Unis.* Philippe Marie Vandermaelen. N.p., n.d. Color, scale 1:1,600,000, 45.5 × 50.5 cm. Sheet no. 56 from volume four of Vandermaelen's *Atlas Universelle,* Brussels, 1827 (Koe Vdm 1). MMNHMC.

Shows Mississippi and large fragments of neighboring Louisiana, Arkansas, Tennessee, and Alabama. (See no. 219 for further information.)

223. *Amér. Sep. Embouchures du Mississipi.* Philippe Marie Vandermaelen. N.p., n.d. Color, scale 1:1,600,000, 45.5 × 50.5 cm. Sheet no. 61 from volume four of Vandermaelen's *Atlas Universelle,* Brussels, 1827 (Koe Vdm 1). Table: the population of the New World, 1823, after Humboldt. MMNHMC.

Shows the Mississippi River Delta. (See no. 219 for further information.)

224. *Amér. Sep. Florides et Iles Lucyes.* Drawn by Philippe Marie Vandermaelen. Lithographed by H. Ode Aout. N.p., 1825. Color, scale 1:1,600,000, 45.5 × 50.5 cm. Sheet no. 62 from volume four of Vandermaelen's *Atlas Universelle,* Brussels, 1827 (Koe Vdm 1). Text: "Florides." MMNHMC.

Shows Florida and the Bahamas. (See no. 219 for further information.)

225. *Amér. Sep. Partie du Mexique.* Philippe Marie Vandermaelen. N.p., n.d. Color, scale 1:1,600,000, 45.5 × 50.5 cm. Sheet no. 65 from volume four of Vandermaelen's *Atlas Universelle,* Brussels, 1827 (Koe Vdm 1). MMNHMC.

Shows the Mexican Gulf Coast. (See no. 219 for further information.)

226. *Amér. Sep. Mérida.* Philippe Marie Vandermaelen. N.p., n.d. Color, scale 1:1,600,000, 45.5 × 50.5 cm. Sheet no. 66 from volume four of Vandermaelen's *Atlas Universelle,* Brussels, 1827 (Koe Vdm 1). Text: "Notes sur Yucatan." MMNHMC.

Shows the Yucatan peninsula and channel. (See no. 219 for further information.)

227. *Amér. Sep. Partie du Guatemala.* Philippe Marie Vandermaelen. N.p., n.d. Color, scale 1:1,600,000, 45.5 × 50.5 cm. Sheet no. 72 from volume four of Vandermaelen's *Atlas Universelle,* Brussels, 1827 (Koe Vdm 1). Table: the annual production of principal Mexican mines. MMNHMC.

Shows Belize, Honduras, and El Salvador, plus part of Nicaragua and Guatemala. (See no. 219 for further information.)

228. *Amér. Sep. Partie de Guatemala.* Philippe Marie Vandermaelen. N.p., n.d. Color, scale 1:1,600,000, 45.5 × 50.6 cm. Sheet 76 from volume four of Vandermaelen's *Atlas Universelle,* Brussels, 1827 (Koe Vdm 1). Table: the annual production of principal Mexican mines. MMNHMC.

Shows southern Nicaragua, Costa Rica, and northern Panama. (See no. 219 for further information.)

229. *Amér. Sep. Partie des États-Unis.* Philippe Marie Vandermaelen. N.p., n.d. Color, scale 1:1,600,000, 45.5 × 50.5 cm. Sheet no. 57 from volume four of Vandermaelen's *Atlas Universelle,* Brussels, 1827 (Koe Vdm 1). Inset: "Iles Bermudes ou Summer's Island." Text on the United States. MMNHMC.

Shows the area around Cape Hatteras. (See no. 219 for further information.)

230. *Plano de la Bahía y Puerto de Galvestown en el Departamento de Tejas.* Alexander Thompson, by order of the Mexican Navy. N.p., 1828. Photostat of manuscript map, scale indeterminable, 59 × 79 cm.; original is in the Barker Texas History Center. Donated by the Gulf, Colorado & Santa Fe Railway Co., 1929.

Thompson was an American, probably a Southerner, who had emigrated to Mexico by 1826. He received a commission in the Mexican navy but quickly became disillusioned by that country's chaotic condition.

At some point, Thompson developed an interest in Galveston and its possibilities. On at least one occasion (1828) he unsuccessfully petitioned the Mexican government to grant him Galveston Island for colonization. He complained bitterly to Samuel May Williams that the Mexican government had promised command of a proposed customs house at Galveston but that revolution had precluded his taking that post. Stephen F. Austin had proposed the customs house in 1825, and it is possible that Thompson knew of the idea before he moved to Mexico. In the same letter to Williams, Thompson remarked that he expected a leave of absence soon and that he planned to return to Texas at that time. (Alexander Thompson to Samuel May Williams, March 16, 1828, no. 23–0002, Samuel May Williams Papers, Rosenberg Library.)

Thompson's leave did not materialize; however, on September 28, 1828, he took command of the Mexican schooner *Luciana,* with orders to draft maps of Galveston Bay (*Archivo General de Mexico,* 310:112). He left for Texas immediately, as his map is dated "Septiembre, Octubre, y Nove de 1828." While in Texas he met Austin, and two topics certainly came up in their conversation. One was Thompson's desire to settle in Texas, particularly in Galveston; the other was his current surveying and chartmaking at Galveston Bay. Austin was nearing the end of the preparation of his own map of Texas, which he also constructed under the direction of the Mexican authorities (see no. 236). There is no evidence that Austin examined Thompson's notes or sketches. At any rate, he failed to incorporate Thompson's information in his own map. Upon Thompson's return to Vera Cruz, he wrote to Austin: "Arrived here only a few days ago & have only now finished my charts of the Bar, Bay, & Rivers of Galveston & need not say in the present state of the Govt. I heartily wish myself back again. I believe however that the commodore who is now here has recommended to the Govt. to remand me" (Alexander Thompson to Stephen F. Austin, December 6, 1828, Stephen F. Austin Papers, Barker Texas History Center).

Thompson was probably referring to his petition to colonize Galveston, which bears the same date as the letter to Austin. Despite the commodore's intercession, Thompson's request was denied. Virtually nothing is known of his life after January, 1829. He may have appeared in Texas in early 1830, but he should not be confused with Alexander Thomson (or Thompson), the surveyor for Robertson's colony.

Thompson's comment that he prepared charts of the bar, bay, and rivers of Galveston may mean that he prepared more than one copy of his chart of Galveston Bay. These copies may have differed slightly in detail. He submitted one chart to the Mexican navy; and publishers, who during the next few years issued printed maps using Thompson's map as an inset, would have needed copies. The only known example, however, is in the Barker Texas History Center. The Library of Congress has a photostat of Thompson's manuscript.

The Barker copy gives Galveston Bay its most accurate configuration of any map since La Harpe's manuscript of 1721; it is also far more accurate than virtually any map published during the next fifteen years. Galveston Island is unnamed and generally featureless, but Fort Point is called "Punta de Culebras." At the approximate site of Laffite's abandoned fort, Thompson locates a well ("pozo"); two additional wells appear on Bolivar Point, just south of Long's fort, close to "Fuerte de Bolivar." Teichman's Point appears as a separate island, with five trees labeled "arboles de venado." Five separate channels extend from the deep water of the Gulf into the gap between Galveston and Bolivar Point. The harbor appears with a depth of up to thirty feet. The Thompson map does not show a channel cutting across the eastern end of the island, as do some other maps (see nos. 204 and 259). Only two settlements appear, Harrisburg and Lynchburg ("Lynch"), although a number of houses belonging to settlers are also indicated. A "Camino a S. Felipe de Austin" leads west from Harrisburg, and two proposed roads run east toward the future San Jacinto battleground site.

Although never separately printed, Thompson's manuscript appeared as an inset on several maps published between 1833 and 1841. These were David H. Burr's *Texas*, 1833 (no. 247); the Galveston Bay and Texas Land Company's *Map of the Colonization Grants to Zavala, Vehlein & Burnet in Texas*, 1835 (no. 249); the anonymous *Plan of the City of Galveston*, 1837 (no. 254); and John Arrowsmith's *Map of Texas*, 1841. How David Burr came upon the manuscript is unknown, but he was probably directly or indirectly responsible for its use on the Galveston Bay and Texas Land Company and Arrowsmith maps. The former shared a mutual engraver and printer with Burr's map (S. Stiles & Co., of New York). Burr and Arrowsmith had a close working relationship during the 1830s and collaborated on *The American Atlas*, London, 1839. Arrowsmith used Thompson's configuration without attribution.

231. *New Jersey.* Engraved by Young and Dellecker. Philadelphia: Anthony Finley, 1828. Color, scale 1 in. to approx. 15.5 mi., 22 × 28.5 cm. Map no. 14 from the 1828 edition of Finley's *A New General Atlas,* Philadelphia. MMNHMC.

The atlas went through many editions, the plates being continually revised to account for new development.

232. *North Carolina.* Engraved by Young & Dellecker. Philadelphia: Anthony Finley, 1828. Color, scale 1 in. to approx. 38 mi., 21.5 × 28.5 cm. Map no. 19 from the 1828 edition of Finley's *A New General Atlas,* Philadelphia. MMNHMC. (See no. 231 for further information.)

233. *Virginia.* Engraved by Young & Dellecker. Philadelphia: Anthony Finley, 1828. Color, scale 1 in. to approx. 40 mi., 22 × 29 cm. Map no. 18 from the 1828 edition of Finley's *A New General Atlas,* Philadelphia. MMNHMC. (See no. 231 for further information.)

234. *North view of Providence: Amérique Septentrionale État de Rhode Island* (title also given in Latin and German). Drawn by Jacques Gerard Milbert. Lithographed by Deroy. Printed by Henry Gauguin. Color, scale indeterminable, 25 × 30 cm. Plate no. 44 from Milbert's *Itinéraire pittoresque du fleuve Hudson et les parties Latérales d'Amérique du Nord,* Paris, 1828–29. MMNHMC.

235. *Map of the Territory of Florida, From its Northern boundary to Lat: 27,'30"N., Connected with the Delta of the Mississippi.* William Henry Swift. Washington, D.C., 1829. Scale indeterminable, 71 × 166 cm. "Annexed to the report of the Board of Internal Improvement dated Feby. 19th, 1829 relating to the Canal contemplated to connect the Atlantic with the Gulf of Mexico." Insets: "Gulf of Mexico"; "Entrance to Mobile Bay"; "Entrance to Pensacola Bay"; "Eastern entrance to St. Rosa Sound"; "Entrances to St. Andrew's Sound"; "Entrance to St. Joseph's Bay"; "Entrance to Appalachicola Bay"; "Main Entrance to St. George's Sound"; "Middle entrance to St. George's Sound"; "Entrance to Ocklockony Bay"; "Eastern entrance to St. George's Sound"; "Entrance to St. Augustine"; "Entrance to St. John's River"; "Entrance to St. Mary's Harbour." MMNHMC.

236. *Map of Texas With Parts of the Adjoining States.* Compiled by Stephen F. Austin. Engraved by John and William W. Warr. Philadelphia: Henry S. Tanner, 1830. Color, scale 1 in. to approx. 25 mi., 60 × 74 cm., folding into octavo leather covers, map badly wormed. Notes giving sources of map information and a general description of Texas. Land grants after 1830 added in manuscript. Milam's grant is marked "waved," which dates the additions after 1835.

This is the first issue of one of the most important maps in Texas history. It is the first large-scale map of Texas, a scale made possible by excluding all of the present-day state west of the 102nd meridian. Austin's use of this format established a precedent followed by many cartographers before 1860.

In 1822 Austin promised the Mexican officials that he would compile topographical material and prepare a detailed and accurate map of Texas. He began work the following year and for six years employed numerous surveyors to plot the state's features. Austin did much of the surveying along the coast, but for the western interior he relied heavily upon the reports of fur traders and trappers.

Several manuscript maps appeared. This printed version, taken from Tanner's copy of one of the manuscripts, shows Austin's colony, Austin's 1827 grant on the Colorado, and De Witt's colony. The new settlements of San Felipe de Austin, Brazoria, Matagorda, Harrisburg, Victoria, Gonzales, and Waco appear for the first time on a printed map.

Austin's more primitive manuscript copy at the Barker Texas History Center includes two additional towns—Monterwine, on the Colorado, and Galveston. The appearance of Galveston may have been a projection of Austin's well-known desire to see a port established at that site, for the island had no permanent settlement until 1838. Although Galveston is absent on this first issue of the printed map, the site's strategic importance was not ignored: "Harbour" appears between Pelican and Galveston islands, the only Texas harbor identified. Tanner added Galveston to the 1836 issue.

Streeter (Bibliography, no. 1115) identifies six issues in all, dated 1830–39, and locates nine copies of this rare first issue, including this Rosenberg Library copy.

237. *St. Thomas.* Lithographed by Johan Friedrich Freyse. Hamburg, ca. 1830. Scale indeterminable, 28 × 42 cm. MMNHMC.

A panorama of the port of St. Thomas, Virgin Islands. Freyse was working in Hamburg in 1830.

238. *Mexico*. London: John Arrowsmith, 1832. Color, scale 1 in. to approx. 100 mi., 48 × 60 cm. From Arrowsmith's *London Atlas*. Inset: "Mexico, Shewing its connection with the Ports of Acapulco, Vera Cruz & Tampico." MMNHMC.

This is one of the first European maps to use Austin's *Map of Texas*, 1830, as a source (see no. 236). The library's collection includes a number of other maps from the *London Atlas*. The first edition of the atlas appeared in 1834; as subsequent editions were published, the maps were frequently revised. The maps in this collection are listed by their copyright date.

239. *West Indies*. London: John Arrowsmith, 1832. Color, scale 1 in. to approx. 90 mi., 48 × 60 cm. From Arrowsmith's *London Atlas*. Untitled inset: southwestern coast of Mexico. MMNHMC. (See no. 238 for further information.)

240. *Brazil*. London: John Arrowsmith, 1832. Color, scale 1 in. to approx. 125 mi., 48 × 62 cm. From Arrowsmith's *London Atlas*. MMNHMC. (See no. 238 for further information.)

241. *Map of the State of Coahuila and Texas*. Engraved by William Hooker. N.p., n.d. Color, scale 1 in. to approx. 90 mi., 27 × 34 cm. From Mary Austin Holley's *Texas*, published by Armstrong & Plaskitt, Baltimore, 1833.

Hooker first issued this map as a separate item, but shortly thereafter it was used, with minor variations, to supplement Holley's book (Streeter, *Bibliography*, no. 1135) and, slightly later, an anonymous work, *Visit to Texas*, 1834 (Streeter, no. 1155). Hooker's map is one of the earliest maps of Texas to show all of Texas to the Arkansas River, including the Panhandle. Four settlements appear on or near Galveston Bay: Harrisburg, New Washington, Anahuac, and "Powhattan," at the mouth of Dickinson's Creek.

242. *Map of the United States Compiled from the Latest and Most Accurate Surveys*. New York: Amos Lay, 1834. Title and cover designed and engraved by Thomas Starling, London. Color, scale 1 in. to approx. 24 mi., 132 × 157 cm., cloth-backed, dissected and folding into marbled boards. Insets: "Florida"; western hemisphere. Tables: populations of the United

States and Canada. Profiles of the Ohio Canal, Erie Canal, Union Canal, and Morris Canal. MMNHMC.

This map gives a wealth of detail on Jacksonian America, including all existing counties, larger towns, roads, native tribes and trails, forts, canals, railroads, proposed railroads. The map shows settled parts of eastern Texas the year before the Texas Revolution. Four land grants (Austin, Burnet, Vehlein, and Zavala) appear, as well as many roads and sixteen towns and forts. The cartographer incorrectly placed Galveston near the site of present-day Anahuac. (Streeter, *Bibliography*, no. 1094).

243. *United States.* London: John Arrowsmith, 1834. Color, scale indeterminable, 48 × 61 cm. From Arrowsmith's *London Atlas.* MMNHMC. (See no. 238 for further information.)

244. *Colombia.* London: John Arrowsmith, 1834. Color, scale 1 in. to approx. 80 mi., 49 × 60 cm. From Arrowsmith's *London Atlas.* MMNHMC. (See no. 238 for further information.)

245. *Peru & Bolivia.* London: John Arrowsmith, 1834. Color, scale 1 in. to approx. 80 mi., 50 × 60 cm. From Arrowsmith's *London Atlas.* MMNHMC. (See no. 238 for further information.)

246. *Virginia.* David H. Burr. N.p., n.d. Copyright by Thomas Illman, New York, 1834. Color, scale 1 in. to approx. 33 mi., 27 × 32.5 cm. Map no. 42 from Burr's *A New Universal Atlas,* New York, 1831–35. Inset: "The Western Part of Virginia." MMNHMC.

247. *Texas.* David H. Burr. Engraved by S. Stiles & Co., New York: J. H. Colton & Co., 1833–35. Color, scale 1 in. to approx. 50 mi., 44 × 54 cm., folding into brown leather covers. Front cover: *Burr's Map of the State of Coha. & Texas.* Inset: "Plan of the Port of Galveston," by Alexander Thompson. MMNHMC.

Streeter (*Bibliography*, no. 1134B) gives an excellent account of this map. Overall, Burr's map represents a great improvement over previous Texas maps. It is the second map to show all of Texas, preceded only by the greatly inferior Hooker map of 1833 (see no. 241).

Burr uses Thompson's configuration of Galveston Bay as the model for the bay on the main map, thereby giving it a better form than do Austin, 1830 (see no. 236), and Hunt and Randel, 1839 (see no. 278). Three settlements appear in the vicinity of the bay: Harrisburg, Lynchburg, and Anahuac. The Bolivar Channel is labeled "Galveston Inlet 14 to 18 feet."

248. *Texas.* Thomas Gamaliel Bradford. Boston, 1835. Color, scale 1 in. to approx. 75 mi., 20 × 26.5 cm. Map no. 64A from Bradford's *A Comprehensive Atlas, geographical, historical & commercial.* MMNHMC.

Locates four settlements in the vicinity of Galveston Bay: Harrisburg, Lynchburg, Liberty, and Anahuac. Evidently not all copies of Bradford's atlas contained this map (see the copy described by Phillips, *Atlases*, no. 770).

249. *Map of the Colonization Grants to Zavala, Vehlein & Burnet in Texas, Belonging to the Galveston Bay & Texas Land Co.* Engraved by S. Stiles & Co. New York, n.d. Original color, scale 1 in. to approx. 55 mi., 23 × 31 cm. From David Woodman's *Guide to Texas Emigrants*, Boston, 1835. Inset: "Plan of Port of Galveston," by Alexander Thompson.

This map locates the three colonization grants controlled by the Galveston Bay and Texas Land Co., which was organized in New York on October 16, 1830. With the repeal of the restrictive Mexican immigration law in 1834, the company began to advertise for colonists. Several promotional pieces, including Woodman's *Guide*, were published. (Apparently Woodman was the company's Boston agent.) This map appeared earlier on a broadside published by the company (Streeter, *Bibliography*, no. 1164).

The map shows an oversized but well-formed Galveston Bay, similar to that on Burr's map of 1833 (see no. 247) and also closely following Thompson's map. Four settlements are located on or near the bay: Harrisburg, Lynchburg, Liberty, and Anahuac.

250. *Mexico and Guatimala.* Drawn and engraved by J. Dower. London: Henry Teesdale & Co., n.d. Color, scale 1 degree to 69 mi., 33.5 × 40 cm. From Teesdale & Co.'s *A New General Atlas of the World*, London, 1835. MMNHMC.

Texas has a panhandle extending north into present-day Wyoming.

251. *Map of Texas, Containing the Latest Grants & Discoveries.* E. F. Lee. Cincinnati: J. A. James & Co., 1836. Color, scale indeterminable, 22 × 31.5

cm. From David Barnett Edwards's *The History of Texas; or, The Emigrant's, Farmer's and Politician's Guide to the Character, Climate, Soil and Productions of that Country.*, J. A. James & Co., Cincinnati, 1836.

According to Streeter (*Bibliography*, no. 1199), the map was probably lithographed as late as January, 1836, for it notes Ben Milam's death in the storming of Bexar by the Texans on December 10, 1835. Lee adapted the map from a later issue of Austin's map (see no. 236), probably the 1835 issue. Only three human features appear on or near Galveston Bay: Harrisburg, Anahuac, and a "Salt Work" opposite Anahuac.

252A. *A New Map of Texas, with the Contiguous American & Mexican States.* Engraved by James Hamilton Young. Philadelphia: S. Augustus Mitchell, 1836. Photostat of printed map, scale (of original) 1 in. to approx. 75 mi., 45.4 × 54 cm. Notes: "Land Grants"; "Remarks on Texas"; "Rivers of Texas."

This is the second of eight issues identified by Streeter (*Bibliography*, no. 1178A). The map shows about the same area as Burr's map of 1833 (see no. 247), but with the extended boundaries claimed by the Republic of Texas in 1836. Four settlements appear on or near Galveston Bay: Harrisburg, Lynchburg, New Washington, and Anahuac.

B. Another issue: same title, publisher, size, and scale, but dated 1843, with changes to the notes and with added cover title, *Mitchell's Map of Texas*. Folds into black leather covers, which are detached but present. Poor condition.

This is Streeter's seventh issue (*Bibliography*, no. 1178F). The twenty-three counties created since 1836 are overprinted on the colonial land grants.

Ten settlements appear in the vicinity of Galveston Bay: Galveston, Virginia, Austinia, St. Leon, New Washington, Houston, Harrisburg, Lynchburg, Anahuac, and Bolivar. The San Jacinto battleground is marked. Streeter located four examples of this issue, including this copy.

253. *A Map of the Extremity of Cape Cod Including the Townships of Provincetown & Truro: with A Chart of Their Sea Coast and of Cape Cod Harbour, State of Massachusetts.* United States Army Corps of Engineers. Executed under the direction of J. D. Graham, 1833–35. Made by order of the U.S. House of Representatives. Engraved by W. J. Stone. Washington, D.C., 1836. Scale 1 in. to ⅙ mi., four sheets forming one 142 × 172 cm. map. Part of House Document 121, 25th Congress, 2d Session, 1836. Notes, references, and "Register of the Tides at High and Low Water." MMNHMC.

254. *Plan of the City of Galveston Situated on the East End of Galveston Island Texas.* Anonymous. Printed by the Lithographic Office. New Orleans, n.d. Photostat of printed map, scale indeterminable, 52 × 81 cm. From the *City of Galveston, on Galveston Island, in Texas: with a History of the Title of the Proprietor, and a Brief Account of all its Advantages,* published by Hotchkiss & Co., New Orleans, 1837, 8 pp. Inset: "Survey of the Port of Galveston," by Alexander Thompson. Diagram showing proposed division of city blocks into lots.

This is the first printed plan of Galveston, predating John Groesbeck's survey and city plan by several months (see no. 259). The accompanying pamphlet was designed to vindicate Michael B. Menard's title to the island and to sell the stock of the fledgling Galveston City Company.

When the depression of 1837 occurred, the City Company abandoned original plans to sell all one thousand shares of stock by subscription. The directors decided instead to survey and plat the city, put the lots up for sale, and divide the stock among members of the company. (See Hayes, 1:256–60, for a full account of early title disputes and promotion schemes.)

The map shows Galveston in a form quite similar to that actually carried out but differing in a number of important respects. It shows a more fully developed metropolis than do the later maps of Groesbeck and Sandusky (see no. 277), though the core of the city is essentially that adopted later. The Gulf shore is farther inland than on any other nineteenth-century map. This map is also unique in showing a grand oceanfront boulevard that corresponds to the modern Seawall Boulevard.

The cartographer divided the city north of Avenue L ("Menard Street") into regular blocks of twelve lots without alleys; and south of Avenue L into oversize outlots. No wharves appear on the map, and locations of public buildings, markets, squares, cemeteries, are quite different from those on any other printed map. Street names are also different, here bearing names rather than letters or numbers.

The compiler of the map and the author of the pamphlet are unknown. Either Menard or Levi Jones, City Company directors, probably designed the map. Hayes implies that Menard and his associates already had a well-formed concept of the plan they wanted for their new city when they hired Groesbeck to conduct the official survey. This anonymous printed plan is probably their original concept, which they later gave to Groesbeck to adapt to the actual townsite. It is unlikely, on the other hand, that Menard wrote the accompanying pamphlet. The text continually refers to him in the third person and misspells his name as "Maynard."

Both the pamphlet and the map are quite rare. Streeter (*Bibliography*, no. 1268) locates only two copies of the pamphlet, one defective. The original from which this photostat was taken has not been located.

255A. *Galveston Island.* R. C. Trimble and William Lindsay. N.p., 1837. Photostat of an 1889 manuscript copy of the 1837 manuscript; the 1889 copy drawn by O. H. Ewet, Texas. General Land Office. Scale (of original) 1 in. to 40 chains, 46 × 69 cm. Donated by the U.S. Army Corps of Engineers, Galveston office, 1929.

B. Another copy: same title, cartographers, date, and scale, but 69 × 90 cm. Photostat of an 1890 manuscript copy of the 1837 manuscript; the 1890 copy drawn by F. G. Blau, Texas General Land Office. Donated by the Gulf, Colorado & Santa Fe Railway Co., 1929.

C. Another copy: same title, cartographers, date, and scale, but 55 × 86 cm. Blueprint of an unsigned, undated manuscript copy of the 1837 manuscript.

There are several differences in ornamentation between this blueprint and the two previous photostats. In addition, the blueprint locates a number of presettlement landmarks discussed in the "General Reference" on the map.

D. Another copy: same title, cartographers, date, and scale, but 54 × 90 cm. Blueprint of an unsigned, undated manuscript copy of the 1837 manuscript. Donated by the Bartholow-Willits Engineering Co., 1917.

Henry C. Ripley overlaid the Hall and Jones sections on the Trimble and Lindsey plots on this copy.

The Trimble and Lindsey survey shows all of Galveston Island but focuses on the portion west of the original city limits. In 1837 the Republic of Texas Congress authorized the sale of west Galveston Island, then in the public domain. Trimble and Lindsey charted all topographical features of note and divided the domain into ten-acre lots. Their survey set the grid pattern for all subsequent development on the west end of the island. If viewed together with John Groesbeck's *Map of the City of Galveston,*

1838, (see no. 259), the map is the first comprehensive survey of the whole island.

The lots were immediately offered for sale at auction, but with little success. In 1839 Edward Hall and Levi Jones located all the unsold lots and resurveyed them. They received a patent to the land in 1840 and offered the lots for sale again.

Among the landmarks indicated on the map are "Eagle Grove" and the "three trees," important guideposts for early navigators.

256. *Map of the City of Austin, on Tres Palacios Bay, Texas.* Printed by Miller Lithograph. New York, ca. 1837. Scale indeterminable, 48 × 65 cm., on tissue paper. Untitled inset of the Matagorda Bay area. From the John Grant Tod Papers.

This plan of Austin was one of a great number of urban schemes promoted in Texas in the euphoric months following the victory at San Jacinto. The town was to be located just north of Oyster Lake, near Palacios, on a small headland jutting into the northeastern corner of Matagorda Bay.

The promoters probably launched their scheme in early 1837, at about the time Matagorda County was established. Place-names provide clues as to the identity of the promoters. One street on the plan is named for New York financier Samuel Swartwout, and "Biddle Square" suggests that Philadelphia money was involved in the project. The site was on land owned by Ralph Wright, about whom little is known.

Austin was to have 178 blocks, each with thirty-two lots. The promoters set aside four additional blocks for a church, a college, and public buildings. There were also four public squares and a "public promenade" running along a part of the waterfront. Although the town never developed according to this ambitious plan, some settlement did take place. The site appears on several nineteenth-century maps, including the 1880 General Land Office *Map of Matagorda County* (see no. 384).

The inset shows a "proposed canal" between the Colorado River and Wilson Creek, with a raft blocking the flow of the river. The canal was completed and the raft removed before 1836, but the raft reappeared periodically. John Grant Tod, among whose papers this map was found, worked on clearing a raft from the Colorado in 1857–60, while he was assistant state engineer for river work.

257A. *Connected Map of Austin's Colony.* Commenced by Stephen F. Austin, 1833. Completed by James F. Perry, 1837. Projected by John P.,

Thomas H., and Gail Borden. Drafted by P. G. Blau. Texas. General Land Office. Austin, 1892. Photostat of an 1892 copy of the 1837 manuscript, scale indeterminable, four sheets forming 208 × 436 cm. map. Tables: "Labors at Mouth of Brazos"; "Labors opposite San Felipe"; "Labors Below San Felipe."

B. Another copy: same title, cartographers, and dates, but blueline on 104 × 109 cm. sheet.

258. *Republique des États Unis du Mexique.* Drawn by Charles V. Monin. Engraved by L. Grenier. Edited by Armand Aubrée. Paris, 1837. Color, scale indeterminable, 45 × 32 cm. Inset: "Guatemala ou Provinces Unies de L'Amérique Centrale."

This map incorrectly shows Coahuila and Texas as separate Mexican states, with the southern border of Texas at the Nueces River.

259. *Map of the City of Galveston Situated on the East End of Galveston Island Texas.* Surveyed and drawn by John D. Groesbeck. 1838. Certified copy by L. H. Bradford & Co. Boston, 1854. Photostat of printed map, scale indeterminable, 55 × 97 cm. Diagram showing the division of city blocks into lots.

John Groesbeck conducted the second survey of Galveston, which was the first under the direction of the Galveston City Company. Though he finished the map in 1838, it did not reach print until 1854; and the company never used it in promotionals. Shortly after Groesbeck completed the map, the company commissioned William Sandusky to prepare a third survey of Galveston. It was the Sandusky map that became the standard view of Galveston in the 1840s.

Groesbeck platted the city site and named streets according to a pattern set by the city of Philadelphia. Avenues ran east and west and were in alphabetical order, beginning at the bay with Avenue A. Streets ran north and south and were in numerical order, beginning on the east with First Street. Two major thoroughfares divided the city: Broadway ran east and west, and Bath Avenue (now Rosenberg or Twenty-fifth) ran north and south. North of Avenue M, Groesbeck platted city blocks measuring 260 × 360 feet and containing fourteen business or residential lots. South of Avenue M, he created outlots, which were four times the size of city blocks and were intended for agricultural use.

In several instances Groesbeck drew lot lines across bayous and bayshores; it was obvious that the City Company planned from the beginning to fill in wetlands and use every available space on the barrier island for human habitation.

Groesbeck located cemeteries on the bay at the far northwestern corner of the city and set aside land for five churches, three schools, three markets, a customs house, and a courthouse. He also showed three wharves and a large park in the harbor area. A channel separated the eastern tip of the island from the city (see no. 204). Groesbeck left this Fort Point area undeveloped but did show an "old fort" and a pilothouse there, among other features.

Original copies of the printed map are in three repositories: the Galveston city archives; Yale University; and the Barker Texas History Center. This photostat seems to have been made from the Barker copy. The original manuscript has been lost since at least the 1890s. In 1898 the Galveston City Company tried unsuccessfully to retrieve from Bradford & Co. either the stone from which the map was pulled or the original manuscript itself.

260. *Swartwout.* Anonymous. Printed by P. A. Mesier & Co. New York, ca. 1838. Scale 1 in. to approx. 885 ft., 50 × 76 cm. From the James Morgan Papers.

Swartwout was on the east bank of the Trinity River in southwestern Polk County at the site of an Alabama-Coushatta village. It was named for Samuel Swartwout, a New York financier, who organized the town with James Morgan, Arthur Garner, and Thomas Bradley. Swartwout was also involved in other Texas real estate projects, including the Galveston Bay and Texas Land Company, the New Washington Association, and the development of Austin on Matagorda Bay (see no. 256). The first Anglo-American settlers came in 1835, and by 1844 Swartwout was described as a "rather considerable village" (Hollon and Butler, p. 315).

The map shows a town with eighty-six blocks, usually with ten lots to a block. Penciled notations, probably in James Morgan's hand, locate lots taken by the first settlers and lots "sold 1st march," 1839. To promote the city, Morgan, Garner, and Bradley had placed an advertisement for "shares or lots" in Swartwout in the Houston *Telegraph and Texas Register,* November 17, 1838 (see Streeter, *Bibliography,* no. 244).

Streeter (no. 1324) locates only this copy of the map. Reps includes a copy of the map in his *Cities of the American West* (fig. 5–19), attributing it to Yale University; Yale actually has a photostat of the Rosenberg copy.

261. *Lower Canada, New Brunswick, Nova Scotia, Prince Edward Id., Newfoundland, and a large portion of the United States.* London: John Arrowsmith, 1838. Color, scale 1 in. to approx. 35 mi., two sheets forming one 48 × 61 cm. map. From Arrowsmith's *London Atlas* (See no. 238 for further information.). Untitled inset of Newfoundland. MMNHMC.

262. *Upper Canada &c.* London: John Arrowsmith, 1838. Color, scale 1 in. to approx. 35 mi., 48 × 61 cm. From Arrowsmith's *London Atlas* (See no. 238 for further information.). MMNHMC.

263. *Plan du Port de Saint Thomas et de ses environs (Iles Vierges).* Drawn by L. J. Rohde, 1822. Soundings augmented by Chrestien de Poly, 1837. Engraved by J. M. Hacq and Chassant(?). Published by order of the French Secretary of State. Paris, 1839. Scale indeterminable, 30.5 × 59 cm. MMNHMC.

264. *South America from Original Documents, including The Survey by the Officers of H. M. Ships* **Adventure** *and* **Beagle.** London: John Arrowsmith, 1839. Color, scale 1 in. to 200 mi., 50.5 × 63.5 cm. From Arrowsmith's *London Atlas* (See no. 238 for further information.). Insets: Patagonia; "Falkland Islands"; "Port San Carlos"; "Galapagos Islands." MMNHMC.

First issued in 1832, this map was revised in 1839 to illustrate the discoveries of the *Adventure* and the *Beagle* for the official narrative of the Darwin expedition.

265. *The Provinces of La Plata, The Banda Oriental del Uruguay and Chile.* London: John Arrowsmith, 1839. Color, scale 1 in. to approx. 70 mi., 51 × 63 cm. From Arrowsmith's *London Atlas* (See no. 238 for further information.). Untitled inset of Patagonia. MMNHMC.

Arrowsmith based this map on reports from Woodbine Parish, British Charge d'Affairs at Buenos Aires.

266. *France.* London: John Arrowsmith, 1840. Color, scale 1 in. to approx. 31 mi., 49 × 59.5 cm. From Arrowsmith's *London Atlas* (See no. 238 for further information.). Insets: "Sketch of France Divided into Provinces"; "Corsica." MMNHMC.

267. *Spain & Portugal.* London: John Arrowsmith, 1840. Color, scale 1 in. to approx. 30 mi., 47.5 × 59.5 cm. From Arrowsmith's *London Atlas.* (See no. 238 for further information.). Inset: "Minorca." MMNHMC.

268. *Carte du Texas. Extraite de la Grande Carte du Mexique.* Adrien Hubert Brué. Revised, following the documents furnished by Frederic Leclerc and Charles Piquet. Paris, 1840. Facsimile of printed map, scale indeterminable, 29 × 33 cm.

The original appeared in both Leclerc's *Le Texas et sa révolution,* Paris, 1840, and Henri Fournel's *Coup d'oeil historique et statistique sur le Texas,* Paris, 1841. This library also has a copy of Fournel's work, complete with the map.

269. *Karte von Texas.* Richard S. Hunt and Jesse F. Randel, 1839. Lithographed by G. Stempfle. Augsburg: Math. Rieger, 1841. Scale 1 in. to approx. 41 mi., 32 × 40 cm., folding map bound into a copy of G. A. Scherpf's *Entstehungsgeschichte unf hrgenwartiger Bustand des neuen, unabhangigen, amerikanischen Staates Texas,* Augsburg, 1841. This book also contains a general map of the southwestern United States, *Karte von Rio Grande und dem West Land am Stillen Ocean,* lithographed by G. Stempfle, published by Math. Rieger, Augsburg, n.d. MMNHMC.

This is a reduced copy of the first issue of Hunt and Randel's *Map of Texas,* 1839 (see no. 278). Only the title and the imprint are in German; the main body of the map is in English. The accompanying map of the Southwest appears as an inset in the American issue.

270. *[Cavallo Pass Entrance to Matagorda Bay.]* Anonymous. Printed by C. F. Cheffins. London, n.d. Photostat of printed map, scale indeterminable, 14 × 23 cm. From William Kennedy's *Texas,* London, 1841. Note on soundings. (Streeter, *Bibliography,* no. 1385.)

271. *Cary's New Terrestrial Globe, Delineated From the best Authorities extant; Exhibiting the late Discoveries towards the North Pole, and every improvement in Geography to the present Time.* G. & J. Cary. London, 1841(?). Papier-mâché globe covered with a map of the world printed on twelve gores, scale indeterminable, 31.5 cm. diameter, mounted on a contemporary wooden stand with a compass positioned between the legs. MMNHMC. (See also nos. 190 and 207.)

272. *[Galveston Island.]* Anonymous. N.p., ca. 1842. Four assembled photographs of a manuscript in the Royal Geographical Society, London, scale 1 in. to 40 chains, 19.5 × 74 cm. Note: "For reference to Introduction to a Geographical account of the Republic of Texas by Wm. Bollaert."

The British Admiralty instructed William Bollaert to examine the coast and interior of Texas, and he did so from 1840 to 1844. The admiralty's chart of *The Coast of Texas,* 1844, in part reflects Bollaert's findings.

This sketch map is probably the "Sketch Plan of Galveston Island" referred to in "Notes on the Coast Region of the Texas Territory: taken during a visit in 1842," *Journal of the Royal Geographical Society* 13 (1843): 226–27. A footnote mentions that this paper was accompanied by four maps, which were prepared by American officers and "which are now preserved in the Society's archives." The "Sketch Plan" is listed without attribution, but it was probably constructed by William Bollaert, not by a U.S. officer.

The sketch is crude and seems to be based on some version of Trimble and Lindsey's map of 1837 (see no. 255), with some hydrographic and topographic details added. The channel connecting Galveston Harbor to the Gulf has a form similar to the configuration of Alexander Thompson, 1828. The map gives few early navigational landmarks (Eagle Grove, the three trees, etc.) and locates two forts, one on the eastern tip of island and the other on the western Gulf shore near present-day Lake Madeline. The following notation appears on west Galveston Island beneath an elongated lake: "Cup-shaped excavations about 8 to (?) feet deep. Supposed to have been made by Indians for retaining rainwater holding about 160 hogsheads." Neither Pelican Island nor Pelican Spit is present, but there is a large shoal where Pelican Spit will appear before 1851.

273A. *Central America II. Including Texas, California and the Northern States of Mexico.* Engraved by J. & C. Walker. London: Chapman & Hall under the superintendence of the Society for the Diffusion of Useful Knowledge, 1842. Color, scale 1 in. to approx. 110 mi., 31 × 39.5 cm. From the atlas published by the society.

B. Another issue: same title, engraver, sponsor, size, and scale, but published by Charles Knight & Co., London, ca. 1850.

274. *Mexico, Mittel America, Texas.* Drawn by A. Theinert. Lithographed, printed, and published by C. Flemming. Glogau, 1842. Color, scale indeterminable, 33 × 42 cm. Key identifying sites by number.

The Nueces River marks the southern boundary of the Republic of Texas.

275. *Mexico & Guatimala, with the Republic of Texas.* Edinburgh: William Home Lizars, n.d. Color, scale indeterminable, 40.5 × 49 cm. Map no. 66 from *Lizar's Edinburgh geographical atlas,* 1842(?). MMNHMC.

276. *North America.* London: Chapman & Hall under the superintendence of the Society for the Diffusion of Useful Knowledge, 1843. Color, scale 1.5 in. to 500 mi., 30.5 × 38.5 cm. From the atlas published by the society.

277A. *Plan of the city of Galveston Texas.* William H. Sandusky. Lithographed by Wagner & McGuigan. Philadelphia, 1845. Scale 1 in. to 600 ft., 70 × 95 cm. Inset: "Chart of Galveston Bar and Harbor." (Streeter, *Bibliography,* no. 1606A.)

B. Another issue: same title, cartographer, date, scale, size, and inset, but lithographed by G. & W. Endicott, New York

Sandusky's plan was the official plat map published by the Galveston City Company to publicize the sale of Galveston lots. Sandusky finished the map in 1839, just one year after Groesbeck's survey (see no. 259). Sandusky followed Groesbeck's general layout for Galveston but changed the earlier plan in several respects. In place of three wharves and a large park on the harbor, he included four wharves. With minor variations the block and lot divisions are the same, but Sandusky used a different numbering system, one that is still in use today. He also moved the city cemeteries to their present location on the south side of Broadway between Fortieth and Forty-second streets. Notations include profiles of churches and public buildings and the names of prominent landowners — Gail Borden, S. M. Williams, T. H. Borden, M. Menard, T. F. McKinney, S. Slater, and J. Love. "Lafitt's Old Fort" appears at Fourteenth and Water streets.

Sandusky's inset shows twelve feet of water over the outer bar. There is no sign yet of Pelican Spit. Groesbeck's channel between Fort Point and the main part of the island is now largely filled with sand. An "Old Fort," a "Sanderson's," and a "Bolivar" appear on Bolivar Point.

278. *Map of Texas, Compiled from Surveys on record in the General Land Office of the Republic.* Richard S. Hunt and Jesse F. Randel. New York:

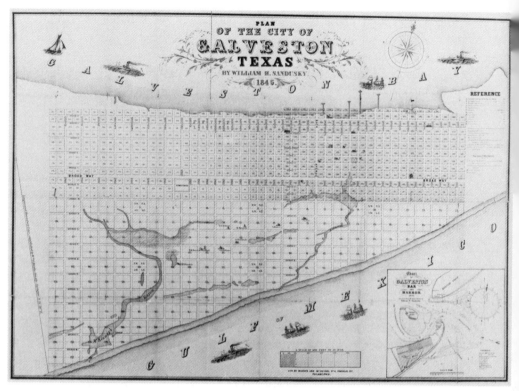

Plan of the City of Galveston, Texas, by William Sandusky, 1845. (See no. 277A.) Executed just six years after the founding of Galveston, the Sandusky map was the standard cartographic reference for the city through the Civil War.

Sherman & Smith, 1845. Copyright by Joseph H. Colton, 1839. Color, scale 1 in. to approx. 20 mi, 61.5 × 80 cm. Extracted from the 1845 edition of Hunt and Randel's *A New Guide to Texas* New York: Sherman and Smith. Inset: "Map of the Rio Grande and the Country west to the Pacific."

Streeter (*Bibliography*, no. 1348) gives an insightful analysis of this map. Apparently this 1845 issue is the first with meaningful revisions: five new counties and several new towns have been added. Twelve settlements appear in the Galveston Bay area: Galveston, Virginia, Austinia, San Leon, Harrisburg, Houston, New Washington, Lynchburg, Allenwood, Liberty, Anahuac, and Port Bolivar. A projected railroad connects Austinia with a second town of Bolivar, on the Brazos River.

A German version of the 1839 issue appeared in G. A. Scherpf's 1841 emigrant's guide to Texas (see no. 269).

279. *Map of Texas from the most recent authorities.* Philadelphia: C. S. Williams, 1846. Copyright, 1845. Color, scale indeterminable, 30.5 × 37.5 cm. From S. Augustus Mitchell's *A New Universal Atlas,* Philadelphia, 1845. Inset: "Texas north of Red River."

The map shows Texas, with the extended borders running to the Arkansas River in the northwest, territory claimed since 1836. Eleven settlements appear in the Galveston Bay area: Galveston, Virginia, Austinia, San Leon, Houston, Harrisburg, New Washington, Lynchburg, Añahuac, Liberty, and Bolivar.

280. *A New Map of Texas Oregon and California with the Regions adjoining. Compiled from the most recent authorities.* Philadelphia: Samuel Augustus Mitchell, 1846. Color, scale indeterminable, 57 × 52 cm., folding into covers, which have been removed but are present; map backed with cloth. Together with the *Accompaniment to Mitchell's New Map of Texas, Oregon and California with Regions adjoining,* Philadelphia, 1846, 46 pp.

Mitchell synthesizes the key explorations and maps of the preceding years—those by Nicollet, Fremont, Wilkes, etc.—and gives one of the best portraits available of western North America on the eve of the Mexican War. Texas appears with the extravagant, claimed boundaries reaching as far west as Santa Fe, as on William Emory's map of 1844.

281. *Map of the north-western Part of Texas received from the general Land Office in 1845.* Lithographed and printed by Maximilien Frommann, Darmstadt. Frankfurt am Main: J. D. Sauerlander, n.d. Color, scale indeterminable, 41 × 51 cm. Folding map bound into a copy of Prince Carl von Solms-Braunfels' *Texas,* Frankfurt am Main, 1846. This work also contains a general map of Texas (see no. 282). MMNHMC.

The first printed map of the hill country shows the area from Smithville (not shown) on the east to the Nueces, Colorado, and Brazos rivers on the west. This is the area of the colony recently established by the Adelsverein, the German emigration society, of which Solms-Braunfels was the principal organizer.

Three areas are bound in color and identified: the lands of the German Emigration Company, Bastrop County, and an oversize Travis County. Twelve settlements appear: Bastrop, Gonzales, Austin, San Marcos, Seguin, Comal Spring, New Braunfels, San Antonio, Castroville, Fredericksburg, Enchanted Rock, and Fort San Saba. This is the first time Fredericksburg (founded May, 1846) appears on a printed map. A number of roads are also shown, including one extending from New Braunfels toward the Gulf.

282. *Karte von Texas entworfen nach den Vermeſsungen der General-Land-Office der Republic.* Printed by Eduard Foltz-Eberlem. Frankfurt am Main: J. D. Sauerlander, n.d. Scale indeterminable, 40 × 47 cm. Folding map, bound into a copy of Prince Carl von Solms-Braunfels' *Texas,* Frankfurt am Main, 1846. Untitled inset of Texas and Mexico. Keys identifying cities, rivers, and counties. MMNHMC.

This general map of the Republic of Texas shows land grants held by the Adelsverein. It is a companion map to no. 281.

283. *Mapa de los Estados Unidos de Méjico, Segun lo organizado y definido por las varias actas del Congreso de dicha Republica: y constuido por las mejores autoridades.* Revised edition. New York: John Disturnell, 1846. Color, scale 1 in. to approx. 120 mi., 74.5 × 103.5 cm., folding into cloth covers that are detached but present. Front cover: "Mexico." Inset: "Carta de los Caminos &c. desde Vera Cruz y Alvarado a Méjico."

According to Lawrence Martin and Walter W. Ristow, "John Disturnell's map of Mexico is of historic importance because it was the official cartographic reference consulted in negotiating the peace treaty of February 2nd, 1848, which terminated the Mexican War and is commonly referred to as the Treaty of Guadalupe Hidalgo. The map actually became a part of the treaty and has figured prominently in settling border disputes." This is the sixth issue and the last dated 1846. Copies of the seventh and eleventh issues were attached to the peace treaty.

Shown in red are the routes of General Taylor (to Monterey), General Wool (to Coahuila), and General Kearney (to Santa Fe).

284. *Map of Mexico, Including Yucatan & Upper California, exhibiting The Chief Cities and Towns, The Principal Travelling Routes &c.* Philadelphia: Samuel Augustus Mitchell, 1846. Color, scale 1 in. to approx. 115 mi., 44 × 64 cm., folding into cloth covers. Front cover: "Mexico." Inset: "The late Battlefield [Monterey, Mexico.]" MMNHMC.

The map shows Texas with a panhandle reaching north into Wyoming (after Emory's map of 1844). Flags mark the battlefields of San Jacinto (1836), the Alamo (1836), Palo Alto (1846), and Resaca de la Palma (1846).

285. *United States and Texas.* Alexander Keith Johnston. N.p., n.d. Color, scale indeterminable, 62.5 × 50 cm. From Johnston's *National Atlas of Historical, Commercial, and Political Geography,* Edinburgh, 1846. Inset: "Sketch of the River Niagara."

Streeter (*Bibliography,* no. 1587) lists a separately issued example of the map that he tentatively dated 1845. This map shows the Republic of Texas extending north to the Arkansas River, including Oklahoma and southern Kansas, even though these regions were then part of the United States and were never claimed by Texas.

286. *Connecticut.* Engraved by G. W. Boynton. N.p. Copyright by Thomas Gamaliel Bradford. 1838. Color, scale 1 in. to approx. 13.5 mi., 29 × 36 cm. Map no. 11 from the 1846 edition of Bradford's *A Universal Illustrated Atlas,* Boston. MMNHMC.

Bradford's atlas was very popular and went through many editions. An 1842 edition also contained this map, with the same copyright date.

287. *Massachusetts.* Engraved by G. W. Boynton. N.p. Copyright by Thomas Gamaliel Bradford. 1838. Color, scale 1 in. to approx. 15.5 mi., 29 × 36 cm. Map no. 13 from the 1846 edition of Bradford's *A Universal Illustrated Atlas,* Boston. MMNHMC.

288. *New Hampshire.* Engraved by G. W. Boynton. N.d., Copyright by Thomas Gamaliel Bradford. 1838. Color, scale 1 in. to approx. 7.5 mi., 29 × 36 cm. Map no. 16 from the 1846 edition of Bradford's *A Universal Illustrated Atlas,* Boston.

289. *Pennsylvania.* Engraved by G. W. Boynton. N.d. Copyright by Thomas Gamaliel Bradford. 1838. Color, scale 1 in. to approx. 22 mi., 29 × 36 cm. Map no. 20 from the 1846 edition of Bradford's *A Universal Illustrated Atlas,* Boston. MMNHMC.

290. *Philadelphia.* Engraved by G. W. Boynton. N.d. Copyright by Thomas Gamaliel Bradford. 1838. Color, scale 1 in. to approx. 1400 ft., 29 × 35.5 cm. Unnumbered map from the 1846 edition of Bradford's *A Universal Illustrated Atlas,* Boston. MMNHMC.

291. *A Map of the United States of Mexico, As organized and defined by the several Acts of the Congress of that Republic, Constructed from a great variety of Printed and Manuscript Documents.* Fifth edition. N.p.: Henry S. Tanner, 1847. Copyright, 1846. Color, scale 1 in. to approx. 83 mi., 57 × 73 cm., folding into cloth covers. Front cover: "Tanner's Traveling Map of Mexico." Insets: "Map of the Roads &c from Vera Cruz & Alvarado to Mexico," showing the advance of the U.S. Army as far as Jalapa; "Harbor of Vera Cruz." Three tables: statistics, distances, and battle dates.

This map first appeared in a quite different form in 1826 (*Streeter Sale*, vol. 1, no. 215). In this 1847 revision eastern Texas is based on Austin's map of 1830 (see no. 236); western Texas is based on Emory's map of 1844. Salt Lake and Utah Lake are joined as on Fremont's map of 1843. Also marked are Kearney's route from Council Bluffs to Santa Fe, Wool's route from San Antonio to Saltillo, Taylor's route from Corpus Christi to Saltillo, and the U.S. Army's route from Matamoros to Veracruz.

292. *A New General Chart of the West Indies and The Coast of America from East Florida to Guayana, including the Gulf of Mexico, Bays of Honduras and the Caribbean Sea, Correctly Drawn from the Latest English French and Spanish Surveys And from various Original Documents.* J. W. Norie. London, 1830. Corrected to 1847. Scale indeterminable, 77.5 × 125.5 cm. MMNHMC.

Norie's chart admirably illustrates the contemporary ignorance of Texas coastal geography. For Texas, Norie still relies on the old configurations first shown on the *Carta Esférica* of 1799, although his renderings of the other areas are quite accurate and up-to-date.

293. *Amérique Septentrionale.* Geography and statistics by Victor Levasseur. Engraved by Laguillermie(?). Illustrated by Raimond Bonheur Pientre. Edited by A. Combette. N.p., n.d. Color, scale indeterminable, 17.5 × 20 cm. map surrounded by a decorative panel, on a 27.5 × 42.5 cm. sheet. From Levasseur's *Atlas universel illustre*, Paris, 1847. Population table and descriptive text. MMNHMC.

The map still shows Texas as a republic. The surrounding decorative panel depicts American flora, fauna, and native inhabitants.

294. *Karte des Staates Texas (aufgenommen in die Union 1846.)nach der neuesten Eintheilung.* Lithographed by Fr. Koenen. Elberfeld: Julius

Badeker, 1849. Photostat, scale indeterminable, 50 × 61 cm. Although separately issued, some copies were also bound into Viktor Bracht's *Texas im Jahr 1848*, Elberfeld, 1849. Insets: "Plan von Neu-Braunfels und Comalstadt"; "Plan von Castroville."

Published to serve the prospective European emigrant to Texas, the map designates in color the colonies of Solms-Braunfels and Henri Castro. Organized counties are outlined in red. The inset plans of New Braunfels and Castroville are among the earliest cartographic records of those two towns (see also no. 281).

295A. *J. De Cordova's Map of the State of Texas Compiled from the records of the General Land Office of the State of Texas.* Compiled by Robert Creuzbaur. Houston, 1849. Engraved by J. M. Atwood, New York. Copyright by Jacob De Cordova, 1848. Color, scale 1 in. to approx. 10 mi., 84 × 92 cm., folding into tan cloth covers. Untitled inset of the southwestern United States. Reference to "Texas Land Districts." Gift of Kate C. Sturgis, 1928.

B. Another issue: same title, compiler, engraver, color, scale, size, copyright date, and reference, but now published 1851, with both the map and the inset slightly revised. This copy is mounted on cloth, with the covers missing.

C. Another issue: same title, compiler, engraver, color, scale, size, and reference, but revised and corrected by Charles W. Pressler, published by J. H. Colton & Co., New York, 1856, copyright by Jacob De Cordova, 1856, folding down into black leather covers. Front cover: "J. De Cordova's Texas J. H. Colton & Co. New York." Untitled inset of the western United States. Donated by Frank Manning Chubb.

Jacob de Cordova came to Texas in 1837 and quicly became one of the new republic's most active promoters. He was responsible for a number of influential pamphlets and guidebooks. Hoping to cash in on the expected land boom following the Mexican War, De Cordova commissioned Robert Creuzbaur, an employee of the Texas General Land Office, to compile this map from that agency's records. The result is a very accurate and detailed map.

Creuzbaur followed Austin's format (see no. 236) and used an inset to show the western part of the state. The inset on the 1849 issue is of particular interest, since it shows the short-lived Santa Fe County. The Texas legislature had created the county in March, 1848, in a vain attempt to keep alive the state's claim to New Mexico.

Periodically revised issues of the map appeared until 1861. All three issues in this collection show the same seven settlements in the Galveston Bay area: Galveston, New Washington, Harrisburg, Houston, Lynchburg, Chambersia, and Anahuac.

296. *Map of the More Immediate Dependencies of the Bay of Matagorda From Actual Survey With the Names of Grantees to Lands in its Vicinity.* Lithographed by J. Manouvrier and P. Snell. New Orleans, 1849. Photostat of printed map, scale (of original) 1 in. to approx. 4 mi., 41 × 53 cm. Donated by the Gulf, Colorado & Santa Fe Railway Co., 1924.

The map locates eleven settlements: Calhoun, Saluria, Port Caballo, La Salle, Port Lavaca, Linnville, Palacios, Matagorda, "Indian Pt.," Victoria, and "Texana" on the Lavaca River. The proposed town of Austin (see no. 256) is absent.

Streeter (1349) locates only one copy of this map, which he tentatively dates 1838; this photostat is from a second copy, location unknown. The photostat is one of many that the Engineering Department of the Santa Fe Railroad donated to the Rosenberg Library. Most of the photostats came from originals in the Barker Texas History Center; however, no copy of this map is in that collection.

The 1849 date on this map may have been added later (it is impossible to tell from the photostat), making it a copy rather than a new issue. According to Edward F. Haas, chief curator of the Louisiana Historical Center, Louisiana State Museum, New Orleans, Manouvrier and Snell worked together from 1841 (or 1846) to 1853 and again from 1860 to 1870.

297. *Chart of the Coast of California from San Blas to San Francisco Drawn chiefly from Spanish Surveys, the Charts of Vancouver &c. the whole much improved by recent observations made by English & French Naval Officers.* James Imray. London, 1849. Scale indeterminable, 67.5 × 139.5 cm. Chart no. 8 in Imray's "series of charts for the navigation of the East and West Coast of America." A note lists the other charts in the series. Insets: "Entrance of San Francisco Harbour"; "Harbour of San Francisco;" "Bay of Monterey;" "Guayman;" "Magdalen Bay;" "Mazatlan."

Published shortly after the American occupation of California, this chart predates by one year the first U.S. Coast and Geodetic Survey charts of that coast. George Davidson, who conducted the government survey, kept and annotated a copy of this chart (Davidson's copy is now in the Bancroft Library at the University of California at Berkeley). Imray published a second, extensively revised version of this chart in 1851, probably to incorporate the findings of the coast survey.

298. *[Galveston Bay.]* United States Coast and Geodetic Survey. Topographical survey by J. M. Wampler. Galveston, 1850–52. Photographic copies of manuscript maps in the Archives of the U.S. Coast and Geodetic Survey. Scale (of original) 1:20,000, ten-map sets, maps of varying sizes.

These are the topographical draft maps from the first federal coast survey work in Texas. The U.S. Coast Survey organized in 1807 to compile an accurate map of every part of the nation's coasts. Work began in earnest in 1832 and expanded to include Texas in 1848. Surveying began with Galveston Bay. Compiling a sea chart for an area involved several different activities: making magnetic and astronomical observations and triangulations (1848), surveying the topography (1848–52), and finally gathering hydrographical data (1851–52). The Coast Survey periodically revised the series of printed charts, best known from versions accompanying the annual reports of the agency (see no. 301).

This set of maps shows the bay shore in great detail, including the names of individual settlers. The maps show Pelican Spit, which is absent from Sandusky's map of 1845 (see no. 277). The map of *Galveston Harbor and City* does show existing buildings but not in enough detail to identify them.

Individual sheets (sheet number): *D. Harris' to Lawrence Cove* (331); *Lawrence Cove to Stevenson's* (330); *Vicinity of Bolivar Point to Rollover Station* (1636); *Galveston East Bay and Bolivar Peninsula* (329); *Galveston Harbor and City* (282); *[Edwards' Point to Virginia Point]* (none); *Highland Bayou to D. Harris'* (283); *Red Fish Bar* (298); *Galveston West Bay and Part of Galveston Island* (328); *Galveston West Bay, Galveston Island & Chocolate Bayou* (374).

299. *A New Map of Nth. Carolina with its Canals, Roads & Distances from place to place, along the stage & steam boat routes.* N.p.: Thomas, Cowperthwait & Co., copyright, 1850. Color, scale 1 in. to approx. 38 mi., 29.5 × 35 cm. Map no. 18 from the 1850 edition of S. Augustus Mitchell's *A New Universal Atlas*, Philadelphia. Insets: New Berne vicinity; "Gold Region." Table of distances. Profile: "Dismal Swamp Canal." MMNHMC.

300. *Preliminary Chart of San Luis Pass Texas.* United States Coast and Geodetic Survey. Triangulation by James S. Williams. Topography by J. M. Wampler. Hydrography by the party under the command of H. S. Stellwagen. Washington, D.C., 1853. Scale 1:20,000, 34 × 43 cm.

Among other features, the map shows the beach road and Follet's Ferry.

301. *Annual Reports. United States Coast and Geodetic Survey.* 43 volumes. 1851–93 [1870 missing]. Approximately 1,250 charts, bound in quarto volumes with cloth covers. MMNHMC.

Each volume reports the progress made in surveying U.S. coasts during the preceding year. Although the agency added or deleted maps from time to time, all volumes generally contain the same charts; and each successive issue illustrates advances in the surveying operations. Besides obvious topographical and hydrographical information, the reports also document the evolution of nautical surveying techniques. See no. 298 for further information on the history of the agency and its work in the Galveston area.

In addition to the bound reports, the library also holds several loose copies of survey maps of the Galveston area. These are individually described (see the index for references).

302. *Mexico, California and Texas.* Drawn and engraved by John Rapkin. Illustrations by H. Warren. Engraved by J. Rogers. Printed by the London Printing and Publishing Co. London, n.d. Scale 1 in. to ca. 220 mi., 21 × 30 cm. Map no. 71 from *Tallis's Illustrated Atlas,* London, 1851. Vignettes: "Ruins at Uxmal, Yucatan"; "Gold Washing"; "Mexican Peasantry."

Shows the newly annexed southwestern United States prior to the Compromise of 1850.

303. *United States.* Drawn by John Rapkin. Illustrations by J. Marchant. Engraved by J. Rogers. London: John Tallis & Co., n.d. Color, scale indeterminable, 24 × 32 cm. From *Tallis's Illustrated Atlas,* London, 1852. MMNHMC.

304. *Map of Texas, Compiled from surveys recorded in the General Land Office.* J. Eppinger and F. C. Baker. N.p., 1852. Photostat of printed map, scale indeterminable, 70 × 60 cm. Inset: "Map of New Mexico, California and Utah."

Following the format established by Stephen F. Austin's map of 1830, this map shows Texas east of approximately the 101st meridian. West Texas appears on a reduced scale in the inset.

The 1852 issue is evidently quite rare; it is not listed in Phillips, is not in Day (except in photostat; see p. 56), and is not listed by Storm. Phillips (*America*, p. 44) lists only the 1851 issue.

305. *Map of the State of Texas.* Engraved by James Hamilton Young. Copyright by S. Augustus Mitchell. 1852. Color, scale 1 in. to approx. 75 mi., 20 × 26.5 cm. Map no. 13 from *Mitchell's School and Family Geography.* Insets: "Map of the Vicinity of Galveston City;" "Northern Texas."

306. *Discoveries in the Arctic Sea up to MDCCCLII.* British Admiralty. Hydrographic Office. London, 1852. Scale indeterminable, 64 × 97 cm. MMNHMC.

This chart incorporates all of the most recent findings in the Arctic.

307. *Mexico & Texas.* Liverpool: George Philip & Son, 1853. Color, scale 1 in. to approx. 90 mi., 51 × 63 cm. MMNHMC.

308. *Carte Générale des Iles Antilles et du Golfe du Mexique Dressée d'après les travaux Anglais et Espagnols.* Aimé Robiquet. Paris, 1853. Color, scale indeterminable, 67 × 117 cm. Insets: "Veracruz"; "San Juan de Nicaragua"; "Port de Chagres"; "Carmen."

The configuration of the Texas coast is primitive, suggesting that the results of the U.S. Coast Survey (see no. 298) were not yet available in France. Only three lighthouses are shown on the Texas coast. MMNHMC.

309. *New Map of that portion of North America, exhibiting the United States and Territories, The Canadas, New Brunswick, Nova Scotia, and Mexico, also, Central America, and The West India Islands.* Engraved and printed by A. Hoen & Co. Baltimore: Jacob Monk, 1853. Color, scale indeterminable, 148 × 158 cm. cloth-backed wall map on rollers. Inset: "New Map of the World on Mercators Projection." MMNHMC.

310. *Mouths of the Mississippi=Die Mündung des Mississippi.* Lithographed by J. Arnz & Co. N.p.: Henry Lewis, n.d. Color, scale indeterminable, 15.5 × 18 cm. From Lewis's *Das illustrierte Mississippital*, Dusseldorf, 1854–58. MMNHMC.

Lewis originally issued the atlas in twenty installments in German. At the same time, he began an English version, which he abandoned after three installments. The parallel English and German titles indicate that this map is from the incomplete English version.

311A. *Map of the State of Texas from the latest Authorities.* James Hamilton Young. Engraved by J. L. Hazzard. Philadelphia: Cowperthwait, Desilver & Butler, 1855. Copyright by Thomas, Cowperthwait & Co., 1850. Color, scale 1:3,400,000, 32 × 39.5 cm., folding into roan leather covers. Front cover: "Mitchell's Map of Texas." Insets: "Map of the Vicinity of Galveston City"; "Northern Texas." Note: "Railroads in Texas." Table (inside front cover): "Population of Texas, by Counties, in 1850."

B. Another issue: same title, scale, size, insets, note, and table, but published by Charles Desilver, 1856, copyright by Thomas, Cowperthwait & Co., 1852. Once owned by A. Parker Porter, "2nd Calvary, Dec. 1st, 1856," who added to the map a few notations relating to west Texas.

The map focuses on railroads. The earlier issue shows the tracks of the Buffalo Bayou, Brazos and Colorado Railroad, then under construction from Harrisburg to Richmond. Four additional proposed lines, including the "Atlantic and Pacific Railroad," appear.

The later issue adds several more proposed lines, including two "Pacific" railroads. A northern "Pacific" line follows the north bank of the Red River, crosses into Texas in Grayson County, then runs west-southwest through "Ft. Belknap" and by Big Springs to El Paso. A southern "Pacific" line runs from San Antonio west to Fort Clark, up the Pecos River, and joins with the northern line just south of the New Mexico line.

312. *Map of Spanish-Texas.* Anonymous. N.p., n.d. Scale indeterminable, 35 × 42 cm. From Henderson Yoakum's *History of Texas*, New York, 1855.

The map shows Texas during the late Spanish period (ca. 1800).

313. *[Virgin Islands.]* Copenhagen: Emmanuel Baerentzen & Co., 1856. Color, scale indeterminable, 23 × 28 cm. MMNHMC.

This is a set of six tinted bird's-eye views of the Danish Virgin Islands: *St. Jan (Partie af det Indre); Cruxbay (St. Jan); St. Thomas (Partie af Byen og Havnen); Parti af St. Thomas; Christianssted (St. Croix); Parti ved Frederikssted (St. Croix).*

314. *Colton's Atlas of the World, illustrating Physical and Political Geography. Vol. II. Europe, Asia, Africa, Oceanica, etc.* Compiled by George Woolworth Colton. Accompanying description by Richard Swainson Fisher. New York: J. H. Colton & Co., 1856. Color, scale varies, forty-four single- and double-paged maps and diagrams bound in folio volume.

315. *Colton's General Atlas, containing One Hundred and Seventy Steel Plate Maps and Plans on One Hundred Imperial Folio Sheets.* Compiled by George Woolworth Colton. Accompanying descriptions by Richard Swainson Fisher. New York: J. H. Colton & Co., 1857. Color, scale varies, contents as described in the title, bound in one-quarter black gilt-stamped morocco. MMNHMC.

Among the contents are city plans of Boston, New York, Baltimore, Philadelphia, Washington, Pittsburgh, Cincinnati, St. Louis, Chicago, Louisville, New Orleans, Savannah, and Charleston, and a small version of Jacob de Cordova's map of Texas (see no. 295).

316. *Italie.* Drawn by Adolphe Hippolyte Dufour. Engraved by Charles Dyonnet. Illustrated by Gillot(?). printed by Cosson & Co. Paris: Paulin & Le Chevalier, 1857. Color, scale indeterminable, 56 × 63.5 cm. Plate no. 24 from Dufour's *Atlas Universel,* Paris, 1857.

317. *Pressler's Map of the State of Texas. Compiled from the records of the General Land Office of the State and various other sources.* Compiled by Charles W. Pressler. Galveston: Jones, Root and Co., 1858. Color, scale indeterminable, 117 × 130 cm., folding into cloth covers, front cover detached. Insets: "[View of the] State Capitol at Austin"; "Map of Original Land Districts"; "Map of the Old Colonies." Table of counties.

Pressler worked as a draftsman in the Texas General Land Office from 1850 to 1899. He established his reputation as a cartographer through his long association with Jacob de Cordova, whose map of Texas he revised (see no. 295). Before compiling this 1858 map of Texas, Pressler also worked with W. Voelker to produce the map included in George M. von Ross's *Der nordamerikanische Freistaat Texas,* an 1851 German emigrant's guide.

Pressler's map is very detailed and accurate. He rejected Austin's format showing west Texas in an inset (see no. 236) and instead depicted the whole state in one view. He also corrected many cartographic errors, particularly regarding the rivers and streams of west Texas.

The "Table of Counties" gives extensive information on the establishment and organization of all existing counties.

318. *Map of Jamaica Compiled Chiefly from manuscripts in the Colonial Office and Admiralty.* London: John Arrowsmith, 1858. Color, scale 1 in. to ca. 6.5 mi., 32.5 × 60.5 cm. From Arrowsmith's *London Atlas* (See no. 238 for further information.). Inset: "Wesleyan Mission Stations in the Island of Jamaica." MMNHMC.

319. *Map of the Leeward Islands; Comprising Antigua, Montserrat, Barbuda, St. Christopher, Nevis, Anguilla, Virgin Islands & Dominica.* London: John Arrowsmith, 1858. Color, scale 1 in. to approx. 14 mi., 45.5 × 59 cm. From Arrowsmith's *London Atlas* (See no. 238 for further information.). Key identifying European possessions by color. MMNHMC.

320. *Map of the Windward Islands; Comprising Barbados, St. Vincent, Grenada, Tobago, St. Lucia & Trinidad.* John Arrowsmith. London, 1858. Color, scale 1 in. to ca. 14.5 mi. From Arrowsmith's *London Atlas* (See no. 238 for further information.). MMNHMC.

321. *Map of British Guiana From the latest Surveys.* Drawn by J. Hadfield, Georgetown, Guyana. London: John Arrowsmith, 1858. Scale 1 in. to approx. 24 mi. From Arrowsmith's *London Atlas* (See no. 238 for further information.). Tables: "Extent of the Parishes in Demerara & Essequibo"; "Extent of the Parishes in the County Berbice." MMNHMC.

322A. *Richardson's New Map of the State of Texas including Part of Mexico. Compiled from Government Surveys and other authentic documents.* Philadelphia: Charles Desilver, 1859. Photostat of printed map, scale (of original) 1 in. to 35 mi. Printed for the 1859 *Texas Almanac.* Inset: "Map showing the proposed Route of the Aransas Railroad (and its) connections with the Eastern Roads." Table of railroads completed and under construction.

B. Another issue: same title, publisher, source, scale, and inset, but corrected by H. Wickland, Galveston, 1860. Photostat of printed map, 62 × 83 cm. The table is revised and expanded.

Richardson's *Almanacs,* except those published in 1857 and 1862–65, contain a general map of Texas. The maps for 1859 and 1860 are described above. The library also has a complete run of the almanacs (except for the Civil War years). Most of the volumes include original maps, though some contain photostats. Winkler and Friend describe almanacs and accompanying maps.

323. *Carte Générale des Îles Antilles, des îles et Bancs de Bahama, des États-Unis de L'Amérique-Centrale, de La Mer du Mexique &a.* A. H. Brué. Revised and augmented by André Vuillemin. Edited by A. Logerot. Paris, 1860. Color, scale indeterminable, 62.5 × 91 cm. Insets: "Détails de Îles Vierges"; "La Martinique"; "La Guadeloupe et Îles adjacentes." MMNHMC.

324. *Birds Eye View of Texas and Part of Mexico.* John Bachmann. New York, 1861. Color, scale indeterminable, 57 × 72 cm. From the *Panorama of the Seat of War* series.

This is one map from the series of bird's-eye views of the southern coast published by John Bachmann during the early months of the Civil War. Each map gives a rough idea of the terrain and locates important towns, forts, and roads. The bird's-eye views also show the federal blockading fleet. The following two maps are others in this series.

325. *Birds Eye View of Louisiana, Mississippi, Alabama and Part of Florida.* John Bachmann. New York, 1861. Color, scale indeterminable, 58.5 × 71.5 cm. From the *Panorama of the Seat of War* series. Table of distances. (See no. 324 for further information.)

326. *Birds Eye View of North and South Carolina and Part of Georgia.* John Bachmann. New York, 1861. Color, scale indeterminable, 56 × 71 cm. From the *Panorama of the Seat of War* series. (See no. 324 for further information.)

327. *The Historical War Map.* Asher & Co. Indianapolis, 1862. Color, scale indeterminable, 58.5 × 61 cm., folding into paper boards. Insets: "Northeast Virginia"; "South-east Virginia"; "Charleston and Vicinity"; "Vicksburg and Vicinity." Accompanied by the pamphlet *The Historical War Map,* Benjamin B. Russell, Boston, 1862, 21 pp., which covers the war to date. The pamphlet also includes maps of Richmond, Virginia; Fort Donelson, Tennessee; the Shiloh battlefield; and the battle of Bull Run. MMNHMC.

The map shows all of the Confederate states except Texas and locates railroads and important sites.

328. *Map of the United States of America.* L. Holle. Wolfenbuttel, Germany, 1861. Color, scale indeterminable, 57 × 87 cm., folding into blue printed wrappers. MMNHMC.

329. *Mapa de la Isla de Sto. Domingo.* Edited by Mariano Bordas. Barcelona, 1861. Scale indeterminable, 37 × 57 cm. map; surrounding border contains a descriptive text, panoramas of "Ciudada de Santo Domingo," portraits of Las Casas, Oviedo, Columbus, Ponce de Leon, and Santana. MMNHMC.

330A. *Johnson's New Map of the State of Texas.* Johnson and Ward. New York, ca. 1862. Color, scale indeterminable, 42 × 62 cm. Insets: "Plan of Sabine Lake"; "Plan of the Northern part of Texas"; "Plan of Galveston Bay." From *Johnson's New Illustrated Family Atlas of the World.* Donated by the Friends of the Rosenberg Library.

B. Another issue: same title, publisher, source, size, and insets, but revised ca. 1864.

C. Another issue: same source, but *Johnson's Texas.* A. J. Johnson. New York, 1866. Color, scale indeterminable, 43 × 59 cm. Inset of Sabine Lake omitted.

Johnson's map of Texas appeared in several revised and updated issues in various editions of *Johnson's New Illustrated Family Atlas of the World* during the period 1859–70. It was probably the most popular map of the state during that time. (See Phillips, *Atlases,* pp. 837, 840, 843, 858).

331. *Eastern and Central Texas.* United States Army Corps of Engineers. Prepared by order of Nathaniel P. Banks. Notes by W. E. Young. Transferred and printed by J. E. Bockler. New Orleans(?), 1864. Scale 1 in. to 20 mi., 58 × 77 cm., cloth-backed. U.S. Army. Department of the Gulf, map no. 14. Table of the rivers of Texas.

The Union army prepared this military map to use in the Red River campaign. The map locates agricultural produce, available water, timber, cattle, type of terrain, in each section of Texas. The Corps of Engineers *Map of Texas and New Mexico*, 1857, is apparently the base map for this map.

The Red River campaign was a complete failure, and Banks held no other active command for the rest of the war.

332. *Map of Galveston Texas. Showing the rebel line of works.* United States Army Corps of Engineers. Surveyed and drawn by order of G. L. Gillespie, under the direction of S. E. McGregory, by Pvt. St. Vignes. Galveston, ca. 1865. Photostat of manuscript map, scale indeterminable, two sheets forming one 44 × 96 cm. map. Original in the National Archives.

A companion to no. 333, this map shows only the immediate city defenses. Like later bird's-eye view and insurance maps, this map shows the outline and site location of every existing building. One of the United States Coast and Geodetic Survey maps (see nos. 298 and 301) probably was the basis for this map.

A line of breastworks surrounds the city. Railroad lines run through the city to supply batteries in the defense line and in outlying forts.

333. *Rebel Defenses of Galveston and Vicinity.* United States Army Corps of Engineers. Surveyed and drawn by order of G. L. Gillespie, under the direction of S. E. McGregory. Galveston, 1865. Blueprint, scale 3 in. to 5,000 ft., 58.5 × 90 cm. Note: "The shore line & contours & soundings in blue are from the coast survey of 1856."

This map shows in red all of the forts, redoubts, and batteries on Virginia Point, Galveston Island east of Teichman's Point, Pelican Island, and Bolivar Point. It ignores all the features within the city of Galveston (see no. 332).

334. *Map of Washington County and parts of the Surrounding Counties Texas.* Anonymous. N.p., ca. 1865. Photostat of printed map, scale indeterminable, 14 × 21 cm. The original was extracted from an unidentified book and later laid down in a manuscript journal by Thomas Affleck.

Affleck's journal, "Description of a cotton Plantation in Texas," was one of several of his writings on the management of Glenblythe Plantation, near Brenham in Washington County. His *Cotton Plantation Record and Account Book* served as a model for other planters.

335A. *Chart of the Gulf of Mexico and Windward Passages including the islands of Cuba, Haiti, Jamaica, Porto Rico and the Bahamas. Compiled Principally from the Surveys made by order of the British, Spanish and United States Governments.* James Imray & Son. London, 1866. Scale indeterminable, 98.5 × 189.5 cm.

Aside from the Galveston Bay area, the Texas coast is imperfectly rendered, with many sections drawn in a broken line. The entrance to the bay is marked "Bar 9ft. L.W. [low water]." There are six lighthouses from Sabine Pass to the mouth of the Rio Grande. (See no. 347 for a similar issue.)

B. Another issue: same title, cartographer, and size, but revised 1874. Insets: "Laguna de Terminos"; "Vera Cruz and Roadstead of Anton Lizardo"; "River Goazacoalcos"; "Galveston."

Eleven lighthouses appear on the Texas coast.

C. Another issue: same cartographer and size, but title omitted, revised 1879 and a fifth inset, "Old Bahama Channel," added.

Nine lighthouses are shown along the Texas coast.

336. *Richardson's Map of Galveston City and Island.* Lithographed by Pessou & Simon. New Orleans, 1867. Scale 1 in. to approx. 1,200 ft., 44 × 48 cm., folding into green cloth covers. Insets: "Map of Galveston Island Lots Surveyed by R. C. Trimble & Wm. Lindsey"; "Map of Galveston Bay from the U.S. Coast Survey." Donated by James T. Huffmaster, 1922.

Many of the streets have unconventional names, usually those of illustrious early Galvestonians. Names of many landowners appear on the outlots, and the island bayous are still the same as on Sandusky's map of 1845 (see no. 277). Richardson shows ten wharves, including the Houston & Galveston Wharf and Press Company facility, the first cotton press built in Galveston after the war and the first to connect to the main track of the Galveston, Houston and Henderson Railroad. Ward boundaries are also included on the map.

337. *Railroad Map of Texas.* Anonymous. N.p., ca. 1867. Photostat of an inset of an unidentified printed map, scale 1 in. to 40 mi. Table of distances.

This map shows railroads "in operation," "under construction," and "contemplated."

338. *Examination & Survey of Galveston Harbor with a view to its preservation and improvement.* United States Army Corps of Engineers. Under the direction of M. D. McAlester, under the supervision of W. S. Stanton. New Orleans, 1867–68 with chart "A" showing the harbor as surveyed by T. A. Craven, 1851. Blueprint with manuscript additions in red and black ink, scale 1:20,000, 86 × 145 cm.

This chart was a preliminary step in the project to reverse the shoaling of the bay entrance. According to Hayes, the harbor was in dire need of attention by 1867. In 1843 there had been thirty feet of water over the bar; by 1867 there were only nine feet. Most of the chart's features come from the coast survey maps (see nos. 298 and 301).

339. *Map of the city of Galveston, Situated on the East End of Galveston Island Texas.* Jackson E. Labatt. Lithographed by Strobridge & Co. Cincinnati, 1869. Color, scale 1 in. to 600 ft., 74 × 106 cm., folding into cloth covers that are detached but present. Front cover: "Map of Galveston." References identifying churches and cotton presses. Three diagrams showing the division of city blocks into lots and one diagram showing the "Main County Road & City R.R. Extension Route."

Like Richardson's map of 1867 (see no. 336), this map shows the city divided into four wards and the same inland waterways as on Sandusky's map of 1845 (see no. 277). Eleven wharves and a city park appear in the harbor area. Labatt's map reflects the division of some outlots into regular city blocks, and the Stonewall Addition lies at the west end of the city.

340A. *Galveston Bay to Oyster Bay Texas.* United States Coast and Geodetic Survey. Trigonometric survey under the direction of A. D. Bache and Benjamin Pierce. Triangulation by J. E. Hilgard et al. Topography by J. M. Wampler. Hydrography by the parties under the direction of T. A. Craven et al. Washington, D.C., 1870. Scale 1:80,000, 82 × 100 cm. Coast chart no. 105. Notes on lighthouses, beacons, tides, winds, etc.

B. Another issue: same title, issuing agency, scale, and size, but revised 1905. Notes on tides, lights, soundings, storm warnings, displays, buoys, etc.

The first issue shows the Galveston Bay entrance prior to any construction of the jetty system. The outer bar is only nine feet deep. The later issue shows the same area shortly after the completion of the jetties (1897) and also marks the damage of the 1900 hurricane. The seawall, completed in 1904, is indicated; and the outer bar is now twenty feet deep. The later chart also locates several new or proposed towns in the area: South Galveston, Virginia Point, Texas City, and North Galveston.

341. *Bird's Eye View of the City of Galveston, Texas.* Drawn by C. Drie. Printed by Chicago Lithographing Co. Chicago, 1871. Color, scale indeterminable, 57 × 86 cm.

Reps identifies this panorama as the earliest bird's-eye view of a Texas city. According to United States census figures, the population of Galveston increased from 7,307 to 13,818 between 1860 and 1870. This happened in spite of virtual abandonment of the city during the Civil War and a yellow fever epidemic and a hurricane that occurred in Galveston in 1867. In addition, major fires destroyed five blocks in the central business district in 1869 and 1870; however, developers speedily replaced the simple wooden structures with substantial brick and iron buildings. Drie recorded the rapid development on this map, which is in striking contrast to the simple city reflected on the 1865 "rebel line of works" map. (See no. 332.) There is, however, virtually no development yet along the Gulf shore, and Hitchcock's Bayou is still prominent. Eight wharves appear.

There are three known copies of this map: this example; one at the United States National Bank in Galveston; and one at the Barker Texas History Center. Little is known about Drie. John R. Hebert's catalog of bird's-eye views in the Library of Congress lists five by "C. N. Drie," dated 1872–73. One, the view of Raleigh, North Carolina, was published in Raleigh and lists Drie as a Raleigh resident. Reps lists additional Drie views of Augusta, Georgia, and Columbus, Mississippi. Both Reps and Hebert feel that C. Drie is the Camille N. Dry who produced the 110-sheet view of St. Louis in 1876. Hebert also regards this Drie view of Galveston as the previously unlocated view mentioned by Pauline A. Pinckney (pp. 154–55) and attributed by her to J. J. Stoner. Although not listed in the imprint on this map, Stoner frequently worked with the printers, the Chicago Lithographing Co.

342. *The Tributary Relations of the United States and Mexico By Distance to Galveston Texas For A Sea Port As Shown by the Leading Lines of Railway Completed and Projected.* Compiled and drawn by S. H. Gilman, Galveston. Engraved and lithographed by Douglas. New Orleans, 1871. Color, scale indeterminable, 50 × 65 cm., upper right-hand corner missing. From Gilman's *The Tributary and Economical Relations of the Railway systems of the United States to the Commerce of Galveston: Considered Geographically, Topographically, and Economically. A Contribution to the Galveston Public, by a Committee of its Citizens,* Galveston, 1871, 6 pp.

This promotional piece reflects the growing competition the port of Galveston was feeling from the inland railroad system and the emerging port of Houston.

The library has two copies of the pamphlet, one with the map and one without it. This loose example evidently belonged to the copy of the pamphlet now lacking the map.

343. *Ross' New Connected County and Rail Road Map of Texas and Indian Territory.* E. H. Ross. St. Louis, 1871. Photostat of printed map, scale indeterminable, 60 × 86 cm. Inset: "Plan of the Western part of Texas."

344A. *Colton's New Map of the State of Texas the Indian Territory and adjoining portions of New Mexico, Louisiana and Arkansas.* Compiled by George Woolworth Colton. New York: G. W. & C. B. Colton & Co., 1872. Photostat of printed map, scale indeterminable, 59 × 68 cm. Table: "Population of Texas By Counties. 1870."

B. Another issue: same title, compiler, publisher, and table, but revised 1875. Color, scale indeterminable, 82 × 92 cm.

Colton lists several sources for his map: Texas General Land Office, A. R. Roessler, Mexican Boundary Commission, U.S. Army Corps of Engineers, U.S. Coast and Geodetic Survey, U.S. General Land Office, Charles Pressler, and various railroad companies. He relied most heavily on Roessler (see no. 349).

345. *Colton's Texas.* New York: G. W. & C. B. Colton & Co., 1872. Copyright by J. H. Colton & Co., 1855. Color, scale 1 in. to approx. 60 mi., 32 × 39 cm., folding into cloth covers. Insets: "Plan of Galveston Bay"; "Plan of Sabine Lake." Donated by W. N. Stowe, 1936.

This map also appeared in editions of Colton's *General Atlas.*

346. *Texas.* Chicago: Rand McNally & Co., ca. 1872. Color, scale 1 in. to approx. 75 mi., 21 × 27 cm. Map no. 19 from *Rand McNally & Co.'s System of Geography.* Insets: "Map of Northern Texas"; "Vicinity of Galveston." Donated by the Friends of the Rosenberg Library.

347. *Chart of the Gulf of Mexico and Windward Passages including the Islands of Cuba, Haiti, Jamaica, Puerto Rico and the Bahamas. Compiled Principally from the Surveys made by order of the British, Spanish and United States Governments.* James Imray & Son. London, 1872. Scale 1 in. to approx. 30 mi., 102 × 187.5 cm. map on 150 × 195 cm. sheet. Insets: "Galveston"; "River Goazacoalcos"; "Vera Cruz and Roadstead of Anton Lizardo"; "Laguna de Terminos." Together with *Caribee Islands,* James Imray & Son, London, 1872. Scale 1 in. to approx. 30 mi., 45 × 102 cm.

Similar to no. 335 but printed on a larger sheet and with the secondary chart.

348. *Bird's Eye View of the City of Houston, Texas.* Drawn by Augustus Koch. N.p., 1873. Photostat of printed view, scale indeterminable, 60 × 78 cm.

Original copies of this view are at the Barker Texas History Center and at the Houston Metropolitan Research Center.

349. *A. R. Roessler's Latest Map of the State of Texas, Exhibiting Mineral and Agricultural Districts, Post Offices & Mailroutes, Railroads projected and finished, Timber, Prairie, Swamp Land, etc.* Compiled and drawn by M. V. Mittendorfer. Printed by Ferdinand Mayer. New York: A. R. Roessler, 1874. Color, scale indeterminable, 96 × 107 cm. Two copies, one folding into cloth covers. Inset: "Map Showing Agricultural Districts and Varieties of Soils in the State of Texas." Table: "Enumeration of the Principal Minerals, Rocks, Soils and Timber Varieties Known to Exist in the State of Texas, Arranged According to Counties." Vignettes: "General Land Office At Austin"; "State Capitol At Austin."

In the twenty years following the Civil War, Roessler produced sixteen county maps and several general maps of Texas (see also nos. 344 and 352). Roessler's maps are the only printed maps that preserve the results of the Shumard survey, the state's first geological and agricultural survey. Roessler worked as a draftsman for the survey in 1860–61, before the Civil War halted the work. During its brief life, the Shumard survey was under constant political pressure, and the importance of its work was questioned. This map incorporates later data with the survey material.

350. *Guide Map of the Great Texas Cattle Trail from the Red River Crossing to the Old Reliable Kansas Pacific Railway.* Kansas Pacific Railway. Kansas City: Kansas City Lithograph Co., 1874. Facsimile set. Illinois: Branding Iron Press, Evanston, 1955, no. 353 of 750 copies, with an essay by Herbert O. Brayer on the production of the original publication. Scale indeterminable, 33 × 48 cm., folding map, bound into octavo pamphlet, *Guide Map of the Best and Shortest Cattle Trail to the Kansas Pacific Railway*, illustrated by Joseph G. McCoy.

351. *Map of Galveston.* Drawn by J. V. Smith. Galveston: John A. Caplen, 1875. Scale indeterminable, 61 × 91 cm., folding into cloth covers. Untitled inset of the Fort Point area. Donated by Mrs. C. B. Lee, 1942.

The map identifies the important sites and buildings of the city. Eight wharves appear, but three have disappeared since Labatt's map of 1869 (see no. 339). The city park on the harbor is absent, though Oleander Park, on the western city limits, is now shown. This park will disappear with the Denver resurvey in 1890.

The map indicates a breakwater, a quarantine station, and a fort on the eastern tip of the island. The completed breakwater is an early stage of the jetty system first proposed in 1867 (see nos. 340, 356, 429, and 447 for further information on the jetties). Smith must have drawn the map before the hurricane of September, 1875, since the document does not show the effect of the storm on the geography of the island's east end.

352A. *New map of the State of Texas.* A. R. Roessler. Lithographed by E. D. W. Welcke, & Bro. New York, n.d. Copyright by A. R. Roessler, 1875. Photostat of printed map, scale indeterminable, 42 × 44 cm. Prepared for the 1876 edition of Albert Hanford's *Texas State Register.* Inset: "Map of the Vicinity of Galveston City." Table giving the latitude and longitude of fourteen points. Note on geological features.

Hanford published the *Texas State Register* from 1856 to 1861 and from 1867 to 1879. In 1880 *Burke's Texas Almanac* absorbed the *Register.* (See no. 349 for information on Roessler.)

B. Another issue: same title, cartographer, and copyright date, but revised 1876 and the name of the printer omitted. Color, scale indeterminable, 44 × 49 cm. Prepared for the 1878 edition of *Burke's Texas Almanac,* Houston. Inset: "Plan of Houston Showing its Rail Road and Water Connections."

This updated version shows the counties in the Panhandle. James Burke and his son, James Jr., were Houston book dealers. The *Almanac* was published from 1856 to 1884.

353. *Plan of Brooklyn.* Lithographed by Miles Strickland. Galveston, ca. 1875. Scale 1 in. to approx. 360 ft., 53 × 60 cm. Key identifying important sites.

The town of Brooklyn was to occupy the area of Corpus Christi now known as North Beach. Development of the site began after the 1873 hurricane destroyed all wharves in the city except those of the Central Wharf and Warehouse Company. To circumvent the monopoly of this company, Norwick Gussett built his own warehouse and wharf on North Beach. Evidently the idea for a town originated at the same time. The area was called Brooklyn as early as 1874 ("Brief History of North Beach," anonymous manuscript. Corpus Christi Public Library). As late as 1951 Bracey's block maps of Corpus Christi label the area "Brooklyn Addition."

Except for Fogg and Market streets, the projected town bears little resemblance to the current form of this part of the city. The plan designates sites for public squares, markets, and parks. Rincon Point is a fragmented archipelago labeled "Skipwith's Resort." Because Gussett's warehouse and wharf are prominently marked, it is probable that he was a major backer of this venture. The scheme was evidently a failure: significant development of the area began only after 1886, and Brooklyn was never incorporated.

There are no other known copies of this map (see no. 354 for the companion map of Corpus Christi).

354. *Map of the City of Corpus Christi with a Condensed Sketch of its Environs.* Lithographed by Miles Strickland. Galveston, ca. 1875. Scale 1 in. to approx. 360 ft., 48 × 64 cm. Untitled inset: plat map of the Corpus Christi area. Key identifying important sites.

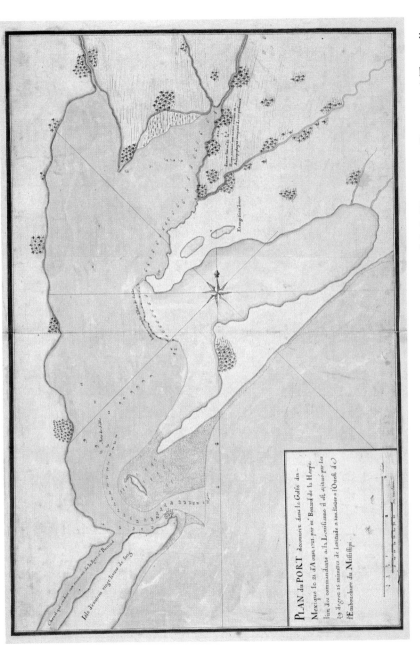

Plan du Port decouvert dans le Golfe du Mexique le 21 d'Aoust 1721, by Bénard de la Harpe, 1725. (See no. 114.) The earliest known map of Galveston Bay. La Harpe discovered the heretofore unknown bay on an expedition to erect a trading post and fort at the "Bay of St. Bernard" (Matagorda Bay).

Bird's Eye View of the City of Galveston, Texas, drawn by C. Drie, 1871. (See no. 341.) The earliest bird's-eye view of a Texas city, this map shows Galveston shortly after the Civil War.

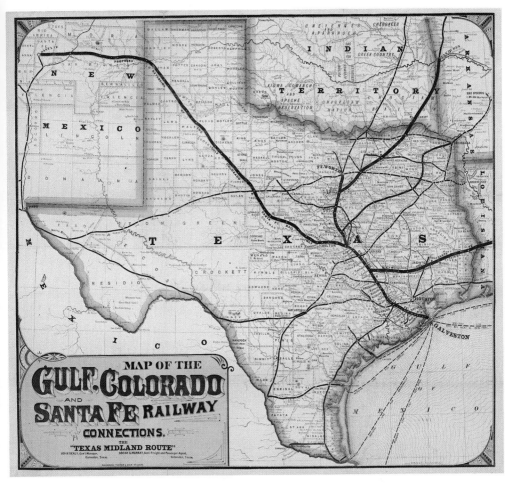

Map of the Gulf, Colorado and Santa Fe Railway and Connections, printed by Rand McNally & Co., 1882. (See no. 388.) Galvestonians chartered the Gulf, Colorado and Santa Fe Railway in an attempt to bypass Houston and connect with the interior of Texas. This map shows the proposed extension to Santa Fe, which was never completed.

Galveston, Texas, drawn by August Koch, 1885. (See no. 393.) This bird's-eye view records the tremendous growth and development of Galveston since Drie's work in 1871. Note the proliferation of brick and iron-front buildings, residential development south of Broadway, and the filling of inlets in the city.

This map's inset shows the "City of Brooklyn" (see no. 353), but the main map does not show the railroad built out of Corpus Christi in 1876. Other than depiction of the Brooklyn area in the inset, this map is essentially the same as the county surveyor's map of 1868 on file at the Neches County courthouse.

The Corpus Christi Public Library also holds a copy of this map.

355A. *Vereinigte Staaten von Nord-Amerika in 6 Blättern.* Augustus H. Petermann. Edited by H. Habenicht. Printed by Eberhardt, Kuhn, Metzeroth and Weiler. Gotha, Germany: Justus Perthes, 1875. Color, scale 1:3,700,000, six 33 × 40.5 cm. sheets, numbered 45a–45f, forming one 66 × 120 cm. map. From *Stieler's Hand-atlas.* Insets: Boston and vicinity; New York and vicinity; southern Texas; southern Florida. MMNHMC.

B. Another issue: same title, cartographer, publisher, source, scale, size, and color, but revised 1879–81 and the sheets numbered 83–88. MMNHMC.

356A. *Map of Galveston & Vicinity.* Compiled by T. A. Washington and Charles F. White. Galveston: Miles Strickland, 1876. Color, scale indeterminable, 87 × 128.5 cm., originally surrounded by a border of pictorial advertizements for local businesses, but the lower border has been trimmed off. Inset: Galveston Bay. Reference: "Churches, Cemeteries, Hotels, Hospitals, Cotton Presses, Banks and Railroads." Table: "Surface Elevations."

B. Another issue: same title, compiler, publisher, date, inset, reference, table, and color, but 69.5 × 108.5 cm., cloth-backed; in poor condition.

C. Another issue: same title, compiler, publisher, date, size (as issue B), inset, reference, table, and color, but folding into octavo cloth covers. Minor variations in the notations on the map. Two copies, one donated by Anna Mosle, 1956, the other by Charles A. Holt, 1924.

Washington and White's map is the first to record the devastation of the eastern tip of the island by the 1875 hurricane. Fort Point appears as fragmented islets, separated from the island by a large channel. The old fort is gone, but the quarantine station remains.

The map also shows the "Gabion Jetty," a novel, submerged breakwater made out of woven reeds. Begun in 1874 and finished in 1877, this jetty system was a complete failure (see nos. 340, 351, 429, and 447 for further information on the jetties). Due to natural tidal action, however, the channel connecting the harbor with the Gulf is now deeper than in 1867. Pelican Spit is more compact and closer to Pelican Island. The long breakwater shown on map no. 351 (1875) has been completely swept away. The Gulf shore also seems to have receded slightly since 1869 (see no. 339).

The map shows eight wharves and extensive landfill added in the wharf area during the 1870s. Outlots have now been divided into regular city blocks as far west as Forty-third Street, and all the inland waterways, except McKinney's Bayou, filled in. The city is divided into twelve wards, in accordance with the charter of 1876.

357. *Map of The Samuel C. Bundick League of Land, Gal. Co. Txs.* J. V. Smith. Surveyed by order of the Galveston County District Court. Galveston, 1876. Photostat of manuscript map, scale (of original) 1 in. to approx. 600 varas, 36 × 43 cm. Copy donated by Thomas Affleck, 1975; original in the possession of Welder T. Hawes.

This plat map of the Virginia Point area shows mainland Galveston County from Highland Bayou (now Jones Bayou) to Swan Lake. It includes the tracks of the Gulf, Colorado & Santa Fe Railway and the Galveston, Houston and Henderson Railroad. (See no. 430 for a later promotional map of this area.)

358. *Kimble Co.* Texas. General Land Office. Austin, 1876. Ink on cloth, scale indeterminable, 46 × 75.5 cm.

Shows sections distributed under the various headright acts and school and railroad lands. At this date, much of the county is still open range in the public domain.

This manuscript map is part of a series of county maps that served as models for the later printed series published by the General Land Office. (See no. 368.)

359. *McCulloch County.* Texas. General Land Office. Austin, 1876. Ink on cloth, scale indeterminable, 49 × 61 cm. (See no. 358 for further information.)

360. *San Saba County.* Texas. General Land Office. Austin, 1876. Ink on cloth, scale 1 in. to approx. 2 mi., 54.5 × 59.5 cm. (see no. 358 for further information.)

361. *Oleander Park Homestead Association's Map of Galveston, Texas.* Oleander Park Homestead Association. Galveston, 1877. Black and white, with some manuscript additions in color, scale indeterminable, 19 × 36.5 cm., mounted on cardboard. On the same sheet with a plat map of the southwest quarter of the addition. Donated by C. G. Sweet, 1922.

Promoters of the Oleander Park addition evidently prepared and altered the map in order to record lot sales. The subdivision was at the west end of the city, on the approximate site of the Stonewall Addition shown on Labatt's 1869 map and on Washington and White's 1876 map (see nos. 339 and 356). The addition took its name from Oleander Park, immediately to the east, which appears on city maps as early as 1875 (see no. 351). The park was probably established in connection with the United States centennial celebration, as it occasionally is named Centennial Park (see no. 409B).

362. *Colton's "New Medium" Map of the State of Texas From the latest and Most Authentic Sources.* New York: G. W. and C. B. Colton & Co., 1877. Copyright, 1872. Color, scale indeterminable, 50 × 66 cm., folding into cloth covers. Insets: "Plan of Matagorda Bay"; "Northern Part or 'Panhandle' of Texas"; "Plan of Galveston Bay"; "Plan of Sabine Lake."

363. *Gray's Railroad Map of Texas Specially Prepared from Official Sources.* O. W. Gray and Son. Philadelphia, 1877. Photostat of printed map; scale indeterminable, 44 × 72 cm. From one of Gray's atlases of the period, probably the *National Atlas.* Inset: "Outline Map of Texas showing the Railroad Connections with New Orleans, St. Louis, etc."

364A. *County Map of the State of Texas Showing also portions of the Adjoining States and Territories.* Drawn and engraved by W. H. Gamble. Philadelphia, n.d. Copyright by S. Augustus Mitchell, 1877. Color, scale 1 in. to approx. 50 mi., 35 × 52.5 cm. From Mitchell's *New General Atlas.* Inset: "Plan of Galveston and Vicinity."

B. Another issue: same title, engraver, scale, source, and inset, but revised, copyright 1878.

C. Another issue: same title, engraver, scale, source, and inset, but revised, copyright 1880.

D. Another issue: same title, engraver, scale, source, and inset, but revised, copyright 1884.

365. *Brazoria County.* F. W. Stevens. Brazoria, Texas: Shapard, Stevens & Co., 1877. Color, scale 1 in. to 6,000 varas, 49 × 52 cm.

366. *Atlantic City.* Anonymous. N.p., 1877. Scale 1 in. to 400 ft., 51.5 × 79.5 cm., folding into cloth covers that are detached but present. Separately issued version of a map that appeared in Harry C. Woolman and T. F. Rose's *Historical and Biographical Atlas of the New Jersey Coast,* Philadelphia, 1878. MMNHMC.

367. *New Map of the State of Texas for 1879.* Drawn, engraved and printed by G. W. and C. B. Colton & Co. New York: Albert Hanford, 1879. Copyright by G. W. and C. B. Colton & Co., 1875. Color, scale 1 in. to approx. 33 mi., 46 × 67 cm. Prepared for Hanford's *Texas State Register.* Insets: "Plan of Galveston Bay"; "Western Portion of the United States"; "Plan of Matagorda Bay"; "Plan of the Northern Part or 'Panhandle' of Texas"; "Plan of Sabine Lake." (See no. 352 for information on the *Texas State Register.*)

368. *Map of Bowie Co. Texas.* Texas. General Land Office. Austin. Lithographed by A. Gast & Co. St. Louis, n.d. Copyright by the General Land Office, 1879. Scale 1:133,320, 40 × 52 cm.

In the late 1870s the General Land Office launched an ambitious program to produce a printed land ownership map for each county. This was an unparalleled undertaking, attempted in no other state.

The General Land Office's interest in such a series was undoubtedly due to the unique character of the state's public lands. Prior to the independence of Texas, Spain and Mexico had issued land grants to promoters, such as Stephen F. Austin, to bring in groups of settlers. When Texas gained independence from Mexico, the new republic took control of all public lands. When Texas joined the Union in 1845, the new state retained this control—the only state ever allowed to do so. The republic, and later the state, disbursed these lands in several ways. Four different headright acts authorized the distribution of vacant lands to settlers. The constitution of the republic granted a league and labor land (approximately 4,600 acres) to all heads of households established in Texas as of March 2, 1836, and a third of a league (approximately 1,500 acres) to single men. A second headright act, passed in December, 1837, conferred 1,280 acres on married men and 640 acres on single men who had settled in Texas between independence and October 1, 1836. In early 1838, a third headright act extended 640 acres to married men and 320 acres to single men who settled in Texas before January 1, 1840. In 1842, a fourth headright act granted the same amount of land as the third act, providing the prospective owner cultivated at least ten acres. Finally, there were special grants. Beginning in the 1850s, Texas granted more than 35 million acres of public domain to forty-one railroad companies to encourage railroad construction.

The first session of the Congress of the Republic created the General Land Office in 1837 to handle the distribution of the public lands. The agency immediately began authorizing surveys and preparing manuscript maps of the areas surveyed (see no. 358).

This map of Bowie County is typical of printed maps issued by the General Land Office between 1879 and 1897. All the maps show boundaries, names of landowners, and dates of the grants of the surveyed and assigned plots.

369. *Map of Burleson Co. Texas.* Texas. General Land Office. Austin. Lithographed by A. Gast & Co. St. Louis, n.d. Copyright by the General Land Office, 1879. Scale, 1:133,320, 41 × 53 cm. (See no. 368 for further information.)

370. *Map of Chambers County, Texas.* Texas. General Land Office. Austin. Lithographed by A. Gast & Co. St. Louis, n.d. Copyright by the General Land Office, 1879. Scale 1:133,320, 48 × 62 cm. (See no. 368 for further information.)

371. *Map of Concho County.* Texas. General Land Office. Austin. Lithographed by A. Gast. & Co. St. Louis, n.d. Copyright by the General Land Office, 1879. Scale 1:133,320, 44 × 58 cm.

Adelsverein lands along the Concho River are outlined in red. The German emigration society had intended to settle the area, but most of the colonists found the conditions unsuitable for agriculture and settled farther west.

372. *Map of Jefferson County Texas.* General Land Office. Austin. Lithographed by A. Gast & Co. St. Louis, n.d. Copyright by the General Land

Office, 1879. Scale 1:133,320, 47 × 54 cm. (See no. 368 for further information.)

373. *Map of Lee Co. Texas.* Texas. General Land Office. Austin. Lithographed by A. Gast & Co. St. Louis, n.d. Copyright by the General Land Office, 1879. Scale 1:133,320, 41 × 53 cm. (See no. 368 for further information.)

374. *Red River Co. Texas.* Texas. General Land Office. Austin. Lithographed by A. Gast & Co. St. Louis, n.d. Copyright by the General Land Office, 1879. Scale 1:133,320, 49 × 59 cm.

Settlers came to this northeastern corner of Texas from Arkansas as early as 1814. Originally Red River County contained all or part of thirty-nine present counties. (See no. 368 for further information.)

375. *Map of Runnels Co. Texas.* Texas. General Land Office. Austin. Lithographed by A. Gast & Co. St. Louis, n.d. Copyright by the General Land Office, 1879. Scale 1:133,320, 46 × 60 cm. (See no. 368 for further information.)

376. *Map of San Jacinto Co.* Texas. General Land Office. Austin. Lithographed by A. Gast & Co. St. Louis, n.d. Copyright by the General Land Office, 1879. Scale 1:133,320, 46 × 60 cm. (See no. 368 for further information.)

377. *Waller County Texas.* Texas. General Land Office. Austin. Lithographed by A. Gast & Co. St. Louis, n.d. Copyright by the General Land Office, 1879. Scale 1:133,320. (See no. 368 for further information.)

378. *Map of Wood Co. Texas.* Texas. General Land Office. Austin. Lithographed by A. Gast & Co. St. Louis, n.d. Copyright by the General Land Office, 1879. Scale 1:133,320, 40 × 41 cm. (See no. 368 for further information.)

379. *Austin County.* Texas. General Land Office. Austin. Lithographed by A. Gast & Co. St. Louis, n.d. Copyright by the General Land Office, 1879. Scale 1:133,320, 51 × 56 cm. (See no. 368 for further information.)

380. *Map of Brazoria Co. Texas.* Texas. General Land Office. Austin. Lithographed by A. Gast & Co. St. Louis, n.d. Copyright by the General Land Office, 1879. Scale 1:133,320, 60 × 66 cm. (See no. 368 for further information.)

381. *Map of Colorado County.* Texas. General Land Office. Austin. Lithographed by A. Gast & Co. St. Louis, n.d. Copyright by the General Land Office, 1879. Scale 1:133,320, 54 × 57 cm. (See no. 368 for further information.)

382. *Map of Grimes Co. Texas.* Texas. General Land Office. Austin. Lithographed by A. Gast & Co. St. Louis, n.d. Copyright by the General Land Office, 1880. Scale 1:133,320, 54 × 57 cm. (See no. 368 for further information.)

383. *Knox County.* Texas. General Land Office. Austin. Lithographed by A. Gast & Co. St. Louis, n.d. Copyright by the General Land Office, 1880. Scale 1:133,320, 47 × 56 cm. (See no. 368 for further information.)

384. *Map of Matagorda County.* Texas. General Land Office. Austin. Lithographed by A. Gast & Co. St. Louis, n.d. Copyright by the General Land Office, 1879. Scale 1:133,320, 61 × 73 cm. (See no. 368 for further information.)

385. *Montgomery County.* Texas. General Land Office. Austin. Lithographed by A. Gast & Co. St. Louis, n.d. Copyright by the General Land Office, 1880. Scale indeterminable, 53 × 61 cm. (See no. 368 for further information.)

386. *Smith County.* Texas. General Land Office. Austin. Lithographed by A. Gast & Co. St. Louis, n.d., Copyright by the General Land Office, 1880. Scale 1:133,320, 48 × 60 cm. (see no. 368 for further information.)

387. *Chart of Galveston Shewing Proposed Greenway Breakwaters To Illustrate the Proposals of Admiral Bedford Pim.* Bedford Pim. N.p., ca. 1885. Based on the United States Coast and Geodetic Survey map of Galveston Bay entrance, corrected to 1883.

As an alternative to James Eads's harbor development plan, Pim, a British naval engineer, proposed a deep-water harbor with railroad jetties extending several hundred yards into the Gulf. Floating Greenway breakwaters were supposed to protect this exposed harbor. This map is accompanied by an 1885 press release by Pim describing the plan (ms. no. 04-0055, Rosenberg Library).

388. *Map of the Gulf, Colorado and Santa Fe Railway and Connections.* Gulf, Colorado & Santa Fe Railway. Printed by Rand McNally & Co., Chicago, 1882. Color, scale indeterminable, 56 × 56 cm., folding into a 10 × 18.5 cm. brochure, with text by John Sealy on the *Texas Midland Route*. Table of distances.

A group of Galveston businessmen, determined to bypass Houston and connect directly to the interior of Texas, chartered the Gulf, Colorado, and Santa Fe Railway in 1873. By 1882 the railroad reached Lampasas. The map shows the proposed extension to Santa Fe.

389. *Gulf Coast from Galveston to the Rio Grande.* United States Coast and Geodetic Survey. Washington, D.C., issued 1883. Hydrography corrected to 1906. Scale 1:400,000, 78 × 102 cm. General chart of the coast no. 21. Notes on lighthouses (also located in yellow), buoys, soundings, tides, weather, signal stations.

390. *Map of Galveston Co.* Texas. General Land Office. Austin, 1883. Photostat of a manuscript map, scale indeterminable, 47 × 68 cm. Donated by the Gulf, Colorado & Santa Fe Railway, 1929. (See no. 358 for further information.)

391. *Military Map of Western Texas.* Anonymous. N.p., 1884. Photostat of manuscript map, scale (of original) 1 in. to 10 mi., 59 × 90 cm.

This map shows the area west of San Antonio and south of Fort Griffin.

392. *Galveston Texas.* New York: Sanborn Map and Publishing Co., 1885. Photostats of printed maps, scale 1 in. to 50 ft., twenty 33 × 55 cm. sheets, originals bound in one volume.

The Sanborn Map Co., incorporated in 1876, was the largest producer of maps for fire insurance underwriters. The company produced maps and atlases covering some twelve thousand cities nationwide. These maps locate existing buildings and give detailed information about the size and material composition of the structures.

This is the second atlas prepared for Galveston. The Sanborn Company had just completed the atlas when a large portion of the area depicted burned to the ground in November, 1885. The company halted publishing plans and compiled a completely new atlas (no. 436; see also nos. 473 and 481 for later editions).

The Library of Congress holds the original copy of this 1885 edition. The Barker Texas History Center also holds several Sanborn editions for Galveston: 1877, 1885, 1889, 1899, 1912, 1918, 1923, and 1948.

393. *Galveston, Texas.* Drawn by Augustus Koch. N.p., 1885. Color, scale indeterminable, 67 × 102 cm. Eighteen vignettes of commercial buildings in Galveston. Key locating sixty-one sites.

This panorama shows Galveston just prior to the November, 1885, fire. Koch worked at least two years on this project and recorded considerable development in the city since 1871. (See no. 341.) Signs of progress include the proliferation of brick and iron-front buildings in the business district, residential development south of Broadway, and the fill of inlets and bayous in the city.

Very little is known about Koch. Pinckney suggests that he may have been a native of La Grange (pp. 154–55). He made panoramas of a number of other Texas cities, including Houston, Austin, Belton, Bastrop, Brenham, La Grange, San Antonio, Fredericksburg, and New Braunfels. He also recorded many cities outside Texas.

394. *Galveston, Texas.* Augustus Koch. N.p., 1885. Scale indeterminable, 64 × 101.5 cm.

A variant of the preceding bird's-eye view (no. 393), differing in several respects: it has no imprint, is smaller, lacks color, omits the vignettes, and shows the secondary detail (shadows, water surface, etc.) differently. The background panorama of the Gulf has been completely redrawn to compensate for the absence of the vignettes. Although faithful to Koch's colored view in all other respects, it is clearly printed from a different stone.

This previously unknown variant is probably a proof state for the colored view. Because bird's-eye views were usually sold by subscription, Hebert has suggested that this issue may be a copy used to promote sales and advertising. Variant states are common among other bird's-eye views, though none is known for any other Koch view.

The quality of workmanship and the drawing style indicate this panorama is also Koch's work, not a copy drawn by someone else.

395. *Diagram of Burnt District Galveston Texas. Great Fire of November 13th, 1885.* Clarke & Courts. Galveston, 1885. Color, scale indeterminable, 25 × 40 cm.

The fire, which began at the Vulcan Iron Works on Avenue A, cut a forty-block corridor across the city from the harbor to Avenue O, between Sixteenth and Twenty-third streets. The devastated area was largely residential; property losses amounted to almost two million dollars, and twenty-five hundred people were left homeless.

The library has seven copies of this map. On one, a few buildings and houses have been marked in pencil.

396. *Birdseye View of the Eastern Portion of the City of Galveston, with the houses destroyed by the Great Conflagration of November 13th, 1885.* Miles Strickland & Co. Galveston, 1885. Color, scale indeterminable, 49 × 61 cm. Key locating important sites.

Strickland has carefully, if rather crudely, copied the central portion of Koch's bird's-eye view (see no. 393). The burnt district is shaded in red.

397. *Morrison & Fourmey's Map of the City of Houston Texas.* Morrison and Fourmy. Revised by William Harkness. Philadelphia: O. W. Gray & Son, 1885. Color, scale 1 in. to 500 ft., 78 × 84 cm.

398. *Map with Names and Locality of residence, of the Principal Inhabitants; Tributary to Galveston Texas.* Compiled and drawn by George W. Grover. Galveston, 1885. Color manuscript, scale indeterminable, 51 × 68 cm.

This carefully drawn map shows approximately three hundred landowners around Galveston Bay, excluding most of the island and the west bay area. It does not indicate property lines but does show major topographical features and existing lighthouses.

399. *The Railroad System of Texas on September 1st, 1887.* Drawn by E. A. Hensoldt for A. H. Belo & Co. Printed by Rand McNally & Co., Chicago.

1887. Scale indeterminable, 50 × 67 cm. Tables: "Railroad Construction in the United States"; Texas towns with a population of more than 1,000.

This map was probably issued as a supplement to the *Galveston Daily News* and the *Dallas Morning News,* both owned by A. H. Belo & Co.

400. *Episcopal Cemetery.* Traced by the Galveston Civil Engineer, 1921. From the copy by Nicholas J. Clayton, Galveston, 1887. Blueprint, scale indeterminable, 60.5 × 82.5 cm. Donated by Charles Harper Anderson, 1924.

A plat map of plot owners, the 1921 copy was taken from Clayton's 1887 copy of the original map. The date of the original is unknown.

401. *Bird's Eye View of Galveston, Texas.* Published for Victor Phillips, Galveston. Copyright by Ward Brothers, Columbus, Ohio, 1888. Photostat of printed view, scale indeterminable, 21.5 × 51.5 cm. Donated by the Gulf, Colorado & Santa Fe Railway, 1927.

This is a modification of Koch's view of 1885 (see no. 393). The cartographer added a few buildings but generally ignored drastic changes caused by the 1885 fire.

402. *Galveston Bay Texas.* United States Coast and Geodetic Survey. Reduced drawing by W. T. Martin, et al. Engraved by E. A. Maedel et al. Washington, D.C., issued 1888. Corrected to 1887. Scale 3 in. to approx. 5 mi., 83 × 102 cm., cloth-backed. Coast chart no. 204. Notations on lights, buoys, tides, soundings, etc. Donated by Henry J. Runge, 1922.

Shows Fort Point still separated from the main body of the island by a wide channel. Interior topographical detail for the island is the same as appears on the first coastal survey of the early 1850s. A submerged jetty follows the course later taken by the south jetty (see no. 429). The depth over the outer bar is eleven feet.

403. *City Cemetery.* Galveston County. Clerk. Galveston, 1888. Blueprint, scale indeterminable, 113 × 76 cm. Donated by the Galveston City Engineer, 1921.

404. *Flake's Map of Hitchcock Galveston County, Texas.* A. Flake. N.p., 1888. Blueprint, scale indeterminable, 43 × 89 cm.

Hitchcock was established in 1873 on the Gulf, Colorado and Santa Fe Railway line. The map shows Flake's addition, on the southern edge of town. A. Flake probably was a member of the Flake family of Galveston, of whom Ferdinand Flake (1822–73), Unionist newspaper publisher, is best known.

405. *Sherman County. State of Texas March 1888. Indian Territory.* Texas. General Land Office. Austin. Lithographed by A. Gast Bank Note and Lithographic Company. St. Louis, n.d. Copyright by the General Land Office, 1888. Scale 1:133,320, 41 × 51 cm. (See no. 368 for further information.)

406. *Wichita County.* J. W. Field, Wichita Falls. Engraved by Moss Engraving Co. New York, 1888. Scale indeterminable, 20 × 28 cm. Descriptive text along right margin. Donated by Henry Runge.

This landowners map was compiled from General Land Office records.

407. *Williamson County.* Compiled and drawn by Herman Pressler. N.p., 1888. Photostat of printed map, scale indeterminable, 37 × 54 cm.

A photostat of a commercially published copy of the General Land Office county map.

408. *Atlas Geográfico de la República Argentina que contiene los mapas de cada provincia, y los del Uruguay y Paraguay compuesto en presencia de los últimos trabajos científicos.* Mario Felipe Paz Soldán. Corrected and augmented edition. Edited by Felix Lajouane. Buenos Aires, 1888. Twenty-nine maps, bound in folio volume, with 113 pages of text.

The maps show Argentina province by province, the Argentinian railroad system, Paraguay, and Uruguay.

409A. *[Galveston.]* Compiled and drawn by E. M. Hartrick, 1877. Revised by H. T. Wilson. Galveston: Clarke & Courts, 1889. Scale indeterminable, 18 × 30 cm. Untitled inset of Galveston Bay. Four diagrams showing the division of the city blocks and outlots into lots. Key to railroads and street railways.

B. Another issue: identical, but revised by C. A. Sias, 1897. Street railways and a few other features are printed in red.

The 1897 revision shows new development—most noticeably, new wharves, changes in street railway lines, the addition of the Denver resurvey and Fort Crockett, and the omission of Centennial Park.

410. *Atlas of Commercial Geography Illustrating the General Facts of Physical, Political, Economic, and Statistical Geography, on which International Commerce Depends.* John George Bartholomew. With introductory notes by Hugh Robert Mill. Cambridge, England: University Press, 1889. Thirty-eight maps on twenty-seven sheets, scale varies, quarto volume bound in cloth with red morocco backstrip.

411. *Topographical Map for Commerce of Galveston Texas.* Baltimore: William A. Flamm & Co., 1890. Scale indeterminable, 41 × 66 cm.

A channel runs across the island at about Sixth Street, separating Fort Point from the city. This channel is not shown on other contemporary maps of Galveston. Virtually all of the city's outlots east of Twenty-ninth Street have been divided into regular city blocks, but there is no sign yet of the Denver resurvey, begun in this year (see no. 412). The area north of Offat's Bayou is named "Poolville."

412. *Map of the City of Galveston Texas.* Compiled by E. A. Hensoldt for the Galveston Land & Improvement Co. of Denver, Colorado. Printed by Rand McNally & Co., Chicago, 1890. Photostat of printed map, scale (of original) 1 in. to approx. 1,000 ft., original in the Barker Texas History Center, Tucker Collection. Key locating important sites. Four diagrams showing the division of the blocks and outlots into lots.

This map was commissioned to show the Denver resurvey, which converted outlots in the western section of the city into city blocks. The blocks were then subdivided into small lots, twenty-four to a block, instead of the normal ten to fourteen lots. The entire project encompassed 276 blocks.

The Galveston Land and Improvement Company, chartered in 1890, organized the project. Most of the directors of the company were Colorado businessmen, but some prominent Galveston businessmen, such as Julius Runge, were involved (Kauffman & Runge Papers, Rosenberg Library).

The general plan of the city shows the blunted east end caused by the

1875 hurricane. The area to the east of Fourth Street was probably a mud flat, which would have been covered at high tide. The city extends in a dotted line to First Street.

413. *Plan of the City of Galveston Texas 1845.* William H. Sandusky. 1845. Revised by H. T. Wilson. Galveston: Clarke & Courts, 1890. Scale 1 in. to 80 chains, 75 × 97 cm. Inset: "Map of Galveston Island Lots Surveyed by R. C. Trimble and Wm. Lindsey."

Revisions of note include sweeping changes along the harbor front, the addition of seventy-two square blocks (in dotted line) east of Seventh Street, the overlay of a new ward system, the electric railway system, and the Denver resurvey. This map, like the preceding one (no. 412) was designed to illustrate that latter development scheme. The division of blocks and outlots outside the Denver resurvey is identical to Sandusky's map, although earlier maps indicate that several outlots east of Forty-fifth Street had also been resurveyed between 1845 and 1890 (see, for example, no. 339).

414. *Map of the County of Galveston Texas.* Printed by Clarke & Courts. Galveston, ca. 1890. Scale 1 in. to 4,000 varas, 47 × 67 cm. Vignettes: "U.S. Custom House"; "Galveston Rope and Twine Co."; "Clarke & Courts' Building"; Galveston Bagging and Cordage Co."; "Lone Star Flour Mills"; "Galveston Cotton and Woolen Mills."

The map shows county landowners.

415. *Public Sale of Town Lots at Arcadia, on Wednesday, March 19th, 1890.* Printed by Clarke & Courts. Galveston, 1890. Color, scale 1 in. to 400 ft., 43 × 60 cm.

Founded in 1889, Arcadia is on the main line of the Gulf, Colorado & Santa Fe Railway, twenty-one miles from Galveston and halfway between the towns of Alvin and Hitchcock. The development's Galveston agents were C. E. Angell and Julius Runge.

416. *Official Map of the City of Houston and Adjoining Surveys. Compiled from the Records of Harris County, Texas.* Porter, Pollard & Ruby. Printed by A. Gast Bank Note and Lithography Co. St. Louis, 1890. Scale indeterminable, 86 × 90 cm.

417. *Map Showing the advantages of the City of Houston as a Commercial, Manufacturing, and Distributing Center and as a Deep-water Port for the Coast of Texas* together with the *Map of the Houston Belt and Magolia Park Railway and Connection With Deep Water at Port Houston.* Printed by Rand McNally & Co., Chicago. Houston: Thomas, Bright and Company, 1890. Scale indeterminable, two maps on one 50 × 76 cm. sheet. Inset on first map: "Map Showing the Relation of the City of Houston, Texas, to the trade of the Gulf of Mexico, West Indies, and Caribbean Sea." Table of statistics on Houston manufacturing and commerce. Donated by Samuel M. Penland, 1905.

This promotional sheet, touting Houston's potential as a port and a marketing center, graphically presents the commercial rivalry between Galveston and Houston. The top map shows the Gulf Coast from New Orleans to Corpus Christi, inland as far as Waco, and traces all existing and proposed rail connections into Houston. The bottom map focuses on the city of Houston and the lower reaches of Buffalo Bayou. Large ships are shown as far inland on the bayou as Harrisburg and the neighboring "Port Houston."

A manuscript note along the lower margin sums up the contemporary Galveston view of such promotionals: "An advertising sheet sent out by the Houston Real estate men to show that Galveston does not exist — note the ships in the prairie near Houston."

418. *Gulf Coast from Atchafalaya Bay to Galveston Bay.* United States Coast and Geodetic Survey. Washington, D.C., 1900. Hydrography corrected to 1905, aids to navigation corrected to 1906. Scale 1:400,000, 77 × 96 cm. General chart of the coast no. 20. Notations on lighthouses (also marked in yellow), buoys, tides, soundings, etc.

419. *Geographically Correct Map of Texas & Indian Territory Showing Lines of the Gulf, Colorado & Santa Fé Ry. And Connections.* Gulf, Colorado & Santa Fe Railway. Designed, engraved, and printed by Matthews, Northrup & Co. Buffalo, New York, ca. 1890. Color, scale indeterminable, on one side of a 64 × 85 cm. sheet that folds into a 10.5 × 22 cm. brochure entitled "The Santa Fe in Texas." Inset: "Western Part of Texas."

The Atchison, Topeka, and Santa Fe Railroad purchased the Gulf, Colorado and Santa Fe in 1886, to satisfy the former company's desire to serve a Gulf port. The proposed connection from Lampasas to Santa Fe never materialized for the Gulf, Colorado and Santa Fe (see no. 338): the western terminus of the line is San Angelo.

420. Map of Stephens County, Texas. Dallas: Daugherty, Connellee & Ammerman, ca. 1890. Lithographed by August Gast, St. Louis, ca. 1890. Scale 1 in. to 4,000 varas, 48 × 52 cm.

A privately published promotional map adapted from the General Land Office's printed county map, this version is modified to locate the plats offered for sale by Dougherty, Connellee & Ammerman.

Dougherty, Connellee & Ammerman adapted this promotional map from the General Land Office's printed map of Stephens County. The company modified the state document to locate plats offered for sale.

421. Map of the County and City of Galveston Texas. Compiled From Original Field Notes and Latest Surveys As Furnished By The Island City Abstract and Loan Co, Galveston, Texas. Copyright by D. W. Ensign & Co., 1891. Color, scale 1 in. to approx. 2 mi. Inset: "Map of the City of Galveston." Text: "Condensed Statistics of Galveston's Temperature, Climate, Health, Population, Improvements, Wealth, etc."

This plat map of Galveston County shows both the original land grants and subsequent subdivisions. Trimble and Lindsey's survey of west Galveston Island appears, with lot numbers given for each of the tracts.

Designed to promote investment and development in the county, the map shows a number of proposed town schemes that were popular in the Galveston Bay area at the end of the nineteenth century: South Galveston (see no. 427), North Galveston (see no. 439), Port Bolivar (see no. 552) and West Galveston. The new town of Arcadia appears (see no. 415), but there is no sign yet of Alta Loma, which was founded about 1893, when it was called Highland. Here, that name is given to the town of La Marque.

422. Map of Highland Park Addition to the City of Galveston Tex. C. A. Sias. Galveston, 1891. Copied by the Galveston County Clerk, Galveston, 1926. Ink on cloth, scale 1 in. to 100 ft., 61 × 61 cm.

This plat map shows a proposed subdivision just west of the city. The presence of street names Colorado and Palmer (William Jackson?) indicate that the developers may have had contact with the Colorado investors involved with the Denver resurvey (see no. 412). The Highland Park subdivision never developed as projected; however, several streets in the area today bear names originally proposed for the addition. Highland Park also appears on Courtney Washington's map of 1928 (see no. 509) and R. W. Luttrell's map of 1902 (see no. 464).

423. *Atlas to accompany the official records of the Union and Confederate Armies.* George B. Davies, Leslie J. Perry, and Joseph W. Kirley. Compiled by Calvin D. Cowles, published under the direction of the United States Secretary of War. Washington, D.C.: Government Printing Office, 1891–95. Color, scale varies, 175 plates bound in three 39 × 45 cm. volumes, red leather covers.

424A. *Galveston Co.* Texas. General Land Office. Austin, 1892. Scale 1:133,320, 47 × 60 cm. (See no. 368 for further information.)

B. Another issue: same title and scale, but compiled and drawn by Charles W. Pressler, n.p., 1891; traced in the General Land Office, 1899; 90 × 126 cm.

425. *Map of Nottingham Galveston Island, Texas.* C. A. Sias. Galveston, 1892. Scale 1 in. to 200 ft., 48 × 93 cm. Text, by Frank L. Dana, describing the subdivision.

Chartered in 1892, the Nottingham Company modeled their development after English industrial villages. The original plan of Nottingham appears here as a rectangle of eighty-five blocks, with the core area set aside for a lace curtain factory and associated industrial plants. The Galveston and Western Railroad runs along the south side of the factory site and bisects the town at a slight angle.

The company issued bonds in October, 1892, and began operation by May, 1893. The 1893 depression weakened the lace market, and in January, 1894, the company defaulted on both the bond principal and interest. Trustees sold the property to one of the company officers. Although the new owner tried to operate the factory, by 1896 he, too, went out of business and sold the property for 10 percent of the original cost. Portions of the factory were then torn down. The hurricane of 1900 destroyed most of what remained. (Houston Archeological Society Newsletter, no. 68, December, 1980).

426. *Map of Nottingham Galveston Island, Texas.* The Nottingham Company. Printed by Clarke & Courts. Galveston, ca. 1892. Scale 1 in. to 240 ft., 70 × 44 cm. Untitled inset: Galveston Island. Text, beginning "Do you want to encourage manufacturing enterprises in Galveston?" describes the subdivision.

This plat map is adapted from the Sias manuscript (see no. 425) and varies only in a few details. The untitled inset shows the proposed rail connections between Galveston, Nottingham, and South Galveston.

427. *South Galveston on Galveston Island.* South Galveston Land Company. Galveston, ca. 1892. Scale indeterminable, 30 × 33 cm.

The South Galveston Land Company, chartered in 1891, purchased all of Hall and Jones section no. 8 on the western part of Galveston island. The land company surveyed and platted the section into blocks and lots, and named the area South Galveston. The proposed town was to be quite substantial, extending across the width of the island. It had a grid plan and radiating boulevards centered on "Alta Loma" park. The company also planned to build an electric railway, the South Galveston and Gulf Shore, to connect South Galveston with Galveston. Although some roadbed was laid, the railroad was never completed. The entire South Galveston project failed; today Galveston Island State Park occupies the site.

428. *[Texas.]* Chicago: Rand McNally & Co., n.d. Color, scale 1 in. to approx. 50 mi., 47 × 65 cm. From Rand McNally's *Indexed Atlas of the World.* Inset: "Southern Portion of Texas."

429. *Galveston Harbor Texas.* United States Army Corps of Engineers. Surveyed by E. M. Hartrick and F. Oppikofer, under the direction of A. M. Miller. N.p., 1893. Blueprint, scale 1:10,000, 103 × 180 cm. Donated by the U.S. Army Corps of Engineers, Galveston Office, 1925.

From 1867 to 1897 the Corps of Engineers worked to prevent shoaling at the entrance to Galveston Bay. Due to sporadic funding and a series of unsuccessful experimental jetty designs (see, for example, no. 356), the corps implemented no permanent improvements before 1890. The passage of the Rivers and Harbors Act that year guaranteed stable funding for the project and allowed the corps to complete it. The finished system consisted of two stone jetties flanking the entrance to the bay. The south jetty, 35,603 feet long, began on the bay side of the east end of the island and ran out into the Gulf. The north jetty extended 24,907 feet from Bolivar Point. The jetties are about 7,000 feet apart (Alperin, pp. 37–57).

This survey records the construction to date and the corresponding hydrographic changes. The south jetty is already virtually complete, but work is just beginning on the north jetty. The map shows the outlines of land masses but no interior detail. E. M. Hartrick was later instrumental in the construction of the Houston ship channel.

430. *Plat of Virginia Point Located in the Samuel C. Bundick League Galveston County, Texas. Owned by Walter C. Jones.* Designed and platted by C. A. Sias. Printed by Robert Clarke & Co. Galveston, 1893. Scale indeterminable, 43 × 56 cm.

This promotional sheet illustrates a plan for a proposed town on Virginia Point (see also no. 357). One side of the sheet is a general map of the site, showing a town of 70 blocks and 214 outlots. The verso is a close-up of the 70 blocks, which occupy the southwest part of the site. Two railroad bridges (the Galveston, Houston and Henderson, and the Gulf, Colorado and Santa Fe) and the Galveston County Wagon Bridge connect the island with the mainland at this point. A proposed pipeline appears in manuscript. The scale for both maps is incorrectly given as 1 in. to 833 ft.

431. *Map of the Town of Clear Creek and about 6,500 acres of adjoining acre property.* Anonymous. N.p., 1893. Blueprint, scale 1 in. to 1,000 ft., 50 × 52 cm. Inset: "Plan of Blocks in Clear Creek."

432. *Clarke & Courts Map of Galveston and Vicinity Embracing the Counties of Brazoria, Galveston, Chambers, Jefferson, Harris, Fort Bend and Liberty and also Portions of Austin, Waller, Wharton and Matagorda.* Copyright by Clarke & Courts. Galveston, 1893. Scale 1 in. to 5 mi., 42 × 55 cm.

Locates operational and proposed railroads, towns, and major topographical features. A few rural railroad depots and towns have been added in manuscript.

433. *Map of Harris County.* Texas. General Land Office. Austin. Lithographed by August Gast Bank Note & Lithography Co. 1893. Scale 1 in. to 3,000 varas, 56 × 80 cm. (See no. 368 for further information.)

434. *Plat of the Edmund Andrews League Brazoria County Texas.* Henry C. Ripley. Galveston, 1893. Ink on cloth, scale, 1 in. to 600 ft., 63 × 95 cm.

435. *Fort Bend County.* Texas. General Land Office. Austin, 1893. Scale indeterminable, 55 × 60 cm. (See no. 368 for further information.)

436. *Galveston, Texas.* New York: Sanborn Map & Publishing Co., 1889. Color, scale 1 in. to 50 ft., sixty-four 52 × 62 cm. sheets bound into folio volume, all sheets with paste-down overlays showing revisions to 1894. (See no. 392 for further information and nos. 473 and 481 for other editions.)

437. *Map of the East Part of the Tom Green County.* Texas. General Land Office. Austin. Lithographed by A. Gast Bank Note & Lithography Co. St. Louis, 1894. Copyright by the General Land Office, 1893. Scale 1:133,320, 54 × 57 cm. (See no. 368 for further information.)

438. *Map of the City of Galveston.* Anonymous. N.p., ca. 1895. Scale indeterminable, 73 × 97 cm.

Although a fragment (probably of a four sheet map), this is nonetheless a large, detailed plat map of the city. Due to the newly completed jetties, the eastern end of the island is much larger than on Hensoldt's map of 1890 (see no. 412). There is also a new wharf and an additional landfill in the harbor.

439. *[North Galveston.]* Minneapolis(?): North Galveston Association, ca. 1895. Color, scale indeterminable, 35 × 41 cm. Descriptive text.

In the 1890s the North Galveston Association sought to develop this area north of Dickinson Bayou. The site had been known as San Leon (see no. 278) and Edward's Point, and it already had some buildings: in 1886 a post office, a church, and a daily stage line served the community.

This promotional map and an accompanying pamphlet, *Nature's Choice: North Galveston, Texas* (in the library's manuscripts collection) tout the site as a fruit and truck-garden center. The town struggled in its early years. Heavily damaged by the hurricane of 1900, North Galveston never attained projected growth. By 1912 the town was again called San Leon (see no. 484); by 1959, the area had only approximately 100 residents; and it has never become a citrus fruit and truck farming center.

The map shows some of the tracks of the North Galveston, Houston and Kansas City Railroad, chartered in 1892. Sixteen miles of track were laid from North Galveston before this railroad was incorporated with the La Porte, Houston and Northern Railroad in 1895.

440. *Alta Loma Galveston County, Texas.* Surveyed and platted by C. A. Sias for the Alta Loma Investment and Improvement Company. Lithographed by Clarke & Courts. Galveston, 1895. Scale 1 in. to 200 ft., 34 × 57 cm. Descriptive text.

Founded in 1893, Alta Loma is another of the railroad towns in southwestern Galveston County (see no. 421 for further information on the founding). This map shows forty blocks of various sizes around the Gulf, Colorado and Santa Fe Railway tracks (see also no. 441).

441. *Plat of Alta Loma Galveston County, Texas Showing Location of 10, 20 and 40 Acre Tracts.* Designed and platted by C. A. Sias for the Alta Loma Investment and Improvement Company. Lithographed by Clarke & Courts. Galveston, ca. 1895. Scale 1 in. to 1,360 ft., 50 × 62 cm. Inset: "Map showing location of Alta Loma, Galveston, State of Texas." Text: "Fruits Flowers Vegetables."

Alta Loma appears on a smaller scale and in far less detail than on no. 440. The map focuses on the surrounding area and shows outlots intended as fruit orchards.

442. *Texas City First and Second Divisions.* Texas City Improvement Co. Lithographed by Clarke & Courts. Galveston, ca. 1895. Color, scale 1 in. to 400 ft., 46 × 57 cm. Inset: "Map Showing Location of Texas City, Texas. Texas City Improvement Company, Props. Galveston, Texas." Vignette: "Texas City Hotel—under construction."

In 1893 the Texas City Improvement Company began to develop the townsite formerly known as Shoal Point, which already had a population of three hundred. The company constructed a four-mile railroad to connect with the Gulf, Colorado and Santa Fe Railway and began port improvements by dredging an eight-foot-deep channel. In 1898 this company sold its interests to the Mainland Company.

The map shows 125 blocks and locates existing buildings. The railroad line appears to be completed, but the channel is still labeled "proposed." Sold lots are marked with an *X*.

The attempt to establish a port at this site was initially a failure. The 1899 Sanborn map for Galveston (see no. 473) shows a portion of Texas City, with the following comments: "No fire apparatus—Boom Town— Buildings scattered, few occupied." The Sanborn map locates the Texas City Hotel ("not completed, work suspended, vacant all sides"), the Texas

City Mill & Elevator Co. ("not running—going to ruins") and the Texas City Compress ("not in operation—going to ruins"). However, a supplementary Sanborn sheet, dated 1906, indicates an improved situation, showing a number of buildings, including the hotel, in use.

443. *Map of Harris County, Texas.* Anonymous. N.p., 1895. Color, scale 1 in. to 4,000 varas, 59 × 79 cm. Inset: "Map of Harris and Adjoining Counties Showing locations of Townsites."

Although similar to the General Land Office map of Harris County (see no. 433), this is a privately published promotional map. Many new features have been added: towns (La Porte, Pasadena, Deer Park, Clinton, Aldine, Genoa, Webster, Stella, etc.), railroads (S.A. & A.P.R.R., La Porte R.R.), and a ship channel cutting across Morgan's Point.

444. *Map of Liberty County.* Texas. General Land Office. Austin. Lithographed by A. Gast Bank Note & Lithography Co. St. Louis, n.d. Copyright by the General Land Office, 1895. Scale 1:133,320, 60 × 65 cm. (See no. 368 for further information.)

445. *Map of Wharton County.* Texas. General Land Office. Austin. Lithographed by A. Gast Bank Note & Lithography Co. St. Louis, n.d. Copyright by the General Land Office, 1895. Scale 1:133,320, 57 × 64 cm. (See no. 368 for further information.)

446. *Rand McNally & Co.'s Texas.* Chicago: Rand McNally & Co., 1896. Photostat of printed map, scale 1 degree to 69.16 mi., 59 × 80 cm. From Rand McNally's *New Business Atlas.* Inset: "Southern Portion of Texas." Keys identifying railroads and the populations of larger cities.

447. *Galveston Harbor Texas.* United States Army Corps of Engineers. Surveyed by E. M. Hartrick and R. B. Talfor, under the direction of A. M. Miller. N.p., 1897. Blueprint, scale 1:10,000, 94 × 152 cm. Donated by the U.S. Army Corps of Engineers, Galveston Office, 1925.

This map shows Galveston's newly completed jetty system and other harbor improvements. Conspicuous is the regular, deep harbor entrance channel attained after two years of dredging by the Corps of Engineers. By 1898 the outer bar would be 25.5 feet deep and the inner bar 26 feet, almost twice the depth across the bars only ten years earlier. The new jetty system has also increased land area on the eastern end of the island.

448. *County Map of Texas.* Copyright by S. Augustus Mitchell. Philadelphia, 1890. Color, scale 1 in. to approx. 70 mi., 27 × 34.5 cm. Inset: "Galveston Bay, and Vicinity."

449. *Galveston Entrance.* United States Coast and Geodetic Survey. Copied from the 1850–51 survey sheets by Andrew Braid. Washington, D.C., 1898. Blueprint, scale 1:20,000, 64 × 99 cm. (See no. 298 for photographic copies of the 1850–51 survey sheets.)

450. *Map of Fort Bend Co.* Copied by O. O. Terrel. N.p., 1914. Blueline, scale 1:133,320, 40 × 54 cm.

A commercially published copy of the General Land Office map of 1898.

451. *Sketch showing possibilities of a Light Draft Navigation from Deep Water of the Gulf of Mexico, to the Coast Country of Texas. Based on approximate information received from local sailing masters.* United States Army Corps of Engineers(?). N.p., 1898. Blueprint, with some color, scale indeterminable, 50 × 58 cm.

This map highlights in yellow the intracoastal areas and lower reaches of rivers where navigation was "now possible," and in red those where dredging was necessary to make the waters passable. It was probably constructed in connection with the continuing proposals for the Gulf Intracoastal Waterway. First surveyed and approved by the U.S. Congress in 1873, the waterway project languished until 1905. At that time Texas and Louisiana businessmen renewed efforts to complete the work. The two-hundred-mile section below Galveston was completed in 1913.

452. *[Fort Point.]* Henry C. Ripley. Galveston, 1897–99. Blueprints, scale indeterminable, eleven 19.5 × 25.5 cm. numbered sheets, disbound.

Ripley was a major in the Army Corps of Engineers and probably first produced these drawings for corps business. A note on one sheet indicates Ripley referred to them during his testimony in the Galveston City Company vs. Walter Gresham et al. case (Galveston County District Court, no. 16,546) in 1904.

453A. *Harris County Texas.* P. Whitty, Houston. Printed by E. P. Noll & Co. 1899. Color, scale 1 in. to 6,000 varas, 44 × 59 cm. Untitled inset: United States. Tables: Houston's taxable wealth, bank clearances, population, and cotton trade.

B. Another issue: same title, cartographer, printer, scale, and size, but revised 1903. Inset and tables omitted, but large blank rectangle added to lower left-hand corner.

454. *[Val Verde County.]* Texas. General Land Office. Austin. 1899. Ink on cloth, scale 1 in. to 2,000 varas, 58 × 54 cm. From the Texas Land and Loan Company records among the C. L. Beissner papers (Rosenberg Library, ms. no. 77-0004).

455A. *Map of Galveston Wharf Co.'s Property Showing location of Wharves Tracks & Buildings.* C. A. Sias for the Galveston Wharf Company. Galveston, 1900. Blueprint, scale 1 in. to 300 ft., 33 × 105 cm.

B. Another issue: same title, scale, and size, but lacking the imprint and revised, 1902.

Between 1900 and 1930 the Galveston Wharf Company prepared a series of plans showing the evolution of the company's property between 1856 and 1929. Those plans dated after 1900 were drawn from actual surveys. Those dated before 1900 are historical maps, compiled by studying other maps, records, etc. (See nos. 510 and 511 for other versions of this map set.)

456A. *The Galveston Storm. Saturday, September 8, 1900.* Anonymous. Galveston, 1900. Scale indeterminable, 36.5 × 44 cm. Keys identifying various levels of damage and thirty-two sites. Decorative border and panels with advertising. Three copies, one donated by Mrs. E. B. Labadie, 1922.

B. Another issue: same title and keys, but 34 × 42 cm., folding into printed paper wrappers. Decorative border and advertising panels omitted. Donated by the Texas Historical Society of Galveston, 1931.

C. Another issue: *Map of Galveston, Showing Destruction By The Storm.* Scale indeterminable, 43 × 51 cm. From the September 27, 1900, issue of the *Houston Post*. Same keys, but some repositioned, with explanatory text added and decorative border and advertising panels omitted.

457. *Map of Galveston Island Lots*. R. C. Trimble and William Lindsey. Lithographed by Clarke & Courts. Galveston, ca. 1900. Scale indetermin-able, 33.5 x 55.5 cm.

A turn-of-the-century printed version of Trimble and Lindsey's manu-script map of 1837 (see no. 255).

458. *Plan for the improvement of Galveston Harbor By Colonel H. M. Robert, Divisional Engineer: U.S. Army*. George W. Grover. Galveston, 1900. Ink on paper, scale 5 in. to approx. 6 mi., 28 × 42.5 cm. Two small manuscript maps on verso: "Geographical outline—Vicinity of East End of Galveston Island"; "Plan for the Improvement of Galveston Harbor—Published in Galv. News May 7, 1900."

This manuscript illustrates Robert's intriguing and ambitious plan to transform the harbor. The plan proposed combining Pelican Island and Pelican Spit into one large "Pelican Territory, 7,000 Acres." The new ter-ritory would connect with Texas City by a strip of landfill capable of carry-ing rail transportation. Galveston Island would also be greatly enlarged around Teichman's Point so that only a narrow channel would separate the island from Virginia Point.

Robert's plan received strong support, as it was hoped that the improved harbor facilities would bring a U.S. Navy yard to Galveston. Grover drew this map for display at the Galveston Public Library. Unfortunately, how-ever seriously the plan may have been considered during the summer of 1900, the disastrous hurricane in September ended all thought of altering the harbor to fit this scheme.

459. *Galveston Bay, Texas, showing proposed improvement of Galveston channel*. United States Army Corps of Engineers. Surveyed by E. M. Hart-rick under the direction of C. S. Riche. Drawn by H. J. Condron. Wash-ington, D.C., 1900. Scale 1 in. to approx. 1,050 ft., 49.5 × 61 cm. House Document no. 264, 56th Congress, 2d session.

This map shows the harbor, a small Pelican Island, Pelican Spit, most of the east end of the island, and part of the city. In the years following this view, the Corps of Engineers discharged dredge material on Pelican

Island and eventually increased the island to its present size, absorbing the former spit.

460. *Correct Map of Winnie Suburbs Chambers County, Texas.* R. W. Luttrell. Galveston: Southwest Co., 1900. Originally published by the Winnie Loan and Improvement Co., n.p., n.d. Color, scale 1:7,200, 37 × 50 cm. Untitled inset: Winnie and vicinity.

461. *Map of Galveston Texas. Compiled from Latest Surveys and Best Authorities.* Baltimore: H. V. Gormley, Union Map & Atlas Co., 1901. Scale indeterminable, 45 × 70 cm., folding into paper covers.

462. *Map of Algoa Suburbs Galveston County, Texas.* B. I. Willcoxon. Printed by Clarke & Courts. Galveston, ca. 1901. Scale 1 in. to 300 varas, 50 × 57 cm. Insets: "Map of the Town of Algoa Galveston County, Texas"; untitled map of Algoa and vicinity.

Another of the Gulf, Colorado and Santa Fe Railway towns, Algoa was named for a British ship driven inland by the 1900 hurricane and not refloated for sixteen months. On the map the Leon & H. Blum Land Co. and the Turnley Real Estate Co. are listed as the owners and general agents, respectively, of the Algoa land. One of these firms probably commissioned Willcoxon to draw this map.

The main map shows the town of Algoa and thirty-eight surrounding outblocks. The large titled inset shows only Algoa, bisected diagonally by the railroad tracks.

463. *Clarke & Courts' Map of Jefferson County and Beaumont and Sour Lake Oil Fields.* G. H. Derrick. Galveston: Clarke & Courts, 1901. Scale indeterminable, 55 × 65 cm.

The copyright date on the map is "May, 1901," meaning it was printed just four months after the first gusher came in at Spindletop, touching off the oil boom in Texas. The map locates approximately one dozen producing wells and an equal number being drilled.

464. *Map of Sections 1, 2, 3 & 4 Galveston Island Galveston County Texas Resurvey of 1901.* R. W. Luttrell. Galveston, 1902. Blueprint, scale 1:10,000, 72 × 142 cm. Inset: "Galveston Island, continued."

Since 1837, when Trimble and Lindsey conducted the original survey of Galveston Island, the contour of the island had changed significantly, necessitating this resurvey. Luttrell preserves the four Trimble and Lindsey sections and their ten-acre lots and lot numbers, though most of the shoreline lots have increased or decreased in size, depending upon shoreline changes. Luttrell also records the Hall and Jones sections of 1839 and many human and topographical details.

465. Maps of *Texas* and *The World.* A. H. Belo & Co. Printed by Rand McNally & Co. Chicago, 1902. Color, scale varies, 67 × 100 cm. sheet, one map on each side. Inset on *Texas:* "Southern Portion of Texas." Census table on each map.

Published as a supplement to the *Galveston Daily News* and the *Dallas Morning News.*

466A. *Map of the City of Galveston Texas.* Compiled by C. G. Wells. Printed by Clarke & Courts. Galveston, 1904. Scale indeterminable, 77.5 × 114 cm. Insets: "Map of Galveston Bay;" three cross sections of the seawall.

B. Another issue: identical, except 41 × 54.5 cm.

Wells's map shows the new Galveston emerging after the 1900 hurricane. Each existing building is outlined, with the more important ones emphasized in black; none are identified. The new seawall runs along the Gulf shore from Thirty-ninth Street to Sixth Street, cuts north across the island, and terminates at the south jetty, just east of the medical school. In the western part of the city, a levee extends north from the seawall as a partial barrier to flooding from the unprotected western end of the island.

467. *Geological Map of a Portion of West Texas Showing parts of Brewster, Presidio, Jeff. Davis, and El Paso Counties, and South of the Southern Pacific R.R.* University of Texas Mineral Survey. Drawn by Benjamin F. Hill and J. A. Udden under the direction of William B. Phillips. Engraved by C. P. Scrivener. Printed by Matthews-Northrup Work, Buffalo, New York, 1904. Color, scale indeterminable, 92 × 127 cm. Key identifying geological formations by color.

This map is based on United States Geological Survey maps and field work by Phillips, Hill, and Udden.

468. *Map of East End of Galveston Island.* United States Army Corps of Engineers. Galveston, 1905. Blueprint, scale 1:10,000, 52 × 52 cm.

469. *Map of Texas City and Vicinity.* C. S. Corrigan, for the Texas City Realty Co. N.p., 1905. Blueprint, scale 1 in. to 2,000 ft., 76 × 81 cm. Untitled inset: Galveston and Texas City vicinity.

470. *Map of Texas City, Galveston County, Texas.* Texas City Company. Printed by Clarke and Courts. Galveston, 1905. Scale 1 in. to 400 ft., 46 × 58 cm. Inset: "Map showing location of Texas City."

471A. *Railroad and County Map of Texas.* Texas. Railroad Commission. Printed by Woodward & Tiernan. St. Louis, 1905. Color, scale 1 in. to 25 mi., 80 × 89 cm.

B. Another issue: same title, issuing agency, printer, and color, but compiled and drawn by R. A. Thompson, 1906. Scale 1 in. to 18 mi., 105 × 110 cm.

C. Another issue: same title, issuing agency, compiler, printer, color, scale, and size (as issue B), but revised 1908.

D. Another issue: *Official Railroad and County Map of Texas.* Same issuing agency, printer, scale, and size (as issue B), but revised 1912.

E. Another issue: Same title (as issue D), issuing agency, printer, and scale (as issue B), but revised 1914, and 106 × 108 cm.

F. Another issue: Same title (as issue D), issuing agency, printer, and scale, but revised 1917, and 106 × 111 cm.

472. *Soil Map. Texas, Houston County Sheet.* United States Department of Agriculture. Bureau of Soils. Surveyed by William T. Carter and A. E. Kocher. Printed by A. Hoen & Co. Baltimore, 1905. Color, scale 1 in. to 1 mi., 91 × 113 cm., cloth-backed. Key identifying soil types.

473. *Insurance Maps of Galveston Texas.* New York: Sanborn-Perris Map Co., 1899. Color, scale 1 in. to 50 ft., 101 52 × 62 cm. sheets, bound in folio volume, all sheets with paste-down overlays showing revisions to 1906. (See no. 392 for further information and nos. 436 and 481 for other editions.)

474. *Kokernot & Kokernot Ranch in Lubbock County Texas.* Surveyed by W. D. Twichell, state surveyor. Drawn by M. J. McCombs, 1907. Blueprint, scale indeterminable, 73 × 88 cm.

475. *Map of Galveston Bay.* Anonymous. N.p., n.d. Scale 1 in. to 2.5 mi., 33 × 38 cm. Together with *Map of Port Bolivar Galveston Co. Texas.* Drawn by R. W. Luttrell. Galveston: the Port Bolivar City Company, n.d. Scale 1 in. to 1,304 ft., 33.5 × 36.5 cm. On 59.5 × 71 cm. sheet, with descriptive text on Port Bolivar on lower panel. Sheet printed by August Gast Bank Note & Lithography Co., St. Louis, published by the Port Bolivar City Company, Galveston, ca. 1895.

Map of Galveston Bay shows Galveston, North Galveston, La Porte, the newly completed jetties, and the proposed city of Port Bolivar. *Map of Port Bolivar* is a close-up view of the projected city.

476A. *Galveston Entrance.* United States Coast and Geodetic Survey. Washington, D.C. First published 1856. Revised 1909. Scale 1:40,000, 39.5 × 53.5 cm. Coast chart no. 520.

B. Another issue: same title, issuing agency, size, scale, and chart number, but revised 1916, with lights, beacons, buoys, and dangers corrected for 1918. Notes on tides and storm warnings.

C. Another issue: same title, issuing agency, size, and chart number, but revised 1931–32. Scale 1 in. to approx. 890 yards. Notes on soundings, tides, improved channels, storm warnings, and radio beacon signals.

477. *Texas.* Chicago: Rand McNally & Co., 1909. Color, scale indeterminable, 66 × 97 cm. Key identifying 103 railroads.

478. *[Houston-Galveston Area.]* Houston; A. B. Mayes & Co., ca. 1910. Scale 1 in. to approx. 4 mi., 44 × 60 cm.

479. *Cram's Superior Reference Atlas: Texas & The Great Southwest.*
George F. Cram. Chicago, ca. 1910. Quarto, 208 pages, cloth binding. Accompanied by folding map in manila pocket on back cover, *Texas and Oklahoma,* corrected and revised by George F. Cram, copyright by the Geographical Publishing Co., Chicago, 1907. Color, scale 1 in. to 26 mi., 65 × 89 cm.

A world atlas with promotional material on Texas, including photographs, maps, statistical tables, and descriptions added in the front. The folding map shows the 1910 congressional districts.

480. *[Seymour, Texas.]* Anonymous. N.p., n.d. Ink and pencil on paper, scale indeterminable, 52 × 74 cm. From the C. L. Beissner Papers.

This map shows the C. C. Mill Elevator and Light Company property in Seymour.

481A. *Insurance Maps of Galveston Texas.* New York: Sanborn Map Company, 1912. Color, scale 1 in. to 50 ft., 115 52 × 62 cm. sheets, bound into folio volume, all sheets with paste-down overlays showing revisions to 1931. (See no. 392 for further information and nos. 436 and 473 for other editions.)

B. Another issue: same title, publisher, and date on title page, but copyright 1948, with overlays showing revisions to 1955 and bound into two folio volumes.

C. Another issue: same title, publisher, date on title page, copyright, and two-volume format (as issue B), but with overlays showing revisions to 1961.

482A. *Revised Map of the City of Galveston.* Compiled by A. T. Dickey. Engraved by E. G. Cain. Galveston: Clarke & Courts, 1912. Scale 1 in. to 800 ft., 46 × 76 cm. Key identifying sixty sites. Four diagrams showing division of city blocks and outlots into lots.

B. Another issue: identical, except 21 × 35 cm.

The map focuses on the Broadway Addition at the western edge of the Denver resurvey.

483. *Easterly End of Galveston Island showing Area for which Patent is Desired from the State of Texas.* United States Army Corps of Engineers. Drawn under the direction of Earl I. Brown. Galveston, 1912. Blueprint, scale 1 in. to approx. 850 ft., 25 × 79.5 cm. Text describing the area. Donated by Mrs. W. B. Lockhart, 1922.

484. *Map of San Leon Farm Home Tracts, Galveston County, Texas.* San Leon Company, San Leon, Texas. Photographs by Wilbert Davis. Printed by Rein & Sons Co. Houston, 1912. Color, scale 1 in. to 1,000 ft., 37 × 40 cm. map on 52 × 78 cm. sheet, surrounded by fifteen photographs and promotional text. On verso: "Houston-Galveston District," bird's-eye view showing the location of San Leon, plus additional photographs and text.

This is the same site that the North Galveston Association promoted just a few years earlier (see no. 439). San Leon varies little from the proposed North Galveston—the agricultural outlots vary slightly (there are 104 instead of 102 on the North Galveston plan), as does the exact positioning of a few streets and the location of proposed and constructed railroads. The developers still touted the site as perfect for citrus farming. Lots already planted in Satsuma oranges appear in orange; those planted in "truck and field crops" are in green.

485. *Conroe, County Seat of Montgomery County, Texas.* Anonymous, n.p., ca. 1912. Blueprint, scale 1 in. to 200 ft., 36 × 53 cm.

This blueprint focuses on a nineteen-block section of Conroe bounded on the south by the Gulf, Colorado and Santa Fe Railway tracks, and on the west by the International and Great Northern Railway. The latter line was officially known by that name between 1911 and 1914. It is now part of the Missouri Pacific System.

486. *Subdivision of Lemuel Smith League, Montgomery Co. Tex.* Anonymous. N.p., ca. 1912. Blueprint, scale 1 in. to 400 ft., 42 × 62 cm. Donated by the J. C. League estate, 1924.

A companion to no. 485, this is a plat map of the area one mile to the east of Conroe.

487. *Sketch Map of Galveston Island.* United States Army Corps of Engineers. Made under the direction of T. H. Dillon, Galveston, 1913. Based on the map made under the direction of C. O. Sherrill, 1911. Blueprint, scale 1 in. to ⅓ mi., three sheets joined into one 35 × 132 cm. sheet.

This map of the central part of Galveston Island, from Twenty-fifth Street west to approximately sixteen miles down the island, provides a wealth of topographic and human detail. The corps probably prepared the plan in connection with federal improvements on Galveston Island following the hurricane of 1900.

488. *Map of San Jacinto Battlefield Reservation.* United States Army Corps of Engineers. Surveyed under the direction of W. L. Guthrie. Drawn by George A. Brown, Galveston, 1913. Blueprint, scale 1 in. to 200 ft., 49 × 120 cm. Key identifying twenty battlefield monuments.

489. *Proposed Extension of Seawall with Railroad access to same, Galveston, Texas.* United States Army Corps of Engineers. Galveston, 1914. Blueprint, scale 1 in. to 400 ft., 70 × 104 cm., poor condition. Diagrams: cross section of seawall and south jetty; "Borings."

This plan shows Galveston Island east of Fourteenth Street. Work on the original seawall began in 1902 and ended in 1904 (see no. 466). In 1913, the corps reported that the original seawall route left the east end flats unprotected. A severe storm may cut a channel across the east end of the island and breach the jetty. By 1914, plans were underway to extend the seawall eastward from Sixth Street to Fort San Jacinto in the east end flats.

490A. *Brazos River Entrance.* United States. Coast and Geodetic Survey, Washington, D.C., 1915, lights, beacons, buoys and dangers corrected to 1916. Color, scale 1:25,000, 76 × 98 cm. Coast chart no. 520. Notes on tides, storm warnings, and soundings.

B. Another issue: same title, issuing agency, scale, size, chart number, and notes, but revised 1932. Note added: "Caution Improved Channel."

491A. *Visitors' Map of Galveston.* Oscar Springer. Galveston, 1915. Scale indeterminable, 48 × 58 cm., folding into stiff paper wrappers. Untitled inset: Galveston Bay area. Text on wrappers: "A Detailed Automobilist's Guide from Galveston to Houston." Key identifying 131 sites.

B. Another issue: same title, publisher, size, and inset, but revised 1921. Pictorial wrappers altered and lacking text.

492A. *Houston Ship Channel.* United States. Coast and Geodetic Survey. Washington, D.C., 1915. Lights, beacons, buoys, and dangers corrected to 1916. Scale 1:25,000, 75 × 78 cm., Coast chart no. 532. Notes on tides and channel.

B. Another issue: same title, issuing agency, scale, size, and chart number, but revised 1932, with lights, beacons, buoys, and dangers corrected to 1926. Channel note also revised.

C. Another issue: same title, issuing agency, scale, size, chart number, and notes (as issue B), but revised 1926, with lights, beacons, buoys, and dangers corrected to 1927.

D. Another issue: same title, issuing agency, scale, size, chart number, and notes (as issue B), but revised 1930, with lights, beacons, buoys, and dangers corrected to 1932.

These four charts, showing the area from Morgan's Point to Houston, provide an excellent summary of the changes that occurred in and around the Houston ship channel from 1915 to 1932. The growth during this period is tremendous. The turning basin has been enlarged; Houston has expanded rapidly southwestward; and new towns, roads, railroad facilities, and oil refineries have developed.

493. *San Luis Pass to Matagorda Bay.* United States Coast and Geodetic Survey. Washington, D.C., 1915. Lights, beacons, buoys, and dangers corrected to 1916. Scale 1:80,000, 81 × 118 cm. Coast chart no. 1281. Notes on tides and storm warnings.

494. *Road Map of Galveston County, Texas.* R. M. Sias. Galveston, 1917. Blueline, scale 1:10,000, 53 × 85 cm. Donated by C. C. Washington, 1925.

495. *Cahill Cemetery.* Anonymous. Surveyed for B. W. Key, Galveston, 1920. Blueprint, scale 1 in. to 20 ft., 36 × 40 cm.

This map of plot owners was compiled before Cahill Cemetery (Evergreen) was improved in 1920–21 (see no. 499).

496. *Birdseye View of the Port of Galveston, U.S.A.* Galveston Commercial Association. Galveston, ca. 1920. Scale indeterminable, 26.5 × 68 cm.

A panorama of Galveston identifying harbor facilities (pier, elevators, mills, etc.).

497. *Washington County.* Compiled by Tom Atlee. Traced by J. Bascom Giles. N.p., 1920. Copied from the General Land Office map. Blueline, scale 1 in. to 4,000 varas, 35 × 53 cm.

498. *Galveston Harbor, Texas. U.S. Harbor Lines. Galveston Harbor, Galveston Channel, Texas City and Port Bolivar.* United States Army Corps of Engineers. Made by J. W. Henderson under the direction of L. M. Adams. Drawn by A. L., Galveston, 1921. Reverse blueprint, scale indeterminable, two sheets forming one 66 × 100 cm. map. Donated by L. M. Adams, 1921.

This technical map shows public works and harbor facilities at Galveston, Texas City, and Bolivar Point. The map locates numerous monuments, giving geodetic points essential to surveys.

499. *Map of the Cahill Cemetery.* Compiled by C. A. Holt. Galveston, 1921. Blueprint, scale indeterminable, 79 × 80 cm. Donated by the Galveston City Engineer, 1929.

Between July, 1920, and March, 1921, Galveston's parks department improved and altered this cemetery (see also no. 495). The map shows plot owners. One copy also has several names added in red pencil.

500. *Map of Trinity Episcopal Church Cemetery, Block No. 100, City of Galveston, Texas.* Surveyed and compiled by E. G. Cain. Galveston, 1921. Blueprint, scale 1 in. to approx. 12 ft., 78 × 93 cm.

501. *Soil Map. Texas. Harris County.* United States Department of Agriculture. Bureau of Soils. In cooperation with the Texas Agricultural Experiment Station. Surveyed by H. V. Gelb, T. M. Bushnell, and A. H. Bauer. Printed by A. Hoen. Baltimore, 1922. Color, scale 1 in. to 1 mi., two sheets forming one 115 × 164 cm. map. Key identifying soil types and topographical features.

502A. *Galveston Bay and Approaches.* United States Coast and Geodetic Survey. Washington, D.C., 1922. Scale 1:80,000, 81.5 × 109 cm. Coastal chart no. 1282. Inset: "Continuation of Galveston Bay [Turtle Bay]." Notes on soundings, tides, and buoys.

B. Another issue: same title, issuing agency, scale, size, chart number, inset, and notes, but revised 1925, with lights, beacons, buoys, and dangers corrected to 1930. Overprinted in red to show cable and pipeline areas. Added note: "Radio beacon signals."

C. Another issue: same title, issuing agency, scale, size, chart number, inset, notes, and overprint (as issue B), but revised 1932.

D. Another issue: same title, issuing agency, scale, size, chart number, and inset, but revised 1945, with lights, beacons, buoys, and dangers corrected to 1949. Now color, but the overprinting is omitted. Notes extensively revised. Table added: "Galveston Bay Channel Depths."

Each issue updates hydrographic information (depth soundings, buoys, beacons and coastal topographic detail (new roads and buildings, alterations in shorelines). Shoreline alterations are often marked, particularly for Pelican Island and Spit, which merge on issue D, and the eastern tip of Galveston Island.

503A. *Oil and Gas Fields of the State of Texas.* United States Geological Survey. Compiled by Lewis B. Pusey under the direction of G. B. Richardson. Washington, D.C., 1924. Color, scale 1:750,000, two 87 × 134 cm. sheets. Key identifying oil and gas symbols.

B. Another issue: same title, issuing agency, scale, size, format, and key, but revised 1925.

504. *New City (Yellow Fever) and New Cahill Cemeteries.* Galveston City Engineer, C. A. Holt. Drawn by John B. Wointon. Galveston, 1925. Blueprint, scale indeterminable, 54 × 75 cm. Donated by the Galveston City Engineer's Office, 1929.

This plat map shows the name of each cemetery plot owner only.

505. *City of Galveston's plat of Subdivisions of Ave K, 40–43 St's, for cemetery purposes only.* Galveston City Engineer, C. A. Holt. For the Galveston Board of Commissioners. Galveston, 1926. Blueprint, scale 1 in. to 60 ft., 26 × 55 cm.

The map legend identifies property conveyed to the Evergreen (Cahill), Hebrew, Catholic, and Episcopal cemeteries. To give these cemeteries more space, the city narrowed Avenue K between Fortieth and Forty-third streets.

506. *[Galveston.]* Drawn by K. H. Kathan. N.p., 1927. Blueline, scale indeterminable, 70 × 105 cm.

507. *Railroads and Prospective Railroads, Freeport Harbor. High Voltage Lines—Natural Gas Pipe Lines.* Compiled by the Freeport Harbor Association. Freeport, Texas, 1927. Blueprint, scale 1 in. to approx. 3 mi., 67 × 77 cm. Donated by the Brazos River Harbor Navigation District of Brazoria County, 1927.

This map locates the high voltage and natural gas lines within a sixty-mile radius of Freeport.

508. *Map of the City of Galveston Texas.* E. G. Cain. Galveston, 1928. Reverse blueprint, scale 1 in. to 200 ft., eleven 40.5 × 72.5 cm. folding sheets, bound together to form one map. Inset: "Map showing location of the City of Galveston on East End of Galveston Island." Five diagrams showing the divisions of city blocks.

This is the most detailed map of Galveston for this period. All subdivisions and additions, including the Denver resurvey, public sites and buildings, important industrial and commercial structures, railroads, wharves, are located and generally identified.

509. *Proposed County Park, Trimble & Lindsey Survey Sec. No. 1 Galveston Island.* Galveston County Surveyor, C. C. Washington. Galveston, 1928. Blueprint, scale 1 in. to 200 ft., 52 × 90 cm.

The map shows "Dredging Company Property," with boundaries marked by hatching. In 1929 Raymond A. Perry, president of the North American Dredging Company, gave this land along Offat's Bayou to the county for development as a county park, later known as Perry Park. The irregularly shaped property borders the Highland Park Addition on two sides. Part of the site is occupied by another subdivision, which is divided into small lots and named Oceanview Addition.

The full park was never built, because of the depression, which stripped development funds; World War II, which brought about the construction of an airfield on the property; and lengthy legal battles concerning land usage. Nevertheless, smaller versions of the park do appear on several later maps, including nos. 523 and 538 (1958). A center of activity in the 1950s, Perry Park is no longer maintained, and its future as a city park is uncertain.

510. *Map of Galveston Wharf Co's. Property Showing Location of Wharves.* Galveston Wharf Co. Compiled by N. J. Anderson. Galveston, 1927. Revised 1929. Blueprints, scale 1 in. to 300 ft., twelve 29 × 105 cm. sheets, bound in manila wrappers. (See no. 455 for additional information.)

511. *Map of Galveston Wharf Co's. Property Showing Location of Wharves.* Galveston Wharf Co. Compiled by N. J. Anderson. Galveston, 1929. Revised ca. 1930. Photostats of blueprints, scale indeterminable, seventeen 22 × 56 cm. sheets, bound in manila wrappers.

The same set as no. 510, but including five additional source maps, dated 1877–1902. (See no. 455 for further information.)

512. *Gulf of Mexico and Caribbean Sea including The West Indies.* United States Navy Hydrographic Office. Washington, D.C., 1982. 104th edition. 1925. Revised 1931. Color, scale 1:3,322,519, 83 × 125 cm. Chart no. 1290. Donated by Harold J. Bellingham, Navy Hydrographic Office, 1932.

513. *Railroad Map of Gulf Southwest showing location of Cotton Compresses and Cottonseed Oil Mills.* United States Army Corps of Engineers. Washington, D.C., 1931. Color, scale indeterminable, 55 × 71 cm.

514. *Sabine Pass and Lake Louisiana and Texas.* United States Coast and Geodetic Survey. Washington, D.C., 1930. Color, scale 1:40,000, lights, beacons, buoys, and dangers corrected to 1932. Coast chart no. 517. Notes on tides, canal beacons, and storm warnings.

515. *Traffic Survey, Galveston, Texas.* Anonymous. Traced by A. T. L. Blueprint, scale 1 in. to 800 ft., 46 × 120 cm.

A general map of Galveston, illustrating the relative volume of traffic on the city's streets.

516A. *City of Galveston, Texas.* Santa Fe Railway Engineering Department. Drawn by R. Neumann. Galveston, 1933. Blueline, scale 1 in. to approx. 800 ft., 64 × 139 cm. Inset: "Galveston Island and Vicinity." Keys identifying important sites. Donated by J. L. Starkie, 1933.

B. Another issue: same title, issuing organization, and keys, but undated, printed, and 40 × 68 cm. Untitled inset: eastern tip of Galveston Island.

C. Another issue: same title, issuing organization, and inset (as issue A), but revised 1950. Photostat of blueprint, scale 1 in. to 1,500 ft., 38 × 80 cm. Extensive manuscript notations and revisions, especially to Pelican Island and the harbor channel.

This map gives good detail of the city's harbor, industrial, and transportation facilities.

517. *Confederate Fortifications, 1865, Galveston & Vicinity.* S. J. Hannig. N.p., 1933. Ink on cloth, scale indeterminable, 61 × 94 cm.

A note on the verso gives the sources of the information in this map. The map shows the shoreline of 1865 (in blue) overlaid with the shoreline of 1933 (in black). The information on Confederate fortifications is chiefly from the 1865 maps nos. 332 and 333, with alternate names for some forts supplied from other sources.

518. *Highway Map of Texas.* R. M. Steve. Published by the *Dallas Morning News.* 1932. Scale indeterminable, 50 × 63 cm. Key: "Guide to Location of State and Federal Highways in Texas." On verso: *A Map of Texas.* Published by the *Dallas Morning News.* Color, scale indeterminable, 80 × 63 cm. Key: "Guide to location of Counties & Railroads." Both maps published for the 1933 edition of the *Texas Almanac and State Industrial Guide.*

519. *Sinclair 1933 Official Road Map, Texas.* Sinclair Oil Company. Copyright by Rand McNally & Co. Chicago, 1933. Color, scale 1 in. to approx. 30 mi., 49 × 67 cm. Insets: "Brownsville Section"; "Panhandle Section." On verso: *Sinclair Pictorial United States,* plus advertising.

520. *East End Flats Owners of Record Dec. 1935.* Galveston. City Engineer, W. B. McGarvey. Galveston, 1933. Blueprint, scale 1 in. to 100 ft., 88 × 92 cm.

This map shows landowners in the area east of Sixth Street and west of the United States Government Reserve on the tip of the island.

521. *Rand McNally Standard Map of Texas.* Chicago: Rand McNally & Co., ca. 1935. Color, scale 1 in. to 25 mi., 66 × 83 cm. Insets: "Western Part of Texas"; "Dallas, Ft. Worth and Vicinity"; "Houston, Galveston and Vicinity." Key Identifying railroads. On verso: *Rand McNally Standard Map of Texas with Air Trails.* Same map overprinted to show airports, flight corridors, and other air traffic features.

522A. *Visitors Guide, City of Galveston Texas.* E. G. Cain. Galveston, 1937. Scale 1 in. to approx. 1,100 ft., 40 × 63 cm., folding into brown paper covers. Keys identifying important sites.

B. Another issue: same title, publisher, scale, and size, but revised 1949, folding into gray paper covers. New keys.

523. *Plat showing development west of city limits in section 1—Trimble and Lindsey Survey of Galveston Island.* Galveston. City Engineer. Drawn by K. H. Kathan under the direction of W. B. McGarvey. 1931. Revised 1939. Reverse blueprint, scale 1:10,000.

This map records the changes in section one of the Trimble and Lindsey survey since Luttrell's resurvey of 1902 (see no. 464). Most important are the municipal airport (Scholes Field); the Galveston Country Club, now the municipal golf course; and the old government airport, later the site of "Jones Addition" and "Island City Homes." Also shown is a "Proposed

City Park 100 acres" (Perry Park) on the site of the "Proposed County Park" shown on no. 509.

524. *Structural Map of Texas.* University of Texas. Bureau of Economic Geology. Drawn by Atlee Manthos under the direction of E. H. Sellards. 2d edition. Printed by Williams & Heintz Co. Washington, D.C., 1939. Key identifying geological feature symbols.

525. *[Gulf of Mexico.]* Anonymous. N.p., ca. 1942. Scale ⅛ in. to 100 mi. Notation showing the "Path of the Tropical Hurricane August 24–30, 1942."

526. *General Highway Map of Galveston County Texas.* Texas. Highway Department. In cooperation with the United States. Department of Agriculture. Bureau of Public Roads. N.p., 1936. Blueline, scale 1 in. to 2 mi., 45 × 60 cm. Key identifying roads, road surfaces, etc.

527. *Fort Travis Showing Modernization Plan.* United States Army Corps of Engineers. Prepared by Joseph W. Westbrook. Approved by A. V. Rinearson, 1944. Scale 1 in. to 100 ft., 60 × 90 cm. Sheet no. 1 of plan no. 175-F.T.

Fort Travis, built in 1898–99 at the southeastern tip of the Bolivar Peninsula, was heavily damaged in the hurricane of July 27, 1943, and had to be rebuilt. This fort, along with Fort San Jacinto on the island, guarded the entrance to Galveston Bay.

528. *Gulf of Mexico.* United States Coast and Geodetic Survey. 12th edition. Washington, D.C., 1945. Reproduction issued by Wreck Charts, Sarasota, Florida, n.d. Scale indeterminable, two sheets forming one 58 × 68 cm. chart. Accompanied by a photostatic copy of "Wreck Information List Compiled by U.S. Hydrographic Office from available sources corrected to March 10, 1945," U.S. Government Printing Office, Washington, D.C., 1945.

529. *Oleander Homes and Addition.* Galveston Housing Authority. Galveston, 1946. Blueprint, scale indeterminable, 51 × 58 cm.

Shows the position of each building in the Oleander Homes housing project.

530. *General Highway Map, Chambers County, Texas.* Texas. Highway Department. In cooperation with the United States Public Roads Administration. N.p., 1948. Revised 1950. Scale 1 in. to 2 mi., 44 × 61 cm. Seven insets of county towns.

531. *City of La Marque.* Drawn and compiled by Houston J. Frederick. Galveston. Revised 1949. Scale 1 in. to 300 ft., 52.5 × 62 cm.

532. *General Highway Map, Harris County, Texas.* Texas. Highway Department. In cooperation with the United States Department of Commerce. Bureau of Public Roads. Blueline, scale 1 in. to 2 mi., two sheets forming 61 × 90 cm. map.

533. *General Highway Map, Jefferson County, Texas.* Texas. Highway Department. In cooperation with the United States Department of Commerce. Bureau of Public Roads. 1948. Revised 1950. Scale 1 in. to 2 mi., 44 × 61 cm.

534. *General Highway Map, Liberty County, Texas.* Texas. Highway Department. In cooperation with the United States Public Road Administration. 1945. Scale 1 in. to 2 mi., two sheets forming 61 × 88 cm. map. Eight insets of county towns.

535. *General Highway Map, Brazoria County, Texas.* Texas. Bureau of Public Roads. 1946. Revised 1951. Scale 1 in. to 2 mi., two sheets forming 60 × 90 cm. map. Eleven insets of county towns.

536. *General Highway Map, Fort Bend County, Texas.* Texas. Highway Department. In cooperation with the United States Department of Commerce. Bureau of Public Roads. 1949. Revised 1951. Scale 1 in. to 2 mi., 45 × 61 cm.

537. *Port Facilities, Port of Galveston, Texas. "America's Port of Quick Dispatch."* Galveston Wharves, E. L. Sembler, 1956. Scale indeterminable, 24.5 × 53 cm. Inset: "[Galveston] Vicinity Map."

538A. *City of Galveston, West Part.* Galveston. Tax Department. Gus F. Jud. Revised 1957. Reverse blueprint, scale 1 in. to 300 ft., 70 × 89 cm.

B. Another issue: same title, issuing agency, scale, and size, but revised 1958.

This is a companion to no. 540 (see no. 523 for a close-up view of this area).

539. *Map of Survey of that portion of Fort Crockett, County of Galveston Texas, lying East of 53rd Street & West of 39th Street, City of Galveston.* Surveyed by order of the United States General Services Administration. By Wallace Fones, A. C. Stimson Land Surveying Co., Houston. Revised 1957. Scale indeterminable, on both sides of a 52 × 85 cm. sheet.

Built in 1879, Fort Crockett fell into disuse after World War II. Most of the fort was auctioned off by the General Services Administration in 1957. The remainder was sold to private interests in 1981.

540. *Map of the City of Galveston, Texas, East Part.* Galveston Tax Department. Gus F. Jud. Revised 1958. Reverse blueprint, scale 1 in. to 300 ft., 72 × 107 cm. Insets: "Map Showing Location of the City of Galveston on East End of Galveston Island"; "Map Showing East End of Galveston Island."

Companion to no. 538.

541. *City Map of Texas City, Texas.* Compiled and drawn by Houston J. Frederick. Fort Worth, 1958. Scale indeterminable, 39 × 46.5 cm., folding into paper cover entitled "Visitors Guide City of Texas City, Texas." Key identifies streets, fire stations, public utilities, parks and playgrounds, churches, schools, etc.

542. *City Map of Texas City, Texas.* Produced for the Texas City Chamber of Commerce. By Houston J. Frederick. Fort Worth, 1960. Scale indeterminable, 34 × 55 cm., folding into paper wrappers.

543. *Central Business District, Galveston, Texas.* Produced for the Galveston Chamber of Commerce. By William D. Alpert. N.p., 1963. Reverse blueprint, scale 1 in. to 40 ft., 95 × 110 cm.

Much like the earlier Sanborn maps, this map gives the dimensions, owner, first-floor occupant, land valuation, and building valuation for each lot in the central business district.

544. *Galveston, Texas.* Galveston Chamber of Commerce. Galveston, ca. 1965. Scale 1 in. to 800 ft., 32 × 83 cm. Key identifying twenty-two sites. Photographs of Galveston on verso.

545. *Zoning District Maps, City of Galveston.* Galveston. Planning & Traffic Department. Printed by Carter & Burgess. Houston, ca. 1968. Scale 1 in. to approx. 425 ft., ninety-two 27 × 43 cm. sheets, bound in oblong quarto volume with stiff paper covers.

This plat book shows the zoning districts established in 1968. Despite its title, the book does cover both the west end of the island and Pelican Island, as well as the area within the city limits of Galveston.

546. *[Galveston Island.]* Anonymous. N.p., ca. 1890. Ink on cloth, scale indeterminable, 31 × 49 cm. Donated by Henry J. Runge.

The map shows proposed railroad bridges connecting with the mainland via Deer Island rather than via Virginia Point.

547. *Plan of the City of Galveston Showing Proposed Sea Wall And Raising of Grade.* Galveston. Board of Engineers. Galveston, 1902. Scale indeterminable, on 40 × 54 cm. sheet together with views of the proposed location of the seawall and cross sections of the city showing the proposed fill levels. Descriptive text on proposed work.

In the aftermath of the September 8, 1900, hurricane that flattened most of the city, the city commissioners appointed Henry M. Robert, Alfred Noble, and Henry C. Ripley as the Board of Engineers to devise a plan for protecting the city against hurricanes. The board submitted its report in January, 1902, suggesting that the city build a seawall and raise the grade level. The general outline of this plan, which was adopted, is shown in this map.

548. *Map showing lands originally granted to the Houston & Texas Central Railway Co. in Harris and Waller Cos., Texas.* Houston & Texas Central Railway Co. Printed by Maverick-Clarke Lithography Co. San Antonio, ca. 1910. Scale, 1 in. to 3 mi., 24.5 × 37.5 cm.

549. *Map of J. K. Ayres Addition to the Town of Conroe, County Seat of Montgomery Co. Texas.* Anonymous. N.p., ca. 1900. Ink on tracing paper, scale 1 in. to 100 ft., 40 × 63 cm.

The map shows the area west of the International and Great Northern Railroad tracks and north of the Gulf, Colorado and Santa Fe Railway tracks.

550. *Map of Part of Hardin County, Copied from Tyler County Map.* Anonymous. N.p., ca. 1890. Ink on cloth, scale indeterminable, 32 × 53 cm.

The map is stylistically quite different from the General Land Office maps, though it is clearly a later copy of a portion of a state map.

551. *Map of Coleman County.* Buffalo, New York: Cosack & Co., ca. 1890. Scale indeterminable, 49 × 63 cm.

552. *Map of Port Bolivar & Galveston Texas Showing Soundings In Harbor Channel, taken from U.S. survey made in 1905.* Bryan & Vauchelet. Beaumont, Texas, ca. 1905. Scale indeterminable, 59 × 100 cm.

A real estate promotional that envisions Port Bolivar as a well-developed city covering the entire tip of the Bolivar Peninsula and having a large port facility with twelve piers. (See no. 557 for a similar promotional.)

553. *Lampasas County Oil Field.* Lampasas, Texas: Southwestern American, ca. 1910. Color, scale indeterminable, 51 × 67 cm.

This is a separately issued broadside, based on the county plat map, that locates producing and exploratory oil wells.

554. *Map of subdivision of west one quarter of Wm Simpson League and parts of east one half of Ira Ingram League in Matagorda County, Texas.* Drawn from official surveys by E. K. Stimson for A. B. Mayes. N.p., ca. 1900. Blueprint. scale 1 in. to 1,600 ft., 34 × 36 cm.

These lands lie along Matagorda Bay, between Little Boggy and Big Boggy creeks, east of Matagorda. The tracts of the Cane Belt Railroad appear in the northwest corner of the map.

555. *[Brazoria County.]* William R. Stockwell. Alvin, Texas, ca. 1890. Scale indeterminable, 32 × 35 cm.

556. *Map of Madison County.* Texas. General Land Office(?). N.p., ca. 1890. Ink on cloth, scale indeterminable, 35 × 51 cm.

Like no. 558, an anonymous manuscript county plat map constructed by a skilled cartographer. It is probably an example of a field or preliminary sketch, from which the final General Land Office manuscripts were prepared. (See no. 358 for an example of these maps).

557. *Port Bolivar Galveston Co. Tex.* The Keynon Company. N.p., ca. 1910. Scale 1 in. to approx. 300 ft., on 60 × 90 cm. sheet, surrounded by photographs.

This real estate promotional shows nearly the same plan for Port Bolivar as does no. 552. The sheet also includes photos of then existing buildings at Port Bolivar, including the lighthouse and the shipyards.

558. *Washington Co.* Texas. General Land Office(?). N.p., ca. 1890. Ink on cloth, scale 1 in. to 4,000 varas, 28 × 69 cm. (See no. 556 for further information.)

ADDENDUM

Carta Esferica que comprehende las costas del Seno Mexicano. Construida de Orden del Rey en el Deposito Hidrografico de Marina: Por disposicion del Éxmo Señor Don Juan de Langara, Secretario de Estado y el Despacho Universal de ella. Año de 1799. [At foot, below neat line:] Fel. Bausa la delineo. Fern. Selma la grabo. [Madrid], 1799. Scale 1 in. to approx. 40 mi., 60 × 93 cm. Purchased 1988.

This is the first issue (of four) of the best general chart of the Gulf of Mexico published to date. It is based on the surveys that Jose de Evia undertook for Bernardo de Galvez during the 1780s, and it is the first printed map or chart of any kind to show Galveston Bay. The Carta Esferica was copied or consulted by such leading cartographic luminaries as Humboldt and Arrowsmith, and it remained the standard depiction for the United States Gulf coast until the publication of John Melish's map of the United States in 1817.

Bibliography

[Alba, Duque de, et al., eds.] *Mapas españoles de América, siglos XV–XVII.* Madrid: N.p., 1951.

Alperin, Lynn M. *Custodians of the Coast: History of the United States Army Engineers at Galveston.* Galveston: U.S. Army Corps of Engineers, 1977.

Archivo General de Mexico. Vol. 310, *Fomento-Colonizacion.* Eugene C. Barker Texas History Center, University of Texas at Austin.

Bagrow, Leo. *History of Cartography.* Rev., enl. ed. Translated by D. L. Paisey. Cambridge, Mass.: Harvard University Press, 1964.

Barker, Eugene C. *The Life of Stephen F. Austin, Founder of Texas, 1793–1836: A Chapter in the Westward Movement of the Anglo-American People.* 1925. Reprint. Austin: Texas State Historical Association, 1949.

Bolton, Herbert Eugene. *Texas in the Middle Eighteenth Century: Studies in Spanish Colonial History and Administration.* 1915. Reprint. Austin: University of Texas Press, 1970.

Bricker, Charles. *Landmarks of Mapmaking.* New York: Thomas Y. Crowell, 1976.

British Museum. *Catalogue of Printed Maps, Charts, and Plans.* 15 vols. London: Trustees of the British Museum, 1967. Reprint.

Brown University, John Carter Brown Library. *Bibliotheca Americana: Catalogue of the John Carter Brown Library in Brown University, Providence, Rhode Island.* 7 vols. 1919–31, 1973. Reprint. Millwood, N.Y.: Kraus Reprint Corp., 1975.

Bryan, James P., and Walter K. Hanak. *Texas in Maps.* Austin: University of Texas Press, [1961].

Campbell, Tony. *Early Maps.* Edited by Phyllis Benjamin. New York: Abbeville Press, 1981.

Carter, John, and Percy H. Muir, comps. and eds. *Printing and the Mind of Man: A Descriptive Catalogue Illustrating the Impact of Print on the Evolution of Western Civilization during Five Centuries.* London: Cassell & Co., 1967.

Castaneda, Carlos E. *Our Catholic Heritage in Texas, 1519–1936.* 7 vols. 1936–58. Reprint. New York: Arno Press, 1976.

Cauwer, Gilbert de. "Philippe Vandermaelen (1795–1869), Belgian mapmaker." *Imago Mundi* 24 (1970): 11–20.

Chueca Goitia, Fernando, and Leopoldo Torres Balbás. *Plano de ciudades Ibero-americanas y Filipinas existentes en el Archivo de Indias.* [Madrid]: Instituto de Estudies de Administracion Local, 1951.

[Church, Elihu Dwight.] *A Catalogue of Books Relating to the Discovery and Early History of North and South America Forming a Part of the Library of E. D. Church: Compiled and Annotated by George Watson Cole.* 5 vols. 1907. Reprint. New York: Peter Smith, 1951.

Clark, Thomas D., ed. *Travels in the Old South: A Bibliography.* 3 vols. American Exploration and Travel, no. 19. Norman: University of Oklahoma Press, 1956–59.

Cumming, William P. *The Exploration of North America, 1630–1776.* New York: G. P. Putnam's Sons, 1974.

————. *The Southeast in Early Maps, with an Annotated Check List of Printed and Manuscript Regional and Local Maps of Southeastern North America during the Colonial Period.* Princeton, N.J.: Princeton University Press, 1958.

Day, James M., comp. *Maps of Texas, 1527–1900: The Map Collection of the Texas State Archives.* Austin: Pemberton Press, 1964.

Delanglez, Jean. "Documents: The Sources of the Delisle Map of America, 1703." *Mid-America* 25 (1943): 275–98.

————. *El Río del Espíritu Santo: An Essay on the Cartography of the Gulf Coast and the Adjacent Territory during the Sixteenth and Seventeenth Centuries.* Edited by Thomas J. McMahon. Monograph Series, no. 21. New York: U.S. Catholic Historical Society, 1945.

————. "Franquelin, Mapmaker." *Mid-America* 25 (1943): 29–74.

Dunn, William Edward. *Spanish and French Rivalry in the Gulf Region of the United States, 1678–1702: The Beginnings of Texas and Pensacola.* 1917. Reprint, New York: Arno Press, n.d.

Fireman, Janet R. *The Spanish Royal Corps of Engineers in the Western Borderlands: Instruments of Bourbon Reform, 1764 to 1815.* Vol. 12 of *Spain in the West.* Glendale, Calif.: Arthur H. Clark Co., 1977.

Fite, Emerson D., and Archibald Freeman, comps. and eds. *A Book of Old Maps Delineating American History from the Earliest Days down to the Close of the Revolutionary War.* 1926. Reprint. New York: Arno Press, 1969.

Folmer, Henry. *Franco-Spanish Rivalry in North America, 1524–1763.* Vol. 7 of *Spain in the West.* Glendale, Calif.: Arthur H. Clark Co., 1953.

French, Benjamin Franklin, ed. *Historical collections of Louisiana and Florida.* . . . New ser., New York: J. Sabin & Sons, 1869.

[Galveston City Company.] *Report [of stockholders].* Printed broadside. [November, 1841]. Galveston City Company papers, Rosenberg Library, #46-0002, ff 1–37.

Ganong, William F. *Crucial Maps in the Early Cartography and Place-Nomenclature of the Atlantic Coast of Canada.* Royal Society of Canada, Special Publications, no. 7. Toronto: University of Toronto Press, 1964.

Garratt, John G. "The Maps in De Bry." *Map Collector,* no. 9 (December, 1979): 2–11.

Goetzmann, William H. *Army Exploration in the American West, 1803–1863.* Yale Publications in American Studies, no. 4. New Haven and London: Yale University Press, 1959.

[Graff, Everett D.] *Fifty Texas Rarities, Selected from the Library of Mr. Everett D. Graff for an Exhibition to Commemorate the Hundredth Anniversary of the Annexation of Texas by the United States.* 1946. Reprint. Austin: Pemberton Press, 1964.

Guillén y Tato, Julio F. *Monumenta Chartográfica indiana.* . . . Madrid: Publicación de la Sección de Relaciones Culturales del Ministerio de Asuntos Experiores, 1942–. Vol. 1, *Regiones del Plata y Magallanica,* 1942.

Hamilton, Peter Joseph. "Was Mobile Bay the Bay of Spiritu Santo?" *Transactions of the Alabama Historical Society* 4 (1901): 73–93.

Harrisse, Henry. *Découverte et évolution cartographique de Terre-Neuve et des pays circonvoisins 1497–1501–1769; essais de géographie historique et documentaire.* 1900. Reprint. Amsterdam: N. Israel, 1968.

———. *The Discovery of North America: A critical, documentary, and historic investigation, with an essay on the early cartography of the New world.* . . . 1892. Reprint. Amsterdam: N. Israel, 1969.

Hayes, Charles W. *Galveston: History of the Island and the City.* 2 vols. Austin: Jenkins Garrett Press, 1974.

Hebert, John R. *Panoramic Maps of Anglo-American Cities.* Washington, D.C.: U.S. Library of Congress, 1974.

Herrera y Tordesillas, Antonio de. *Historia general de los hechos de los castellanos en las islas i tierra firme del mar oceano.* . . . 4 vols. Madrid: En la Emplenta [*sic*; Imprenta] Real, 1601-15.

Hodge, Frederick W., and Theodore H. Lewis, eds. *Spanish Exploreres in the Southern United States, 1528–1543*. . . . 1907. Reprint. New York: Barnes & Noble, 1977.

Hollon, W. Eugene, and Ruth Lapham Butler. *William Bollaert's Texas.* American Exploration and Travel, no. 21. Norman: University of Oklahoma Press with the Newberry Library, 1956.

Holmes, Jack D. L. *José de Evía y sus reconocimientos del Golfo de México, 1783–1796*. Colección Chimalistac de libros y documentos acerca la Neuva España, no. 26. Madrid: Ediciones José Porrua Turanzas, 1968.

[Homem de Mello.] Marcondes Homem de Mello, Francisco Ignacio, barão Homem de Mello, and Francisco Homem de Mello. *Atlas do Brazil.* . . . Rio de Janeiro: F. Briguiet & Cia., 1909.

Howes, Wright. *U. S.iana (1650–1950): A Selective Bibliography in Which are Described 11,620 Uncommon and Significant Books Relating to the Continental Portion of the United States.* Rev., enl. ed. New York: R. R. Bowker Co. for the Newberry Library, 1962.

Howse, Derek, and Michael Sanderson. *The Sea Chart: An Historical Survey based on the Collections in the National Maritime Museum.* Newton Abbot, England: David & Charles, 1973.

Humboldt, Alexander von. *Political Essay on the Kingdom of New Spain.* . . . Translated by John Black, 4 vols. 1811. Reprint. New York: AMS Press, n.d.

Johnson, Adrian. *America Explored: A Cartographical History of the Exploration of North America.* New York: Viking Press, 1974.

Kapp, Kit S. *The Early Maps of Colombia up to 1850.* Map Collectors' Series, no. 77. London: Map Collectors' Circle, 1971.

———. *The Early Maps of Panama up to 1865.* Map Collectors' Series, no. 73. London: Map Collectors' Circle, 1971.

———. *Printed Maps of Central America up to 1860.* Pt. 1, *1548–1760.* Map Collectors' Series, no. 103. London: Map Collectors' Circle, 1974.

———. *Printed Maps of Central America up to 1860.* Pt. 2, *1762–1860.* Map Collectors' Series, no. 106. London: Map Collectors' Circle, 1975.

———. *The Printed Maps of Jamaica up to 1825.* Map Collectors' Series, no. 42. London: Map Collectors' Circle, 1968.

Karpinski, Louis C. *Maps of Famous Cartographers Depicting North America: An Historical Atlas of the Great Lakes and Michigan, with Bibliography of the Printed Maps of Michigan to 1880.* 2d ed. 1931. Reprint. Amsterdam: Meridian Publishing Co., 1977.

Kielman, Chester V., comp. and ed. *The University of Texas Archives: A Guide to the Historical Manuscripts Collections in the University of Texas Library.* Austin: University of Texas Press, 1967.

King, William F. "George Davidson and the Marine Survey in the Pacific Northwest." *Western Historical Quarterly* 10 (1980): 285–302.

Koeman, Cornelis, comp. and ed. *Atlantes Neerlandici: Bibliography of Terrestrial, Maritime, and Celestial Atlases and Pilot Books Published in the Netherlands up to 1880.* 5 vols. Amsterdam: Theatrum Orbis Terrarum, 1967–71.

———. *Joan Blaeu and His Grand Atlas.* Amsterdam: Theatrum Orbis Terrarum, 1970.

Koenig, Virginia, and Joan Cain, trans. *Historical Journal of the Settlement of the French in Louisiana.* USL History Series, no. 3. Lafayette: University of Southwestern Louisiana, 1971. (A translation of Bénard de la Harpe, *Journal historique de l'éstablissement des Français à la Louisiane* [see La Harpe].)

Kohl, Johann Georg. *Die Beiden ältesten General-Karten von Amerika.* Weimar: Geographisches Institut, 1860.

———. *A Documentary History of the State of Maine.* Portland: Maine Historical Society, 1869.

[La Harpe, Jean Baptiste Bénard de.] *Journal historique de l'établissement des Français à la Louisiane.* New Orleans: A. L. Boimare, 1831.

Lauvrière, Émile. *Histoire de la Louisiane française, 1673–1939.* Romance Languages Series, no. 3. Baton Rouge: Louisiana State University Press, 1940.

Leader, John Temple. *Life of Sir Robert Dudley . . . Followed by the [Anonymous] Italian Biography of Sir Robert Dudley. . . .* Amsterdam: Meridian Publishing Co., 1977.

Leighly, John B. *California as an Island: An Illustrated Essay.* San Francisco: Book Club of California, 1972.

Leite, Serafim. *História da Companhia de Jesus no Brazil.* 10 vols. Rio de Janeiro: Civilização Brasileira, 1938–50. Vol. 4, 1943.

Lelewel, Joachim. *Géographie du Moyen Âge.* 5 vols. 1845, 1852–57. Reprint (5 vols. in 3). Amsterdam: Meridian Publishing Co., 1966–67.

Leonard, Irving A. *Don Carlos de Sigüenza y Góngora, a Mexican Savant of the Seventeenth Century.* University of California Publications in History, vol. 18. Berkeley: University of California Press, 1929.

———, ed. and trans. *Spanish Approach to Pensacola, 1689–1693.* 1939. Reprint. New York: Arno Press, 1967.

Lorenzana, Francisco Antonio. *Historia de Nueva-España, escrita por su Eclarecido Conquistador Hernan Cortes, Augmenta con otros Documentos, y Notas por El Ilustrissimo Señor Don Francisco Antonio Lorenzana, Arzobispo de México.* Mexico City, 1770.

Lowery, Woodbury. *The Lowery Collection: A Descriptive List of the Maps* of the Spanish Possessions within the Present Limits of the United States, 1502–1820. Edited by Philip Lee Phillips. Washington, D.C.: U.S. Government Printing Office, 1912.

McGechaen, Alexander, and Coolie Verner. *Maps in the Parliamentary Papers by the Arrowsmiths: A Finding List.* Pt. 1. Map Collectors' Series, no. 88. London: Map Collectors' Circle, 1973.

Margry, Pierre, ed. *Découvertes et établissements des Français dans l'ouest et dans le sud de l'Amérique Septentrionale (1614–1754). Mémoires et documents originaux.* . . . 6 vols. Paris: D. Jouaust, 1876–86. Vol. 6, *Exploration des affluents du Mississippi et découverte des montagnes Rocheuses (1679–1754,* 1886.

Martin, Lawrence, and Walter W. Ristow. "John Disturnell's Map of the United Mexican States." In *À la Carte: Selected Papers on Maps and Atlases,* compiled by Walter W. Ristow, pp. 204–21. Washington, D.C.: U.S. Library of Congress, 1972.

Martin, Robert S. "Maps of an Empresario: Austin's Contribution to the Cartography of Texas." *Southwestern Historical Quarterly* 85 (1982): 371–400.

Mason, Sara Elizabeth. *A List of Nineteenth Century Maps of the State of Alabama.* Birmingham, Ala.: Birmingham Public Library, 1973.

Matos, Luís de. *No. IV Centenário de fundação do Rio de Janeiro.* Lisbon: Fundação Calouste Gulbenkian, 1964.

Melish, John. *A geographical description of the United States, with the contiguous British and Spanish possessions, intended as an accompaniment to Melish's map of these countries.* 2d ed. Philadelphia: John Melish, 1816.

Modelski, Andrew M. *Railroad Maps of the United States.* Washington, D.C.: U.S. Library of Congress, 1975.

Morison, Samuel Eliot. *The European Discovery of America.* 2 vols. New York: Oxford University Press, 1971–74.

Museo Nacional de Arquelogía, Historia y Etnografía, México D. F., Sección de Archivo, Secretaría de Fomento. Expediente no. 17. Legajo no. 4, 1829.

National Maritime Museum [Greenwich, England]. *Catalogue of the Library.* 5 vols. London: Her Majesty's Stationery Office, 1968–76. Vol. 3, *Atlases and Cartography,* 1971.

Nordenskiöld, [Nils] A. E. *Facsimile-atlas to the early history of cartography with reproductions of the most important maps printed in the XV and XVI centuries.* Translated by Johan Adolf Ekelöf and Clements R. Markham. 1889. Reprint. New York: Dover Publications, 1973.

———. *Periplus: An Essay on the Early History of Charts and Sailing-*

Directions. Translated by Francis A. Bather. Stockholm: 1897. Reprint. New York: Burt Franklin & Co., [1967].

Nuñez Cabeza de Vaca, Alvar. *La relación y comentarios del gouernador Alvar Nuñez Cabeça de Vaca de lo acaescido enlas Jndias. . . .* Zamora: Impresso por Augustin de Paz y Juan Picardo, a costa de Juan Pedro Musetti mercader de libros, vezino de Medina del Campo, 1542.

Nunn, George E. *The Geographical Conceptions of Columbus: A Critical Consideration of Four Problems.* 1924. Reprint. New York: Octagon Books, 1973.

————. *The Mappemonde of Juan de la Cosa: A Critical Investigation of Its Date.* Jenkintown, Pa.: George H. Beans Library, 1934.

————. "The Three Maplets Attributed to Bartholemew Columbus." *Imago Mundi* 9 (1952): 12–22.

Ortroy, Fernand Gratien van. *Bibliographie de l'oevre de pierre Apian.* 1902. Reprint. Amsterdam: Meridian Publishing Co., 1963.

Osley, A. S. *Mercator: A Monograph on the Lettering of Maps, etc. in the 16th Century Netherlands with a Facsimile and Translation of His Treatise on the Italic Hand and a Translation of Ghim's "Vita Mercatoris."* London: Faber & Faber, 1969.

Palmer, Margaret. *The Printed Maps of Bermuda.* Map Collectors' Series, no. 19. London: Map Collectors' Circle, 1965.

Parry, John Horace. *The Discovery of South America.* New York: Taplinger Publishing Co., 1979.

Peters, Harry T. *America on Stone: The Other Printmakers to the American People. . . .* 1931. Reprint. New York: Arno Press, 1976.

Peterson-Hunt, William S., and R. Philip Hoehn. *Union List of Sanborn Fire Insurance Maps held by Institutions in the United States and Canada.* Rev. ed. 2 vols. Santa Cruz, Calif.: Western Association of Map Libraries, 1976–77. Vol. 2, *Montana to Wyoming,* by William S. Peterson-Hunt and Evelyn L. Woodruff, 1977.

Phillips, Philip Lee. *A List of Geographical Atlases in the Library of Congress, with Bibliographical Notes.* 4 vols. 1909–20. Reprint (4 vols. in 2). Amsterdam: N. Israel, 1971.

————. *A List of Maps of America in the Library of Congress, Preceded by a List of Works Relating to Cartography.* 1901. Reprint. New York: Burt Franklin & Co., n.d.

Pike, Zebulon Montgomery. *An account of expeditions to the sources of the Mississippi, and through the western parts of Louisiana, to the sources of the Arkansaw, Kans, La Platte, and Pierre Juan, rivers; performed by order of the government of the United States during the years 1805, 1806, and 1807. And a tour through the interior parts of New Spain,*

*when conducted through these provinces, by order of the captain-general,
in the year 1807.* Philadelphia: C. & A. Conrad, & Co., 1810.

Pinckney, Pauline A. *Painting in Texas: The Nineteenth Century.* Austin
and London: University of Texas Press for the Amon Carter Museum
of Western Art, 1967.

Public Records Office [Kew, England]. *Maps and Plans in the Public Records Office.* London: Her Majesty's Stationery Office, 1967–. Vol. 2,
America and West Indies, edited by P. A. Penfold, 1974.

Raines, Cadwell Walton. *A Bibliography of Texas . . . with an introductory essay on the materials of early Texan history.* 1896. Reprint. Houston: Frontier Press, 1955.

Reps, John W. *Cities of the American West: A History of Frontier Urban
Planning.* Princeton, N.J.: Princeton University Press, 1979.

————. *Cities on Stone: Nineteenth Century Lithograph Images of the
Urban West: Accompanying Exhibition Presented at Amon Carter Museum of Western Art, Fort Worth, August 27–October 10, 1976. . . .*
Fort Worth: Amon Carter Museum of Western Art, 1976.

Rich, Obadiah. *Bibliotheca americana nova; or A catalogue of books in
various languages relating to America, printed since the year 1700.* 2
vols. 1835–46. Reprint. New York: Burt Franklin & Co., n.d.

Ristow, Walter W. "John Melish and His Map of the United States." In
A la Carte: Selected Papers on Maps and Atlases, compiled by Walter W. Ristow, pp. 162–82. Washington, D.C.: U.S. Library of Congress,
1972.

Robinson, Adrian Henry Wardle. *Marine Cartography in Britain: A History of the Sea Chart to 1855.* Leicester: University Press, 1962.

Roukema E. "A Discovery of Yucatan prior to 1503." *Imago Mundi* 13 (1956):
30–37.

Royal Geographical Society [London, England]. "Notes on the Coast Region of the Texas Territory: taken during a visit in 1842." *Journal of the
Royal Geographical Society* 13 (1843): 226–27.

Sabin, Joseph, Wilberforce Eames, and R. W. G. Vail. *Bibliotheca Americana. A dictionary of books relating to America, from its discovery to
the present time.* 29 vols. 1868–1936. Reprint (29 vols. in 2). Metuchen,
N.J.: Scarecrow Press, 1966.

Scaife, Walter B. *America: Its geographical history 1492–1892 . . . with a
supplement entitled Was the Rio de Espiritu Santo of the Spanish geographers the Mississippi?* 1892. Reprint. New York: AMS Press, n.d.

Schilder, Günter. *Australia Unveiled: The Share of the Dutch Navigators
in the Discovery of Australia.* Translated by Olaf Richter. Amsterdam:
Theatrum Orbis Terrarum, 1976.

Schwartz, Seymour I., and Ralph E. Ehrenberg. *The Mapping of America.* New York: Harry N. Abrams, 1980.

Schwartz, Seymour I., and Henry Taliaferro. "A Newly Discovered First State of a Foundation Map, *L'Amérique Septentrionale.*" *Map Collector* 26 (1984): 2–6.

Severin, Timothy. *Explorers of the Mississippi.* New York: Alfred A. Knopf, 1968.

Sewell, Gerald, and Mary Beth Rogers. *The Story of Texas Public Lands: A Unique Heritage.* [Austin]: Texas General Land Office & J. M. West Texas Corp., [1973].

Shirley, Rodney W. *Early Printed Maps of the British Isles, 1477–1650: A Bibliography.* Pt. 1 (1477–1555). Map Collectors' Series, no. 90. London: Map Collectors' Circle, 1973.

Skelton, Raleigh Ashlin. *Decorative Printed Maps of the 15th to 18th Centuries.* 1952. Reprint. London: Spring Books, 1965.

———, ed. *Claudius Ptolemaeus. Geographia. Strassburg, 1513. With an Introduction by R. A. Skelton.* Theatrum Orbis Terrarum, ser. 2, vol. 4. Amsterdam: Theatrum Orbis Terrarum, 1966.

———, ed. Cornelis Wytfliet. *Descriptionis Ptolemaicae augmentum, sive Occidentis notitia brevis [sic] commentario [illustrata].* Louvain, 1597. *With an Introduction by R. A. Skelton.* Theatrum Orbis Terrarum, ser. 1., vol. 5. Amsterdam: N. Israel, 1964.

———, comp. *County Atlases of the British Isles, 1579–1850.* Pt. 2 (1612–46). Map Collectors' Series, no. 14. London: Map Collectors' Circle, [1964–65].

———, ed. G[erard] de Jode. *Speculum orbis terrarum. Antwerpen, 1578. With an Introduction by R. A. Skelton.* Theatrum Orbis Terrarum, ser. 2, vol. 2. Amsterdam: Theatrum Orbis Terrarum, 1965.

———, ed. *Lucas Jansz. Waghenaer. The Mariners Mirrour. London, 1588. With an Introduction by R. A. Skelton.* Theatrum Orbis Terrarum, ser. 3, vol. 2. Amsterdam: Theatrum Orbis Terrarum, 1966.

Stephenson, Richard W., comp. *Land Ownership Maps, a Checklist of Nineteenth Century United States County Maps in the Library of Congress.* Washington, D.C.: U.S. Library of Congress, 1967.

Stevens, Henry. *Historical and geographical notes on the earliest discoveries in America, 1453–1530; with comments on the earliest charts and maps. . . .* 1869. Reprint. New York: Burt Franklin & Co., n.d.

Stevens, Henry Newton, and Roland Tree. *Comparative Cartography.* Map Collectors' Series, no. 34. London: Map Collectors' Circle, 1967.

Stevenson, Edward Luther. *Early Spanish Cartography of the New World with Special Reference to the Wolfenbüttel-Spanish Map and the Work of Diego Ribero.* [Worcester, Mass.?]: N.p., [1909?]

————. *Maps Illustrating Early Exploration and Discovery in America 1502–1530.* . . . New Brunswick, N. J.: E. L. Stevenson, 1903–[1906?].

————. *Marine World Chart of Nicolo de Caneiro Januensis, 1502 (circa): A Critical Study, with Facsimile.* . . . Hispanic Society of America, publication no. 14. New York: [American Geographical Society?], 1907–1908.

————. *Terrestrial and Celestial Globes: Their History and Construction.* . . . 2 vols. 1921. Reprint. New York: Johnson Reprint Corp., 1971.

Stokes, Isaac Newton Phelps. *The Iconography of Manhattan Island, 1498–1909.* . . . 6 vols. New York: R. H. Dodd, 1915.

Storm, Colton, comp. *A Catalogue of the Everett D. Graff Collection of Western Americana.* Chicago: University of Chicago Press for the Newberry Library, 1968.

Streeter, Thomas Winthrop. *Bibliography of Texas, 1795–1845.* 5 vols. Cambridge, Mass.: Harvard University Press, 1955–60.

————. *[Catalogue of] The Celebrated Collection of Americana Formed by the late Thomas Winthrop Streeter, Morristown, New Jersey: Sold by Order of the Trustees.* . . . 7 vols. New York: Parke-Bernet Galleries, 1966–69.

Taylor, Virginia H. *The Spanish Archives of the General Land Office of Texas.* Austin: Lone Star Press, 1955.

Thacher, John Boyd. *The Continent of America: Its Discovery and Its Baptism.* 1896. Reprint. Amsterdam: Meridian Publishing Co., 1971.

Thomassy, Raymond. *Cartographie de la Louisiane.* New Orleans: R. Thomassy, 1859. Separately published extract from *Géologie pratique de la Louisiane* (New Orleans, 1859), pp. 205–26.

Tooley, Ronald Vere. *California as an Island.* Map Collectors' Series, no. 33. London: Map Collectors' circle, 1967.

————. *French Mapping of the Americans: The De l'Isle, Buache, De Zauche Succession.* Map Collectors' Series, no. 33. London: Map Collectors' Circle, 1967.

————. "Maps in Italian Atlases of the Sixteenth Century." *Imago Mundi* 3 (1939): 12–47.

————. *Maps of Africa: A Selection of Printed Maps from the Sixteenth to the Nineteenth Century.* Pt. 2. Map Collectors' Series, no. 48. London: Map Collectors' Circle, 1968.

————. *Printed Maps of America.* Pt. 1. Map Collectors' Series, no. 68. London: Map Collectors' Circle, 1971.

————. *Printed Maps of America.* Pt. 2. Map Collectors' Series, no. 69. London: Map Collectors' Circle, 1971.

————. *A Sequence of Maps of America.* Map Collectors' Series, no. 92. London: Map Collectors' Circle, 1973.

————. "The Strait That Never Was." *Map Collector,* no. 2 (March, 1978): 2–7.

————. *Tooley's Dictionary of Mapmakers.* New York: Alan R. Liss, 1979.

True, David O. "Some Early Maps Relating to Florida." *Imago Mundi* 11 (1954): 73–84.

United States Department of Commerce. Coast and Geodetic Survey. *Availability of Original Hydrographic and Topographic Surveys.* N.p., n.d.

United States General Services Administration. National Archives and Records Service. *Civil War Maps in the National Archives.* National Archives Publication no. 64–12. Washington, D.C.: U.S. Government Printing Office, 1964.

Varnhagen, Francisco Adolpho de. *Vespuce et son premier voyage; ou, Notice d'une découverte et exploration primitive du Golfe du Mexique et des côtes des États-Unis en 1497 et 1498. . . .* Paris: L. Martinet, 1858.

Vigneras, Louis-André. *The Discovery of South America and the Andalusian Voyages.* Chicago: University of Chicago Press for the Newberry Library, 1976.

Villiers du Terrage, Marc, baron de. *L'Expédition de Cavelier de La Salle dans le Golfe du Mexique (1684–1687).* Paris: A. Maisonneuve, 1931.

Vindel, Francisco. *Mapas de América en los libros españoles de los siglos XVI al XVIII (1503–1798).* Madrid, 1955.

Wagner, Henry R. *The Cartography of the Northwest Coast of America to the Year 1800.* 1937. Reprint. Amsterdam: N. Israel, 1968.

Walter, Frank K., and Virginia Doneghy. *Jesuit Relations, and Other Americana in the Library of James F. Bell: A Catalogue.* Minneapolis: University of Minnesota Press, [1950].

Warner, Deborah J. *The Sky Explored: Celestial Cartography, 1500–1800.* New York: Alan R. Liss, 1979.

Webb, Walter Prescott, and H. Bailey Carroll, eds. *The Handbook of Texas.* 3 vols. Austin: Texas State Historical Association, 1952–76.

Wedel, Mildred Mott. "J. B. Bénard, Sieur de la Harpe: Visitor to the Wichitas in 1719." *Great Plains Journal* 10, no. 2 (Spring, 1971): 37–60.

Wegelin, Oscar, comp. *Books Relating to the History of Georgia in the Library of Wymberly Jones De Renne, of Wormsloe, Isle of Hope, Chatham County, Georgia.* Savannah, Ga.: The Morning News, 1911.

Wheat, Carl I. *Mapping the Transmississippi West.* 6 vols. San Francisco: Institute of Historical Cartography, 1957–63.

————. *The Maps of the California Gold Region, 1848–1857: A Bibliography of an Important Decade.* San Francisco: Grabhorn Press, 1942.

Wheat, James Clements, and Christian F. Brun. *Maps and Charts Published in America before 1800: A Bibliography.* New Haven and London: Yale University Press, 1969.

Wieser, Franz R. von. "Die Karte des Bartolomeo Colombo über die vierte Reise des Admirals." Ergänzungsband 4, pp. 488–98. Vienna: Universität, Institut für österreichische Geschichtsforschung, Mitteil, 1893.

Williams, Samuel May. Papers. In Rosenberg Library, Galveston, Texas.

Winkler, Ernest W., ed. *Check List of Texas Imprints, 1846–1860.* Austin: Texas State Historical Association, 1949.

Winkler, Ernest W., and Llerena B. Friend, eds. *Check List of Texas Imprints, 1861–1876.* Austin: Texas State Historical Association, 1963.

Winsor, Justin. *The Kohl Collection (Now in the Library of Congress) of Maps Relating to America.* Washington, D.C.: U.S. Government Printing Office, 1904.

————, ed. *Narrative and Critical History of America.* 8 vols. 1884–89. Reprint. New York: AMS Press, n.d.

The World Encompassed, an Exhibition of the History of Maps Held at the Baltimore Museum of Art, October 7 to November 23, 1952. Baltimore: Trustees of the Walters Art Gallery, 1952.

Wroth, Lawrence C. "The Early Cartography of the Pacific." *Papers of the Bibliographical Society of America* 38, no. 2 (1944): 87–268.

Yoakum, Henderson. *History of Texas from its first settlement in 1685 to its annexation to the United States in 1846.* 2 vols. New York: Redfield, 1856.

Yonge, Ena L. *A Catalogue of Early Globes Made Prior to 1850 and Conserved in the United States.* New York: American Geographical Society, 1968.

Index

This index, like the map descriptions, concentrates on Galveston and Texas subjects. Only the most outstanding features of non-Galveston and Texas maps are indexed. Numbers are page references except under the subentry "maps," where they are catalog numbers.

The spelling of known place names is adjusted to reflect current usage. Cartographer's names follow the preferred form given in Ronald V. Tooley's *Dictionary of Mapmakers*. Because Tooley generally drops articles, most cartographers file under the first substantive element in their last name (Fer, not de Fer). There are some exceptions to this rule (De Soto, not Soto). Only European cartographers are indexed by nationality.

The geographic descriptors reflect the focus of each map. Regional maps and globes bear more general headings (World, Central America, Caribbean, etc.); local maps bear more specific headings (Havana, Cuba; Yucatan; Galveston County; etc.). A regional map with insets or with a particular focus has both general and specific descriptors.

Blome, Richard: maps, 52
Bluefields Lagoon, Nicaragua: maps, 172
Bolivar Peninsula: maps, 204, 298, 340, 398, 421, 527. *See also* Port Bolivar
Bolivia: maps, 245
Bollaert, William, 16; maps, 272
Bordas, Mariano: maps, 392
Borden, Gail: maps, 257
Borden Survey of Galveston Island, 16
Boston, Massachusetts: maps, 154, 194
Boston Harbor: maps, 123
Bougainville, Louis Antoine de: maps, 162
Bowen, Emmanuel: maps, 137, 150
Bowie County: maps, 368
Bowles, Carington: maps, 158, 179
Bowles, John: maps, 158
Bowles' New and Accurate Map of North America and the West Indies: maps, 179
Bradford, Thomas Gamaliel: maps, 248, 286, 287, 288, 289, 290
Brasilia Generis nobilitate, armorum et litterarum Scientia prestant: maps, 34
Brazil: maps, 34, 38, 118, 155, 240
Brazoria County: maps, 365, 380, 432, 434, 478, 535, 555
Brazos River: maps, 202
Brazos River Entrance: maps, 490
Breton Sound, Louisiana, 10
Brewster County: maps, 467
Bridgetown, Barbados: maps, 111
Broadway Addition: maps, 482
Brooklyn, Texas: maps, 353
Brown, Christopher: maps, 111
Brue, Adrien Hubert: maps, 268, 323
Bry, Theodore de: maps, 16, 18
Bryan and Vauchelet: maps, 552
Buache, Phillip: maps, 118, 130, 173
Buffalo Bayou: maps, 204, 230
Buffalo Bayou, Brazos, and Colorado Railroad: maps, 311
Buffalo Bayou Entrance: maps, 298
Bundick, Samuel C.: maps, 357
Burke's Almanac: maps, 352
Burleson County: maps, 369

Burr, David H., 15; maps, 246, 247, 252
Cabanas, Cuba: maps, 153, 172
Cabo Frances Viejo, Dominican Republic: maps, 172
Cahill Cemetery: maps, 495, 504, 505
Cain, E. G.: maps, 500, 508, 522
Calcasieu Lake, 5
California: maps, 54, 93, 137, 273, 280, 297, 302
Camp Hawley: maps, 458
Canada: maps, 93, 99, 174, 186, 261, 262
Caneiro, Januensis, 3, 4; maps, 2
Cantino, Alberto, 3, 4
Capassi, P. Domingos: maps, 116
Cape Cod: maps, 46, 75, 127, 216, 253
Cape Hatteras: maps, 229, 326
Cape Horn: maps, 183
Capitol building: maps, 317
capitulacion, 4
Caribbean (*see also* specific countries and islands): maps, 2, 16, 18, 23, 37, 49, 54, 59, 69, 78, 85, 87, 90, 91, 93, 99, 100, 105, 106, 111, 125, 134, 140, 148, 149, 153, 154, 167, 173, 174, 179, 180, 185, 188, 193, 239, 292, 308, 319, 320, 323, 335, 347, 512
Carmen, Mexico: maps, 308
Carolina Newly Described: maps, 63
Carpinetti, Joao Silverio: maps, 161
Carta Esferica, 13, 15; maps, 193, 197, 200, 202, 292, 558
Cartagena, Colombia: maps, 29, 71, 100, 123, 153, 154, 172, 182
Carta General del Oceano Atlantico ú Ocidental desde 52' de Latitud Norte hasta el Equador: maps, 192
Carta particolare che comincia con il capo Mogera in Portogallo è Finisce con il capo di Coriano in Ispagna: maps, 41
Carta particolare che comincia con il capo S. Andrea è finiscie con il capo Matas d'America: maps, 35
Carta particolare della Brasilia, che comincia con il capo S. Antonio et